"E.W. Jackson's new book, *Sweet Land of Liberty*, is a perfect expression of the mission pursued by Fidelis Publishing. America's only hope for returning to 'one nation, under God, indivisible, with liberty and justice for all,' is defined and explained with clarity and self-evident truth. We share backgrounds as Marines and on a much deeper level as brothers in Christ and I can recommend no author or book more highly."

—LtCol Oliver North, CEO of Fidelis Publishing and Fidelis Media, best-selling author of more than twenty books

"*Sweet Land of Liberty* is an eye-opening deep dive into American history. E.W. Jackson approaches the subject of liberty through the lens of a Christian and biblical worldview. While not engendering bitterness and division, this book unifies Americans with a spiritual understanding of our history. If every American would read it and take it to heart, our country would be the better for it. The Scripture says 'where there is no vision, the people perish.' *Sweet Land of Liberty* offers a vision for America that seeks a unified, secure, and prosperous nation."

—Alveda King, PhD, Christian evangelist and activist

"E.W. Jackson is one of the premier voices for sanity in our world today. He not only has a scriptural foundation but is also well versed in true American history which exposes 'woke' ideology for what it is, a lie. The Lord has anointed E.W. with boldness and clarity to be a true prophet of our day. We need to take heed to what the Lord is saying through this man of God. It's my honor to call E.W. a good friend, and I highly endorse *Sweet Land of Liberty*."

—Andrew Wommack, founder and president of Andrew Wommack Ministries

"Bishop E.W. Jackson is a man who started life with the disadvantage of being in a foster home until he was ten years old. He had every reason to be an angry young man, yet today he is one of the boldest, most patriotic, and most courageous evangelical leaders in America. This book is a captivating story of his life and how he sees the current condition of the nation. He gives a brilliant analysis of the Marxist movement in America and discusses how it should be dealt with before it destroys our country. He also takes on the national racial climate with a perspective I promise you have not heard before. This is such a good book! It will enlighten you and encourage you."

—LTG (RET.) Jerry Boykin, EVP Family Research Council, and author of *Strong and Courageous*

"*Sweet Land of Liberty* is the perfect book title for E.W. Jackson because he lives and breathes its message. Never in my life have I known someone so filled with overwhelming gratitude and praise for his country. This doesn't come from a background of privilege, but from a tapestry of trouble and triumph. E.W. is as eloquent on the page as he is in spell-binding person. I am so very proud to call him my friend and colleague. Read and be inspired!"

—Sandy Rios, director of governmental affairs for American Family Association, host of *Sandy Rios in the Morning* on AFR Talk

"I highly recommend my good friend Bishop E.W. Jackson's new book, *Sweet Land of Liberty*, to those who subscribe to the American ideal of being a Victor. The progressive socialist, Marxist, left in America is pushing the delusional and dangerous concept of victimization. The one demographic that is their consistent target is the Black community. Bishop Jackson shares with us his story, which is an American story, of generational triumph from tragedy, which is what slavery was in America. It is time we stop chanting 'We Can Overcome' and get busy *living* a belief that 'We Can Overcome.' And that is possible for any and all here in this Sweet Land of Liberty."

—Lieutenant Colonel Allen B. West (U.S. Army, Retired), member, 112th U.S. Congress, former chairman, Republican Party of Texas

"Bishop E.W. Jackson is a clarion voice in a wasteland of godless, America-hating Marxists. Like John the Baptist, he is calling all who will listen to stand up and take note of what is coming. *Sweet Land of Liberty* is just the book America—and all mankind—needs today!"

—David Barton, founder, WallBuilders; and Tim Barton, president, WallBuilders

"No better time for E.W. Jackson's book—*Sweet Land of Liberty*. After pseudo-scholarship like Critical Race Theory and pseudo-history like the 1619 Project, comes a book of personal history and reflection that shows the truth of America. This patriot, this descendent of slaves, trumpets his gratitude for the legacy of freedom that is the inheritance of every American. *Sweet Land of Liberty* unifies, inspires, and proves that the American dream is very much alive. As long as there are Americans like E.W. Jackson, the dream will never die."

—Bob McEwen, U.S. House of Representatives, former member from Ohio, 1776 Presidential Commission

"*Sweet Land of Liberty* is a well-reasoned defense of America's uniqueness and value, but it is the book's subtitle that gives insight into what makes Jackson's work so authentic and gripping: *Reflections of a Patriot Descended from Slaves*. His biography—from foster care, to juvenile delinquency, to the U.S. Marines to Harvard Law School and beyond—is an American journey. Like few communicators you will ever experience, E.W. Jackson will inform, inspire, and motivate every reader who opens his book."

—Dr. Alex McFarland, educator, author, broadcaster

Sweet Land of Liberty

Reflections of a Patriot Descended from Slaves

E.W. Jackson Sr.

FIDELIS
PUBLISHING

FIDELIS PUBLISHING ®
ISBN: 9781956454208
ISBN (eBook): 9781956454192

SWEET LAND OF LIBERTY
Reflections of a Patriot Descended from Slaves
© 2023 E.W. Jackson Sr.

Cover Design by Diana Lawrence
Interior Design by Xcel Graphic
Edited by Amanda Varian

Order from www.faithfultext.com for discounted books. Email info@fidelispublishing.com to inquire about bulk purchase discounts.

All Scripture is taken from the New King James Version® (NKJV). Copyright © 1982 by Thomas Nelson. Used by permission. All rights reserved.

Fidelis Publishing, LLC Sterling, VA • Nashville, TN
www.fidelispublishing.com

Fidelis Publishing, LLC Sterling, VA • Nashville, TN
www.fidelispublishing.com
Manufactured in the United States of America
10 9 8 7 6 5 4 3 2

I dedicate this book first to my beloved father, the late William Jackson, who instilled in me hope for America, rather than bitterness and hatred. I also dedicate it to the memory of America's Founding Fathers. They created a nation that became far greater than anything they could possibly have imagined. They pledged their "lives, fortunes and sacred honor." I am a beneficiary and heir of their courageous stand. My great-grandparents, Gabriel and Eliza Jackson of Orange County, Virginia, could not have known their great-grandson would experience the blessings of being a free American. Their hardship was for me, and this book is also dedicated to them.

I once had a vision of an ancestor of mine in slavery praying for those who would follow. For all I know, that was Gabriel, praying for me and all who would be born after him. Gabriel and Eliza endured and survived so I could thrive in the greatest nation in history.

My great-grandfather and great-grandmother were born not so long after Thomas Jefferson penned the words "that all men are created equal . . . endowed by their Creator with certain unalienable Rights, that among these are Life, Liberty and the pursuit of Happiness."

They did not live long enough to see the promise fulfilled in their country. Yet they had hope—American hope. Three generations later, that hope passed to me. My wife and I have passed it on to our children. To every veteran and active-duty serviceman and woman who has taken the oath to our Constitution and donned a military uniform, and to those who gave the last full measure of devotion for our country and our people, thank you. This book is also dedicated to those brave souls who have defended the freedom we all enjoy.

May this book honor all Americans who have gone before us, no matter their ancestry. To all my fellow citizens, those who agree with me and those who do not, may we be unified in gratitude as one family. May we never forget we are "the land of the free" because we are "the home of the brave."

CONTENTS

INTRODUCTION

WHY I WROTE
THIS BOOK

I sometimes wonder what my life might be had I been born some place other than the United States of America.

Would I be living in some village mud hut with no running water? Would I be living in a country like China, where I could lose my freedom for declaring my faith in Jesus Christ? Being the outspoken person I am, would I be sitting in a concentration camp or prison for disagreeing with the policies of my government? Or would I already be dead, buried in some region of the world where the rule of law has completely broken down?

Thank God I experienced none of these nightmare scenarios because I am blessed to be an American. I am an heir to the ingenious experiment in self-government we call the United States. Our Founders thought of it as a miracle, and I am part of that miracle.

While I am filled with joy at the privilege and potential my birth affords me, I write this book with a degree of sadness and anger. I am saddened by the efforts of some of our misguided citizens to fundamentally transform this miracle into another kind of nation. I am angered because some political leaders are intentionally trying to rob me and my posterity of the last best hope on earth and pass on to us the social and fiscal ruins of a once-great nation. Like me, most Americans are deeply troubled at the direction of our country

1

and believe unless things change, a future generation, perhaps the next, will face the utter collapse of the America we have known and loved.

Government spending is out of control. Traditional marriage and family are in precipitous decline. The church, once the most culturally influential institution in our country, is under constant attack from without and within. Pop culture sexualizes our children at the earliest possible age. The public schools have joined in the madness. Even our military has become a laboratory for bizarre socio-sexual experimentation. Our Judeo-Christian values are regularly denounced as racist or ignored as irrelevant. Churches and pastors have been shut out or opted out of political discourse. Most of our news and information comes from people who see the world very differently from most of middle America—90 percent of reporters are liberal secularists, if not declared atheists. This is a far cry from our Founding Fathers' vision for America.

Our Founders believed in God, and most of them were Christians. John Adams said, "Our Constitution was made only for a moral and religious People. It is wholly inadequate to the government of any other."[1]

Slavery was a glaring contradiction to the principles upon which our nation was founded, but most of the Founders knew it. They held fast to the belief that all human beings are created equal and worthy of human dignity in spite of the incongruity of slavery.

The majestic words of the Declaration would serve as the conscience of our country and the death sentence of slavery. It was the vision of our Founders that everyone in America would have life, liberty, and the opportunity to pursue happiness. However, they also understood it would be up to each individual to seize that opportunity. Prosperity would not be given or guaranteed, but earned, often with great struggle and sacrifice.

The idea that your future does not depend upon your class, color, or national origin is unique to the United States. There are literally millions of Horatio Alger success stories, and I am only one of them.

In this nation, people often start out in crushing poverty and go on to achieve affluence. Many become staggeringly wealthy. Aside from the criminal class, success in America has come because people—individuals and families—have been willing to work hard, take risks, invest, innovate, and provide value to others.

One of the great tragedies of the American experience is the lack of progress among descendants of former African slaves—Americans of African descent. This is not due to any lack of intelligence, talent, or giftedness. The existence of inner-city pockets of persistent poverty, violence, and drug addiction is the result of a terrible lie. It is a deception directly from *The Communist Manifesto* and Saul Alinsky's organizing blueprint, *Rules for Radicals*. Sadly, it has been embraced by much of the self-appointed leadership of the black community. They are buying into the lie that individual achievement is not possible or does not matter, and prosperity can only be acquired through collective effort. Individual achievement is meaningless in their view because it leaves behind "the masses." This lie is captured in the phrase I've heard used from Leftist politicians recently— "the myth of merit." It was set forth by former President Barack Obama in his infamous statement, "you didn't build that."

The idea is our society is so inherently unjust and racist that those who reap the benefits do so only as beneficiaries of the injustices perpetrated against others. By this thinking, it is only a myth that you have achieved or earned anything by individual effort. You have succeeded only by exploiting others or as a result of "white privilege." This is the American racial version of Marxist class warfare. It originated with European social and economic theorists like Marx and Engels and has spread like a cancer throughout the world. In spite of all America has accomplished and the high standard of living Americans enjoy, this communist/socialist thinking has infected our country as well and is spreading fast under a variety of guises. Marxist influence is behind the seemingly innocent ideas taking root in youth sports: Everyone should receive the same trophy, no score should be kept, and competition should be eliminated so no one feels bad about losing. This masquerades as sensitivity, but the real motivation is to attack and undermine the ethic of competition so fundamental to free enterprise.

One would think the Americans most likely to resist Marxist ideas would be black citizens. But self-appointed black leaders, propped up by the liberal media, are leading black people into a system of slavery with a worse track record than the Atlantic slave trade of the seventeenth and eighteenth centuries. Marxism is inherently dangerous because the individual has no value. The commitment to a collectivist utopia means it is moral to eliminate those who get in the way of this dream, even by mass murder. Slavery was brutal and horrific, but one of the most important restraining influences built into American slavery was the market value of each slave.

It was counter to the economic interests of slave traders and slave masters for slaves to be killed. Communism has no such restraint.

After slavery ended, the black community was entrepreneurial and independent because it had to be. Then the Great Society programs came along in the '60s, breaking down the black family. The American black community became plagued with out-of-wedlock pregnancies, abortion, and black-on-black crime. Most of my adult life I have worked with black youth from poor backgrounds. They need a message of hope, opportunity, and faith—in God and themselves. Instead, they are being told the insurmountable nature of "systemic racism" and the absence of "social justice" make it impossible for them to prosper and grow. They are discouraged from aspiring to great things because "they won't let you."

Riots are justified even when they destroy businesses and property owned by black Americans. The murder epidemic in our cities is generally ignored by media and politicians because black-on-black crime doesn't fit the preferred paradigm of racial injustice and oppression.

Black Americans must wake up to the fact that liberals and the Democrat Party are keeping them in a state of dependence and subsistence. Black Christians in particular are being manipulated out of the biblical thinking that should guide them. They are indoctrinated to believe racism, not God, determines their destiny. It is the Democrat Party, not God, which will supposedly save them from the racists who want to put them back into slavery.

Fear is used to manipulate them to ignore the liberal genocide against black babies through abortion mills strategically placed in or near black neighborhoods. In spite of the desperate need to rebuild the black family, Democrat liberals instead promote homosexuality as the equivalent of being black. They liken the history of black Americans' struggle for civil rights with the radical LGBTQ sexual agenda.

Today's Democrat Party is virulently secularist and wants nothing to do with God. For example, Rep. Bobby Scott of Virginia campaigns in black churches while opposing America's national motto "In God we trust" as offensive. He actually led the effort to prevent putting that motto on the wall of the Congressional Visitors Center.

The moral values of the black church community are in stark contrast to the values of the Democrat Party. Yet in election after election, blacks vote for Godless liberals in overwhelming numbers. It is psychological and spiritual bondage, and the time has come for the black community to be free.

It is not the history of slavery or Jim Crow perpetuating a large underclass of poverty in the black community. It is bondage to the Democrat Party. Trillions of dollars have been spent purportedly to end poverty, but in fact those government programs function to maintain poverty and the myth of collective deliverance.

However, upward mobility is based on individual effort. Family often works together, but each individual must be a responsible contributor or be left behind. There is no government program capable of lifting any individual or group out of poverty. The "War on Poverty" only serves to undermine the only true antidote to poverty—individual determination to achieve a better life.

The federal government's continued efforts to end poverty are nothing more than what Thomas Jefferson called, "taking from labor the bread it has earned." Today, it is called wealth redistribution. An ethnic group rises only as individuals in that group rise. When the mass of individuals makes the personal decision to better themselves, the whole group becomes more prosperous. The best the group can do is establish and reinforce positive cultural norms which lead to productivity and reject those which are self-destructive.

In America, there is no such thing as a caste system relegating certain people to low income or subservient status in life. Yet the Left sells this propaganda to justify their failure to deliver. Racism is blamed not only for the Left's inability to end the wealth gap, but for every black individual's failure and grievance—whether rich or poor. If you are looking for someone else to blame for your condition in life, the Left is happy to oblige by pointing their finger at "white people." This is pure demagoguery used to keep Democrats and Leftists in power.

If Americans ever return to their historic values, it will mean the end of the Democrat Party in its present incarnation. It will either have to become a very different party or cease to exist. The Republican Party would likewise be forced to live up to its creed and platform or suffer the same fate.

In a free market society, there will always be inequality of results. Those with the determination to pursue their dreams will always have more than those who do nothing. The Founding Fathers understood this. They never dreamed of equality of results, only equality of opportunity.

One of my daughters, as a young professional, became disenchanted with a position she held for five years. She started looking for a new job, and within a month had two offers paying more money than the job she was leaving. She is well educated, has marketable skills, and a strong work ethic. Finding a new job required effort, of course, but she is able to add significant value to a company because her skills are needed.

When my son was disenchanted with his level of income in law enforcement, he set out to retrain himself to be a computer systems engineer. He achieved his goal and is being financially rewarded for his initiative. Once he decided to take action to improve his circumstances, nothing stood in his way—including the boogeyman of "systemic racism." The Left believes where there are wage disparities, the government can and should fix them. Because inequality of results abounds, ever more government, higher and higher taxes, and more intrusive regulations are necessary to correct these disparities. In other words, the way to utopia is maximum government control. It may be appealing to call it "social justice," but it is actually the slithering evil of totalitarianism. This is a very slippery slope, and unless we get off it, we will slide into the abyss of pure statism. Instead of a shining city on a hill, we will become a dispirited, impoverished once-great nation, a rotting corpse on the dung heap of history.

Patriots do not pretend America is a perfect country. We have at times been on the wrong side of history, but we have never stayed there. I can say without reservation or apology we live in the greatest nation the world has ever known, not merely because of our economic and military might but because America has provided more freedom and opportunity to fulfill one's God-given potential than any nation in history. Our country has done more to defend the dignity and worth of the individual than any nation that ever existed. Yes, evil happens in America, but we are not an evil nation. More goodness emanates from the United States than from any other nation on earth.

We have done more worldwide to confront AIDS, poverty, hunger, and genocide than all other nations of the earth combined. And that ethic of goodness and giving is not only something we do as a nation; Americans are the most charitable people in the world. Personal generosity outstrips all other nations combined. Sharing, and self-sacrifice are in our spiritual and intellectual DNA because of our Judeo-Christian heritage and culture.

Consider the selfless and heroic acts by Americans. When the passengers of United flight 93 were confronted with terrorists who wanted to use that airplane as a missile against the Capitol, they decided to give their lives to stop those terrorists from carrying out their plans. They would die on their own terms as Americans.

Mike Monsoor and his unit of Navy Seals were assigned to combat in Ramadi, Iraq. While he was in a sniper position, a grenade suddenly landed on his chest and rolled off. Instead of jumping away from the grenade to save himself, he jumped on the grenade to save his fellow Seals. He was near an exit and had the best opportunity to escape, but he chose to give up his life and save the lives of his fellow warriors. His comrades in arms all lived.

America exalts firefighters and law enforcement officers who run toward danger while others run away, just as they did in New York on 9/11.

America responded first when Haiti was hit with a massive earthquake.

America responds any time there is a disaster in any part of the world.

This is the America we know and love.

A nation offering so much to so many does not owe the world an apology.

Liberals look at us as a balkanized nation. They see nameless, faceless special interest groups with our hands out. That is not who we are. We are a nation of individuals and families. Most individuals are good and decent people who evaluate others by the content of their character, not the color of their skin. We are Americans not because of our appearance, national origin, or religious affiliation, but because of our shared national character and destiny.

While I am saddened and angered by some of what is happening in our beloved land, it is my hope this book will encourage a resurgence of American patriotism. We need to restore our national pride. I am an American, descended from slaves, and I have an intense love for my country. It is my intent to persuade every American—regardless their ethnic background, black or white, rich or poor, Republican, Democrat, or Independent—that we have much for which to be grateful. Every American should be a patriot. We must let go of the anger and bitterness based on the past, and work together to build an even brighter future for our country.

America is a gift God has given us and the world. We must all be willing to stand for it and fight for it. America must remain the country God ordained, our Founding Fathers intended, and our Constitution mandates.

Our country is deeply divided, and many of our citizens are confused. We must appeal to the conscience of our nation to return to the values that made America great. Only by reaffirming our historic values will we save our beloved republic. Sincere and patriotic Democrats, Republicans, Independents, and Libertarians should be able to unite around these foundational principles. Those who want a fundamentally different America—be they presidents or protesters—need to find another country.

Those principles and ideals are self-evident truths, and they are why this country has grown and prospered for more than 245 years.

Facts change, and circumstances change, but truth never changes. Truth comes from nature's God and His Word. The Founders called it natural law, a higher order than the subjective whims of human beings.

As fundamental truth is rejected, our Constitution and our culture are being eroded. The Obama Administration was accused by some in President Obama's own party of violating the Constitution in attacking Libya without congressional consent. The administration sought the approval of the UN, not Congress.

The healthcare legislation known as Obamacare was rammed down the throats of the American people, for our own good of course. The administration sought the approval of the Democrat Party in a party-line vote, but not the American people. As a result, the legislation was never popular with the majority.

Our Founding Fathers understood absolute power in the hands of one human being or institution is despotism. They experienced it and wanted to make sure we never would. Beware when the government does things against our will because it is for our own good. It's usually for the good of those in power.

Over the last decade, by the end of the Obama administration the size of the federal government grew by 25 percent, adding 200,000 people to the federal payroll at an average salary of $120,000 per year—twice the average in the private sector. There are already more people working in government than in manufacturing. Is this our future? It is time to say, "enough!" It is time to draw a line in the sand and push government back into its proper constitutional role. It is time to say, "You have gone too far, and we will not allow you to go another step further in this very dangerous direction." President Donald Trump shared this sentiment, and he rolled back regulations at an unprecedented rate. That's one reason the economy boomed under Mr. Trump's leadership.

So, while I am angry and saddened, I am also full of hope. The United States of America is not an accident of history. We are a providential nation. We were founded on godly principles that have withstood the test of time. We are free, and by the grace of God and an engaged citizenry, we will remain free.

Our country is in throes of a mighty conflict between good and evil, freedom versus tyranny, and individualism versus totalitarianism. Freedom must be preserved at all costs.

I say that as a patriot descended from slaves. My heritage is the bitterness of ancestral bondage and the blessing of unparalleled freedom. I will never forget where my ancestors came from or what they endured. The sacrifice of their suffering paved the way for my liberty. Neither they nor the Founding Fathers could have dreamed of the freedom and opportunity that would inure to their descendants. Had they gotten a glimpse of the future, it surely would have made their toil more bearable and their hope more tangible.

There are many places where I might have been born—Africa, the Caribbean, South America, or even Europe. But I was born an American. Therefore, I am an heir to the spiritual and intellectual giants who birthed and shaped this nation: George Washington, Thomas Jefferson, James Madison, Patrick Henry, Frederick Douglass, Abraham Lincoln, Booker T. Washington, George Washington Carver, and Martin Luther King Jr. That is only a sample of the Americans who paved the way for us.

I trust this book will sound the clarion call for us to come together around that shared legacy and vision of a sweet land of liberty— "one nation, under God, indivisible, with liberty and justice for all."

PART I

MY HISTORY: A PATRIOT DESCENDED FROM SLAVES

My history is part of the American story. There is no history, personal or national, that does not include some sin, failure, and ugliness. Yet in the life of every person and every nation there is beauty, goodness, and success. We need only choose to see it. It is my conviction, that America is the unique and exceptional nation because we have done more to advance good over evil than any nation in history. That is part of my motivation for writing this book.

I am an American descended from slaves, and I have a deep love and respect for my country. What is it about this nation that would make someone whose ancestors were brought here in chains cherish it? I hope this book will help my fellow Americans better understand and cherish our country, especially those of African descent whose ancestors were slaves.

CHAPTER 1

AMERICAN HISTORY IN CONTEXT

O ne of the harshest criticisms levied against the USA is our history of slavery. For those on the Left, it is irrefutable proof that America is a fundamentally unjust country, a racist nation. They call slavery America's "original sin." That is a terrible analogy revealing the prejudice of its proponents. Adam and Eve committed original sin because they were created in perfection. They rebelled and fell from their perfect state.

America was not born in perfection, but in the sinful context of the time. The Portuguese were trading in African slaves nearly 200 years before the Jamestown settlement and the Pilgrims' landing at Plymouth Rock. They began transporting slaves across the Atlantic in the 1460s. By the time America declared independence, that "peculiar institution" was not peculiar at all. America didn't invent slavery. Neither did the Portuguese or any other Europeans. Slavery has been practiced by every racial group on every continent. It is intrinsic to human history.

The practice goes back thousands of years. One of the opening epics of the Bible is the liberation of the Jews from Egyptian slavery. Muslims were enslaving Africans and Europeans long before the European slave trade was conceived. Arab Muslims have been enslaving sub-Saharan Africans for generations and continue to do so.

However, they did not invent slavery. It has been a sickness of fallen humanity for all of human history. The American experience must be seen in the context of this reality. By the time the Founding Fathers were born, the Atlantic slave trade had been in existence for 250 years. It was started by Arab Muslims who brought sub-Saharan Africans to the Iberian Peninsula in the early 1500's. Before the dangerous middle passage across the Atlantic, Africans endured the even more deadly trek across the Sahara desert driven by African slave traders.

This in no way diminishes the evil of owning and selling human beings. It merely allows us to see it as part of the panorama of human history and development. On this continent, a miracle occurred on July 4, 1776. My slave ancestors, who came in terrible circumstances, would bequeath to their heirs the benefits of that miracle.

The biblical story of Joseph illustrates this point perfectly. He was sold into slavery by his own brothers. When they were forced to confront what they did, Joseph forgave them, saying, "you meant evil against me; but God meant it for good" (Genesis 50:20). I feel the same way about America's intersection with slavery. There were those who meant it for evil, but the Supreme Planner meant it for my good. I am not obsessed and have absolutely no resentment over how my ancestors got here. I am instead very glad they got here. My destiny is here. I am an American.

My great-grandfather Gabriel Jackson and my great-grandmother Eliza Jackson were slaves in Orange County, Virginia. They are listed in the 1880 census. When the war ended and slaves were set free, they became sharecroppers and he later, a laborer.

My genealogy shows that my ancestry in this country goes back to at least 1798, the year my great- grandfather was born. That is one year before George Washington died. America's international slave trade officially ended in the late 1700s. That means my great-grandfather was born in America, probably in Virginia. My ancestors were likely here during the Revolutionary War.

I am not ashamed of my African ancestry, but after at least two centuries of history in this country, it is indisputably true I am an American. I am an American by destiny, but I remain an American by choice. I have the freedom to leave, renounce my citizenship, and find another country to call home. That will never happen because I am proud of my country and grateful to be an American.

Those who feel differently should leave. Those who seek a socialist "paradise" should find their fortunes elsewhere. We who believe in our country and its fundamental values should defend our heritage, with our lives if necessary. If forced to do so, we will fight for those principles. It has been fifty years since I took an oath to the Constitution as a United States Marine. I am as committed to that oath now as I was the day I took it, perhaps more-so because of the great internal threat to our freedom and way of life.

Whether our ancestors came as indentured servants, slaves, refugees seeking religious liberty, or starving escapees of war and famine, we Americans are a strong, pioneering people. I am in awe at the strength of my ancestors, who survived the brutal middle passage, endured slavery for generations, and then carved out a life for themselves in harsh social and economic conditions.

Every group emigrating to America in the seventeenth and eighteenth centuries faced extreme hardship. Popular history has focused almost exclusively on the struggles of native Americans and African slaves. Their circumstances were no doubt brutal. However, we cannot understand America if we don't also acknowledge that most of our forefathers and mothers no matter their ancestral home, carved a life through a wild, lawless wilderness and suffered hardship, starvation, sickness and even violent deaths.

Of course, there was racism. But it was not limited to white against black. There was ethnic hatred between Americans who came from Europe. The WASPs hated the Irish. The Irish hated the Italians. They all hated the Chinese and Japanese, and these fellow Asians hated each other. The Jews, like blacks, were generally disliked. On it went with each group looking down on the other for whatever reasons they could conjure.

Our schools and colleges should be teaching the truth about how our ancestors were no different from any other group of human beings—full of frailty and sin. They often exploited each other for personal or group advantage. Under the right circumstances, they could all be ruthless.

However, they were also building a country like no other. They were not inherently better people, but they founded our nation on better principles than any that had ever existed. In that context, despite our fallen humanity, the better angels of Americans always ultimately prevailed.

We established the inherent worth and value of life, regardless race or creed. We established the inherent equality of men and women. We recognized wealth should not compromise the principle of equal treatment under the law. Are we perfect? No, but we continue to work at it. The Left has perverted the American thirst for equality and justice into an irrational cult-like, regressive, and anti-freedom hysteria. Nonetheless, most Americans are committed to our highest ideals, and they support a reasonable approach to equal justice and equality of opportunity.

We have come far since the days of our founding. When I read our history, a history most Americans unfortunately aren't taught, it is clear from the very beginning, slavery was a hotly contested issue. Early Americans knew slavery was doomed. Jefferson warned it could precipitate a national crisis, pitting brother against brother. The moral core of the nation could not be reconciled with the purchase and enslavement of human beings. Sooner or later, justice would prevail.

The Founding Fathers struggled with it. John Adams would have nothing to do with it. Washington freed all his slaves on his deathbed. Slavery had to end, not because of external forces, but because the conscience and internal values of the country could never rest peaceably in the cradle of slavery. Slaves were as inspired as other Americans by Jefferson's immortal words: *"We hold these truths to be self-evident, that all men are created equal . . ."* The mere whiff of freedom emboldened many slaves to escape. Jefferson lost slaves—runaways from his plantation—as a result of the Declaration.

This should be of particular note to Americans of African and slave heritage. Jefferson was an extremely intelligent man. He understood the implication of his words. Unfortunately, most black Americans do not understand the tension and division slavery created. Far from being an institution enjoying the support of most

Americans, it was the most divisive issue on the continent since the day the first African servants arrived.

The narrative Americans have been mistaught is Europeans came under idyllic circumstances and had the red carpet rolled out for them, while Africans came on slave ships and immediately faced a lifetime of slavery. Many Europeans came under horrendous circumstances and died during the voyage. Many Africans came as indentured servants and earned their freedom. It is true the law eventually declared Africans to be slaves for life, a status passed on to the children of slave mothers.

What we are not told is making slavery a racial classification was part of the strategy of dissuading the average white servant from unifying with black servants. In fact, this happened during Bacon's Rebellion, where white and black servants and small landowners fought together against mistreatment by large landowners. When the rebellion was finally put down, the elites never wanted anything so frightening to happen again. To prevent a repeat, slave codes were implemented. These codes demonstrate there was no consensus among average colonists that slavery was the justifiable status of black people. It had to be given the force of law, which was meant to enculturate blacks and whites to believe black subservience was the natural order of things.

Those who traffic in racial politics sell a narrative intended to addict black Americans to anger and bitterness and white Americans to guilt and obligation. They want all Americans to see our country as a terrible place—unfair, unjust, and racist. I see America as a nation struggling to transcend the context of the times in which she was founded. That struggle caused division from the moment the first slaves arrived. It continued up to a Civil War costing 625,000 lives. Wrestling with our most painful social issue helped paved the way toward justice for all Americans, not based on skin color. It is time to recognize that although our ancestors may have come on different ships, we are all in the same boat now. We are two and a half centuries into the journey. Some of us want to repair and strengthen this seaworthy ship of state; others want to punch holes in it until it sinks.

CHAPTER 2

A BROKEN HOME

My mother's and father's marriage was over by the time my umbilical cord was cut. My father got control over baby Jackson by default because my mother's life was chaotic.

For the first fourteen months of my existence, I was bounced around to be cared for by my father's network of friends who provided "foster care."

It was he who arranged my permanent placement with Rebecca and Willie Molet. I know they were friends, but I'm not sure how close. Oddly, I never heard my father call my foster mother by her first name. He called her "Miss Beck." Willie was simply "Willie." There was no indication they socialized except for my dad visiting for dinner occasionally. My guess is they were friendly acquaintances. My father liked and trusted them and somehow learned Rebecca wanted children but could have none of her own. She fostered other children after I was in the home, but they never stayed long. I was the only "permanent" child.

I do not know how the transaction happened or what the legalities were, if any. When, at the age of ten years old, my father removed me from their custody rather abruptly, I was present for the conversation. Rebecca implied there were legal requirements to be met. My father took the position I was his son and that was it.

There was nothing more to be said. I do not believe he faced any legal ramifications, but if he did, he kept it from me. His decision prevailed.

I was a toddler when I went to live at 226 Pennell Street in Chester, Pennsylvania. Rebecca Molet became "Mom." She was the only mother I knew.

In my early years, I saw my mother seldom and never in a planned visit. However, at the age of fourteen, something happened, and I was permitted to spend the night in her home once a week on Friday nights. I was about 17 years when I called her Mom for the first time. Until then, I called her "Virginia" because I did not relate to her as my mother. When I did see her, it was like talking to a distant relative. You know the person is related, but it seems more technical than real.

At theme she is ninety-one years old. I visit her when I can, but I often found myself jealous of the men who had a wonderful and affectionate relationship with their mothers. I never had that, and it bothered me more than I realized. In fact, it bothered me enough to that by the age of forty I felt it was absolutely imperative that I talk to her about my childhood and our relationship or the lack thereof.

She was living in Tennessee at the time, and I made a special trip to see her. In a conversation that went on for much of the night, she explained to me about her upbringing by her grandparents being cold and distant, without physical affection. She inherited their relational model. She never knew her own father.

That explained a lot. I never witnessed the tender moments you might expect to see in mother-child interactions with my siblings whom she raised—Ted and Faith.

I always loved her, and wanted to be close to her, but it never happened. To my father's credit, he never poisoned my attitude toward her although he had more than his fair share of resentment. I had no anger or hostility toward her I can ever remember, but she played no important role in my childhood.

I remember seeing her standing in front of a liquor store with the Watchtower magazine of the Jehovah's Witnesses, selling her "literature" for a nickel or a dime—whatever the price was in those days. There was never any tearful reunion or expression of joy at seeing each other. She was just there, and I knew she was my mother. Although we must have spoken, I do not remember her leaving her post to acknowledge me. As I grew older, I realized it affected me, but at the time, I accepted it as normal.

This is in stark contrast to my childhood memories of seeing my father. He was a figure of towering importance in my life for as long as I do not remember her. Growing up in the home of the Molets, I saw my father only when he visited. I'm not sure how often this was, but it was not often enough for me. Sometimes it is difficult to distinguish real memories from things we are told about our earliest years. Nonetheless, I do have a recollection of my father's visits. I especially recall hysterically crying when the time came for him to leave. In those early years they would give me something to distract or occupy me when it was time for him to go. But eventually, I would look for him and, realizing he was gone, I cried uncontrollably. On the other hand, my father was my best friend as a child and remained my best friend until he left this earth in June 2002.

Even my adult relationship with my mother has been complicated. She and I have had some animated discussions. I am always respectful, but I do not hesitate to make clear my disapproval of Jehovah's Witnesses as a pseudo-Christian cult. It has ruined the lives of many and cost the lives of innocent children denied blood transfusions because they irrationally considered the unforgivable sin. That may have changed now, but that was one among their many strange beliefs. I believe she would have been a better mother to all of her children had she not joined that cult, but she is still my mother and I love her and pray for her.

This is the group that predicted the end of the world nine times on specific dates and had their adherents give up their livelihoods and educations because the world was about to end. The world didn't end. These claimed "followers of Jesus" forgot Jesus said no one would know the day or the hour of His return.

When you have lived in deep deception for so long, breaking out can precipitate a psychological crisis. Yet people do come out, for with God, all things are possible.

To his everlasting credit, my father absolutely forbade my mother to expose me to Jehovah's Witnesses. He knew the Watchtower Society for what it was and guarded me against it. That became important as I got older and eventually had more frequent contact with my mother. I'll explain that later.

CHAPTER 3

MY YEARS IN
FOSTER CARE

My foster parents—Rebecca and Willie Molet—were poor, illiterate people. She was born in Farmville, Virginia and raised in South Carolina. He was from Alabama. Willie could not read. He made an X in place of his signature. Rebecca could write her name and read a little. That was the educational atmosphere in which I grew up.

When I was a child, Willie seemed a gigantic man, an intimidating figure. His skin was black as coal, and his hands thick from the sand blasting work he did at Sun Ship Building and Dry Dock Company. His eyes were always red, but he never drank—not a drop. I remember seeing wine in the house, but none ever crossed his lips.

As a sandblaster, he blasted silicon onto the hulls of ships to get rid of excess metal. In Willie's Day, they actually used sand for the job, but medical science discovered it causes lung disease. Now they use other materials. He had a deep voice and spoke in the broken English of an uneducated Southern black man. "Going" was pronounced "gwine." Children was pronounced "childrings." The instruction to get ready to go on an errand sounded like this, "Git own up from 'dare boy. W'gwine to da stow." That's how Willie and Miss Beck said, "Get up. We're going to the store."

23

To my embarrassment, I must also admit I had more than a few laughs at their expense. Their pronunciations could be quite hilarious. I was never mean-spirited or ridiculing, but at times I could not help but laugh at what I heard come out of their mouths, particularly Willie. His limited vocabulary compelled him to make up words. He did not merely mispronounce actual words. He made up his own—completely self-generated. At times, I would laugh until I hurt from his verbal gymnastics.

Of course, as a youngster, I was learning my speech from them. My father told me my word for "crying" was "cry-nin." That was how Willie and Miss Beck pronounced it, and that was how I learned to pronounce it. As in many things, my first lessons in proper grammar also came from my dad.

When I was growing up in their home, the Molets' illiteracy seemed normal. It was not until after I went to live with my father that I realized they were illiterate. My father had only a sixth-grade education, but he was well read, highly intelligent with good grammar and a good vocabulary. He later earned his GED—High School Equivalency Certificate. I often wondered what he would have made of himself if he had the opportunities I enjoyed.

I never thought of Willie as a father, and never felt love for him. I respected him as an authority figure, but I had little interaction with him. He worked the second shift, which meant he left home about 3 p.m. and returned about midnight. During the school years when I lived there, I only saw him on weekends. It was "my Momma"—Rebecca Molet—who captured my heart. She was loving, kind, spoiled me rotten, and I would have done almost anything for her, except of course obey her rules. I never openly disrespected her, and I always paid lip service—"yes ma'am, no ma'am." Once I hit the age of about eight, I obeyed her only if it was something I wanted to do. My demeanor was one of compliance, but my behavior was absolute rebellion.

She tried to discipline me, but once I developed enough size, strength, and speed, she could not catch me. I was not willing to take my punishment for what I did wrong. I would run, hide, and sometimes spend the night at a friend's house leaving everybody worried. Of course, I lied to friends' parents and said I had permission. I was always found out, but I negotiated my way out of punishment. I only returned with the promise of amnesty—no consequences. It was not the right lesson for a rebellious young boy.

That had to be frustrating for the Molets, and it may have led to the only instance of physical abuse I ever experienced as a child. It was in the middle of the day one summer. Willie was sleeping as he usually did before getting ready for work. For some reason on this particular day, I was told not to leave the front of the house. I don't recall why except I'm certain I was being restricted for some infraction. Most of the time, I was free to roam not only around the neighborhood but around the city. It was a different era.

On this occasion, a friend of mine and I decided we were going to go to a corner store two blocks away. I figured we could go and get back before Willie woke up. He would be none the wiser. It was no big deal in my mind, even though I was clearly forbidden to do it. We made our quick trip, got what we wanted, and came back. It couldn't have taken more than fifteen to twenty minutes.

Shortly after returning I walked into the house to find Willie was up. I thought nothing of it because I figured he would not know I went to the store.

I encountered him in the little dining room. Even had I known what was coming, there was no room to maneuver or run. Willie confronted me in the narrow space between the dining table and the wall. He said to me, "Boy, didn't I tell you not to leave the front of this house?" Before I could respond, I saw a flash of light. When I realized what happened I was on the floor. I must have been knocked out for a few seconds. When I came to, my eye was swollen. Willie hit me with one of those gigantic sand blaster hands. It was only one blow because I could easily have been killed had he pummeled me. That one smack was enough to send me into the twilight zone.

It was over in a split second. Willie then dressed and went to work without saying another word. I didn't cry, and there wasn't much pain as I recall, but my eye looked terrible. After Willie went to work, I went outside again, swollen eye and all. My friends reacted with shock. I don't know whether they assumed Willie hit me, but they knew something happened while I was in the house.

When they asked, I told them without hesitation. I wore it as a badge of honor.

There was no social service department to investigate child abuse. My only recourse was to tell my father when I saw him. By the time I told my dad, it looked much better. He listened and seemed concerned. I was there when Willie lied and told him I fell into a tricycle while running through the house. That let me know he was either afraid of my father or of the consequences for what he did.

I think my father believed me, but there weren't many options. Should I have been placed in another foster home? I certainly wouldn't have wanted that. I was eight or nine years old at that point, and at least I knew Momma was going to look out for me. That was the first and only time Willie ever laid hands on me. From that point on, he would have had to catch me asleep. My father later told me the incident only confirmed that he needed to have me come live with him.

What Willie did was wrong. He could have hurt me much worse or even killed me accidentally. He was a big, strong man. However, I never held it against him. He was frustrated by a kid who would not obey. He finally got one good lick in, but he never tried another one. The incident did not deter me one bit. I continued the same pattern of delinquent behavior.

My foster mother Rebecca was a domestic for an Italian family who owned a florist shop a few blocks from where we lived. Momma was an attractive woman with a brown complexion. Although she spoke in the dialect of the Deep South, she tried to put a genteel patina over her broken English. She could read and write a little and sign her name. At church she actually knew the words of the hymns. Willie just mumbled. As a child, I could not understand why he had not learned the hymns after hearing them over and over again. I must admit that even today it makes me laugh. After years listening to the same hymns again and again, he seemed not to know a single verse of the simplest song. Music tends to adhere to the memory. My memory is still vivid of him standing in church, hands clasped in front him as the music played, mumbling through every lyric and butchering every melody. So much for the stereotype that all black people can sing and have rhythm. He's not the only black person

I've known who couldn't hold a tune or keep rhythm if their lives depended it on. Perhaps I should not have laughed at Willie's musical disability, but it made me howl. God is forgiving.

That aside, Willie and Rebecca were Christian people who took me to church every Sunday and often during the week as well. They owned a small, two-bedroom shot gun house. If you opened the front and back doors, you could literally aim a shotgun and shoot straight through front door, the back door and into the little backyard.

Two bedrooms were at the top of the stairs. There was no indoor bathroom. We used a "slop bucket." For those who never experienced country living before flush toilets and septic tanks, a slop bucket was the "bathroom," so you didn't have to walk to the outhouse in the middle of the night. It was white with a red stripe around the rim and a matching top. It needed a lid for obvious reasons. There was also a handle. As I grew older, I was charged with dumping it every morning into the outhouse, which sat in the middle of a 500-foot-backyard where Willie raised chickens. It wasn't far to the outhouse, but it felt like miles. The Molets were very much country folks living in an urban community. The little house is still standing at 226 Pennell Street at this writing but boarded up. I expected it to be torn down by now. Sooner or later, it will be, or it will fall down on its own from age and decay.

The small house had square rooms and low ceilings. That proved to be a saving grace in one instance that could otherwise have resulted in my severe injury. Like many children in the late '50s and early '60s, I was enthralled with Superman. I was sure that if he could fly, so could I. At about six years old, I had a tenuous ability to distinguish between fact and fiction. I was convinced if I jumped from the right height with the right cape, I would fly. So, with a couple of friends in the house, while Willie was asleep, I donned something that served as my cape. I ascended the stairs with certainty that history was about to be made. My plan was to fly to the store and reward myself with some candy to celebrate my first flight. I had not thought about what my next career move would be.

At the top of the stairs, I yelled "SUPERMAN!" and leaped. The top step was not very high, but high enough that I landed so hard my knees hit my chin.

Thank God I did not reside in a big house with a high second floor. I might not have lived to tell this story. Maybe my six-year-old mind reasoned those steps were just high enough to prove my theory without hurting or killing me. More likely it was God's mercy protecting me from an overactive imagination. Rest assured; I never reasoned my flight failed because the jump wasn't high enough. I was forced to face the disappointing realization I could not fly. To this day, I still occasionally dream I can, but airplanes will do quite well. I still love a good Superman movie, though.

When I ran for lieutenant governor of Virginia, the *Washington Post* sent a reporter to Chester with the mission of proving the house I grew up in as a foster child was a "middle class" home with an indoor bathroom. They questioned my background because they did not like my politics. The whole process caught me off guard, and I will talk about that experience in some detail later. I expected the press to examine my policy approaches. Instead, they went after my character. Undermining my life story was one way to do that. They found a foster child who lived there years after I was gone who claimed they had an indoor bathroom. That may be true. What I know is that while I lived there, I picked up the slop bucket most mornings, transported it outside, and poured the contents in the outhouse.

Only an idiot would make up a slop bucket story to "embellish" a resume. The mainstream media lie so much in furtherance of their Leftist agenda they probably think everybody lies like they do. My motive for telling some of the humbling facts of my life is not to make myself look great, but to show the greatness of our country. No matter who you are or where you come from, you can succeed in our nation. It's not just the story of E. W. Jackson. It's the story of Americans.

Unfortunately, many reporters are such determined Leftists that they want to destroy public figures who have a conservative perspective. While writing this book, I witnessed the campaign to eviscerate Brett Kavanaugh during his nomination and confirmation to the Supreme Court. I understood exactly what he was going through. The Left cannot win arguments based on facts because the facts are not on their side. They cannot demolish conservative arguments because the truth has a power of its own. They instead seek to destroy the messenger.

The Left has a particular antipathy for black conservatives because we are seen as traitors to their liberal cause. Indeed, they practically demand black Americans and other minorities be Leftists, and unwillingness to do so can mean loss of livelihood, reputation, and even worse. Dinesh D'Souza went to prison for what normally would have meant a fine or a regulatory slap on the hand. He's a naturalized citizen from India, or in politically correct nomenclature—a "person of color"—who dared to make films exposing the unflattering truth about Barack Obama and Hillary Clinton. He was a convicted felon until receiving a full pardon from President Trump.

Totalitarian regimes distort truth and revise history to further their own ends. Thank God we do not live under such a government, but our culture is becoming increasingly totalitarian. While the press still expresses irrational hysteria about former President Trump, many Americans believe it is the mainstream media that pose an existential threat to our constitutional republic. They tried to overthrow the expressed will of the American people and topple a duly elected president, and then worked feverishly against his re-election. Every day, they abuse their constitutional privileges and protections to serve their far-left ideology. They are indeed, as Mr. Trump has labeled them, "enemies of the people." They are not purveyors of news and information—they are a propaganda organ of the Left and the Democrat Party. They have become so arrogant they no longer even pretend to objectivity. This must change if we are to remain a free, peaceful, and prosperous nation.

CHAPTER 4

MEDIA ATTACKS ON MY BIOGRAPHY

During my campaign for Virginia lieutenant governor, the *Washington Post* implied that since they couldn't prove I did not have an indoor bathroom in the foster home where I lived, it must be a made-up story. If that was a fabrication, they suggested, maybe everything about me was made up. Maybe I wasn't in the Marine Corps. Maybe I didn't graduate from Harvard Law School or attend Harvard Divinity School. Maybe I never served as a chaplain for the Boston Red Sox. Nevertheless, I did all those things, and every word of my biography is true.

One would think liberals would celebrate an accomplished black American. To the contrary, they hate outspoken black conservatives. As I have said many times and will probably repeat again and again in this book, liberals are like the nineteenth-century slave masters. They believe they have an inherent right to dictate how black people should think. They believe black people owe their very existence to liberals. You can see it in liberal, white Tom Arnold's reaction to Candace Owens. Candace is a young, black conservative who is prominent on social media and worked with Turning Point USA and now Prager University.

Here's Candace's tweet in response to a post in which Arnold criticized her:

When @PerezHilton @TomArnold and @ShaunKing, 3 white men, rush to viciously attack the freedom of two black people who refuse to be pawns to a leftist ideology—it should ring as a wakeup call to the world about who the real racists are. None of you white men own my blackness.[2]

This is how Arnold responded (please forgive the language, but I want you to feel the full force of the hatred this liberal expresses for independent black women):

That's a lot of extra words @RealCandaceO so you can suck racist d--- by trying to insult an actual hero @Shaun King hahahaha.[3]

Notice his response is not to disabuse her of the idea that he hates her. Far from it. He confirms that he harbors vile, contemptuous hatred.

There is no way to explain the angry liberal reaction to this beautiful young lady without reverting to the slave and slave master relationship imagined somewhere in the twisted mind of Arnold. His extreme anger suggests she struck a chord when she talked about these white liberals acting as if they "own" her blackness. In his mind, she dared to run off the plantation. She dared to think for herself, to question the slave system, and to assert her own equality and independence of thought. In the liberal mind, that is forbidden. The least hint of deviation from their prescribed pattern of thought and behavior deserves severe punishment. Instead of refuting accusations of his presumed right to dictate how black people think, Arnold doubled down and suggested he owned her sexually as well, which slave masters did 160 years ago. Candace was right about who the real racists are today. They are the direct intellectual descendants of the slave masters and supporters of slavery—the Democrat elites, whether in the North or the South.

The liberal attacks on Candace were so vicious that Kanye West, of all people, came to her defense, and has been on the warpath against liberal attempts to intimidate and silence black conservatives.

The most insidious and toxic form of racism in America today is practiced by white liberal elitists who believe they have the right to define what it means to be black. Like slave masters of the past, they want to severely punish black folks who do not adhere to their view of what a "good" black person is.

Liberal elites are so disconnected from the lives and experiences of most Americans they cannot believe successful black Americans have not been their beneficiaries. The *Washington Post* tried to pick apart my background because, in their minds, the success I've achieved is the result of their heroic effort on my behalf. It cannot be possible I could be instead the beneficiary of the greatness of America, which even in the '60s offered hope and opportunity to a foster child living in a home without indoor plumbing.

With no indoor toilet, bathtub, or shower, country folks had a tradition of bathing once a week on Saturday night to get ready for church on Sunday morning. That's not a black or white experience, but an American experience. I have told that story all over the country to nods and knowing laughter. We took those baths in a galvanized tub filled with water heated on the stove. In my foster home, as I suspect for others, it was completely impractical to fill that tub more than once for a bath. Imagine what that water looked like after three or four people bathed in the same tub. As the youngest, I was always the last person—third or fourth—to take the dip. Once I was old enough to be repulsed by the scum from other people's bodies, I could not do it. I learned instead to splash the water around with my hand pretending to take a bath. I was not about to get into that filthy water. I probably was a very fragrant kid as the weeks wore on. The *Washington Post* or any other media can say what they want, but that was my life as a child in foster care. I laugh about it now. My only resentment is against the liberals who are apparently so jaundiced that they felt the need to slander me as someone who would make up such stories. It reveals who they really are—hateful, destructive people.

CHAPTER 5

BISCUITS AND SYRUP

My foster parents were employed, but they had financial problems because at times there was no food in the house. On those occasions, my foster mother would bake biscuits and pour syrup on a plate. We would sop up the syrup with a couple of biscuits, and it was actually quite satisfying. Less filling, but still tasty were mayonnaise sandwiches. I thought mayonnaise sandwiches and biscuits and syrup was what everybody ate. I had no conception of how tight money was. I was too young to understand. I remember going to Madeline's Supermarket, which wasn't "super" at all. My foster parents had a running tab, and I remember being sent to pick up a few groceries. The owner, Miss Madeline, would say to me, "Tell your folks they need to come see me." I came to understand that meant they owed her money, and she wanted them to pay the bill.

As I grew older, I remember wondering why I didn't have the nice clothes and other things the kids on TV had. My socks and my pants often had holes in them. That started to make me dream of a better life, with nicer things. The sense of deprivation made me want more. I knew a better life was possible because I could see it all around me. At the time I had no idea how to go about getting it.

CHAPTER 6

CRISIS IN FOSTER CARE

I loved my foster mother and knew without a doubt she loved me. I cannot make the same declaration about her husband, Willie. As I approached adolescence, Willie seemed to resent my growing up. I changed too. My relationship with them became more problematic. I felt abandoned and unwanted by my parents and resented the authority of these people who had no right to govern me. I was an angry kid. All the wrong influences were in the neighborhood to turn me into a juvenile delinquent, and that is what I became.

On my street, I started a little gang called the Eagles, a.k.a. the Pennell Street Gang. Our job was to "protect" our street from other kids. That's how it starts. We made sure the guys from Lamokin Street—one block over—couldn't come onto Pennell without our permission. They had their own gang to protect themselves from us. We had many fights, but we stuck to fists. I remember bits and pieces of the last fight in which I tried to gouge out the eyes of my opponent. That fight was so vicious neither of us wanted any more of it, which resulted in an uneasy peace. By the time I was nine years old, that was my life on the mean streets of Chester, Pennsylvania. Thank God I was rescued from that dead end before we graduated to knives and guns.

We did not pose the threat to public safety that gangs are today in the inner city. There were no older gangs organized to enculturate us into drug dealing, violence and other crimes. Yet we were on the path. We engaged in petty theft, threw rocks at commuter trains as they went by, and treated school as a distraction from the "fun" of the streets. During warm seasons, we hung out in the streets of Chester instead of going to school.

In the early fall and late spring, we swam in dangerous Chester Creek. One of my friends who lived across the street from me drowned in that creek. I was not there when it happened, but I will never forget the stern lecture I got from my foster mother about how this could happen to me. I hadn't yet learned to swim anyway, but the incident persuaded me never to wade into that creek again. I was wild, but Putney Koger's death scared me.

By the age of nine I was acting out. My biological father wasn't around to control me, and my foster parents couldn't. As a result, I did whatever I wanted to do. What happens when a boy of nine or ten years old is unleashed to follow his impulses with little or no parental guidance and restraint? Nothing good. One time, I and a group of friends stole my foster father's car. It was an old DeSoto with the shift on the steering column. I knew nothing about driving a car except what I observed. Working a stick shift on the column was a complete mystery. I was just tall enough to see over the steering wheel. Still, I took Willie's keys and somehow managed to get the car started and drove it about two blocks before it stalled. We left it there and I pretended someone stole it. He probably knew I was the culprit, but I was never punished for it.

In hindsight, I think Rebecca mistook leniency for love. Willie on the other hand emotionally detached himself from me. I was no longer the cute baby, but the budding young man. He probably perceived that I viewed all attempts to correct me as illegitimate because after all, they weren't my real parents. I had reached the stage where there was little they could do to rein me. I didn't fear them, and I was old enough to run rather than face discipline

After my father took custody of me, it was a very different story. He did not tolerate disobedience, let alone disrespect or rebellion. I also learned early on he could outrun me, so running was not an option. In fact, he warned me that if I ever ran, it would be worse when he caught me. I never ran from my father.

It still amazes me how dramatically my life changed after going to live with my father. While in foster care, I was on a very dangerous road. I was a young adolescent in desperate need of discipline. I was committing petty crimes. We used to go into predominantly "white" middle income neighborhoods where the houses had nice front porches and manicured lawns. We would surveil the porch to spot unattended pocketbooks or other valuables. Then we would sneak quietly on to the porch, grab the booty, and sprint away. It was the early '60s when I engaged in these criminal shenanigans. Most people still left their front doors open, particularly in the neighborhoods we targeted. They were easy marks.

Another of our escapades was robbing milk trucks. A milk delivery company sat at the edge of Crozer Park in Chester. It was surrounded by a high fence, but the back of the property, where they kept the trucks, abutted the park. Milk men did a lot of business in coin, and the glove compartments were filled with quarters and other change. We would climb over the back fence, far from the front office. The doors on both sides of the trucks were open, and they were parked closely enough that you could jump from truck to truck. We leaped like cats through those open doors, filling our pockets with coins as we went. The last trucks were not far from the entrance gate of the property, and it was always open. There was a large garage door in the front of the building left raised in warm weather. A few workers typically sat outside. I can imagine their shock when four or five kids streamed out of a truck, bolting for the open gate.

We did this more than once, but with enough time between hits, they never seemed to expect us. We were always spotted but were out of the gate before they could catch us. We disappeared into the city. No one was ever caught. Thank God the statute of limitations has run out.

One of my partners in these crimes was Gregory Hanes. I was pretty fast, but he could run like the wind. After one of our milk truck operations, I arrived back at my foster home, pockets heavy with coins. My foster mother heard the jangling as I walked into the house. I concocted a lie to explain it. I said we earned the money after school by helping a man clean his yard and haul away trash. I was nine, maybe ten at the time. I should have been in school getting an education, but I was in the streets getting into trouble.

My foster mother confronted me about the money, and I told her my story. She seemed satisfied with that explanation, but there came a knock on the door. It was Gregory's mother with him in tow. She interrogated him and he cracked under the pressure. I can't remember what my punishment was, so it could not have been much. The money was taken from me. I do not know if my foster mother returned it or kept it. What I do know is I was never held accountable. By that age I knew my foster mother would protect me at all costs. That incident certainly reinforced it. She could not have children of her own. To her, I was not a foster child. I was her baby. She had taken care of me since I was an infant, and the bonding was as strong as a mother-child connection can be. I thought of her as my mother and maintained a relationship with her even after I left the home. I preached her funeral service when she died some twenty-five years later.

As for Gregory, his mother made him scarce. He never participated in another caper with me, and we never hung out together again. We weren't exactly robbing Lufthansa or Bank of America. But we were committing real crimes that probably would have escalated had we continued down that road.

Another of our pastimes was hanging out at the railroad tracks, only a block from where I lived. The tracks on Pennell Street were separated by a walking bridge people crossed regularly. On the other side was a wide-open field with some trees and brush. It was dark and forbidden territory at night. I remember crossing that bridge once during the day to find an unconscious man. I thought he might have been dead because he was not moving, and he was exposed. I saw him in the neighborhood later and realized he probably just passed out from drink or drugs.

Once you got across that field, the neighborhood was nicer, with well-painted row houses and nice lawns. Where I lived, there was no lawn. There was a cement sidewalk, and you went up two or three steps to walk into our house.

My friends and I liked to hang out under the bridge. All over the track bed were black stones, not too large to throw, but big enough to be deadly if you were hit by one. We would stack those stones on the railroad tracks to see if the trains would crush the stones or be thrown off the rails. The train ran through a small valley at that section. We would also sit up on the hillside and throw those stones at trains as they went by.

You will be relieved to know we never derailed a train. No one was ever hit. Thank God we weren't accurate enough to throw a rock through one of the windows, but we tried. We had no concept of the injury we could have caused another human being. What I do recall is some men dressed in suits who were railway police, or something showed up at my foster home to warn my foster parents that I should stay away from the tracks.

I was not a juvenile John Gotti, but the things I was doing could easily have landed me in reform school as it was then called. It was jail for juvenile incorrigibles. There I could have learned how to commit more serious offenses and graduate into adult crime. That was not to be my destiny.

CHAPTER 7

A DRAMATIC RESCUE

That's when one of the most dramatic turning points in my life happened. I was standing on the corner of Third and Pennell Streets in August 1962, smack in the heart of the ghetto. The only places in Chester as rough were some public housing projects. These were mean streets, and I was quite comfortable there at a young age.

As I hung out there with my gang, my father drove up. He rolled down the window and called me over. Over the years I expressed a yearning to live with my father. I cannot explain it. Children are not sophisticated thinkers. I doubt that I could have explained what I was feeling. I knew I felt abandoned and unwanted. I was angry and rebellious. Every time I saw my father, I wondered why I didn't live with him.

What led to this dramatic moment on this particular day, I do not know. I came to learn my father was a determined man. Once he made a decision, he would move heaven and earth to follow through. He had clearly made up his mind he was going to take me in. My life was about to undergo revolutionary change.

As I walked to his car, always glad to see him, I said, "Hi Dad." He got right to the point. "Son, you still wanna come live with me?"

Without hesitation I said, "Yes!" And he said, "Well get in." It never crossed my mind he meant immediately. The gravity of this moment did not hit me when I got into my father's car. Maybe I thought he would begin a process that at some point might culminate in leaving foster care to be with him.

After I was grown, my dad explained to me how he came to the realization that if he did not take custody, he would lose me to the streets. He could see exactly where I was headed and felt strongly he was the only one who could change that. He said as much to Miss Beck, as he called her, on the very day he removed me from her care.

It was a dramatic moment, charged with emotion. My father was always a presence in my life, and there had been a bond between us for as long as I can remember. He was my father. I belonged with him, and I knew it. As he recounted it, as soon as I was old enough to articulate my desires, I began to ask if I could live with him. I don't recall actually asking, but I definitely remember it being a powerful desire in my life.

He occasionally ate Sunday dinner with the Molets and me and stopped by at other times as well. I remember racing him down Pennell Street, convinced I could outrun him. I found out my father was athletic. I ran as fast as I could, but he was faster.

Before he took custody, perhaps the greatest bonding moment with my father was a week-long trip to Wildwood Amusement Park in New Jersey. For that entire time, I was the center of his attention. That experience taught me my safety and security were my father's top priority. During that week, he never left me alone. I went to sleep with him in the room watching me, and when I awoke, he was there. There was plenty of adult entertainment in Wildwood, but he shunned those opportunities and focused completely on me.

This was my father's character, and he was consistent. It is one of the many reasons I not only loved him but came to admire and honor him as I grew up. From the time I went to live with him up to the day I left for Marine Corps boot camp, he never allowed a woman to stay in our apartment. I never awoke to find a girlfriend in his bed. He later told me he never wanted me to feel uncomfortable or that anyone was intruding on my comfort and security. My father was an extraordinary man.

Suddenly and dramatically, he changed my destiny. I got into his car, and he drove a block or so to my foster home. When we walked into 226 Pennell Street that day, I had no idea what was going to happen. He spoke to my Momma respectfully, always calling her "Miss Beck."

"I think my son is at a stage in life where he needs to be with his father," he told her. "So I am taking him to live with me . . . now." He didn't mean next month or next week or even tomorrow. He meant that moment.

Her reaction was strong, bordering on hysteria. There were tears. She threatened legal action, saying, "The court hasn't given you permission to do this." My father was unyielding. He shot back, "My son doesn't belong to any court. He belongs to me and it's time for him to be with me, now." She even tried to negotiate and stall for time, saying, "Well, let me pack some things for him."

My father said, "I'll come back and get anything he needs." It was a passionate conversation, but not hostile. Nor did it last long. My father never sat. He stood at the edge of the dining room. Rebecca was in her small kitchen. I was also in the kitchen between the two of them. I never said a word. He said what he had to say, summoned me to go to his car and we walked out the door together. A new phase of my life began, and he never looked back or expressed a hint of regret. That was my father: strong, decisive, and unmoved by opposition.

He later told me the only reason he didn't take me earlier was I was too young to be at home alone while he worked. Once he reached the conclusion that I was ready, he acted on it immediately. There would be no bargaining or compromise. It was a matter of principle for him. I have never known a more honorable, trustworthy man. I have tried to model the very best I saw in him.

My father lived on the first floor of a three-story building originally designed as a house. The person who lived on the third floor had to walk through the hallways of the first- and second-story apartments. When we arrived at his apartment, he walked me into a combination bedroom and sitting room, which was where he slept. I learned right away my career as a juvenile delinquent was over.

He must have thought about this moment for a long time because he seemed to know exactly what he wanted to say. "Son, every day with me can be like a day of heaven on earth or every day I will tear your behind all to pieces. It's up to you." I will never forget those words. He did not speak them in anger. It was very casual, but very firm. There are several other things he told me from the very beginning. He made clear he had two major expectations, and if I did those two things, we would get along. The first thing was to obey him. He made crystal clear that failure to do so would have consequences. The second was that I would do well in school. My education was a top priority for him. Therefore, school attendance, homework, and study were expected to be a top priority for me. I remember him saying, "My job is to work and take care of you. Your job is to do well in school so that one day you will be able to take care of yourself." His job was work. My job was school. That's the way he put it.

He surely knew about my spotty attendance and poor performance record in fifth grade. I was now under a different regime, and my school record was to reflect that. It did. I went from an F student in 5th grade living in foster care to an A student in 6th grade living with my father. It did not take a government program or midnight basketball to turn my life around. It took a responsible, loving, and firm father.

One other thing worth noting. My father's apartment had an indoor bathroom. It was in the basement of his first-floor apartment, and I found it a little scary down there, but he laid down the law. I was to take a bath every night in the summer and two to three times a week in the winter. In the winter I was to wash up every morning. He was very specific about what that meant and how it was to be done.

At the time, my feet were several shades darker than they should have been because as I explained earlier, they had not been washed in a very long time. I remember with some amazement how the color of my skin lightened when I applied a washcloth and soap to them. Before long I knew what it was like to feel clean, and I liked it. I began to brush my teeth every morning, something I was not made to do in foster care. Several of my teeth were extracted during my childhood because I was taught nothing about dental hygiene until moving in with my dad.

To use the bathroom, I had to go down the stairs and across a poorly lit area. At night, it was foreboding. Flying water bugs occasionally fluttered by as I crossed the chasm between the bottom of the stairs and the light of the bathroom. To my fertile imagination it felt like a journey of a thousand miles. Even though I was a tough street kid, I was still a kid, and the dark basement held terrors for me.

My father would sit outside the bathroom to make me feel safe while I took a bath. My children today say I always made them feel safe. I must have learned that from their grandfather because he always did that for me. Within a year we moved to the upstairs apartment in the same building and basement bathing was over. We had no money, but my father was elevating my life in more ways than one.

CHAPTER 8

MY FATHER'S BACKGROUND

It is hard to account for character. Some people are raised in the most horrendous circumstances and emerge with impeccable character. Some people are raised in idyllic circumstances and become monsters. Perhaps it is a matter of the little decisions we make day by day leading us to decency or degeneracy, those small forks in the road which take us in one direction or the other. My father knew hardship. His mother died when he was five, and my grandfather, growing up in Orange County, Virginia, shortly after the end of Civil War, was raised in harsh circumstances. In fact, my grandfather had the reputation of being one of the meanest people you would ever meet, dangerously mean.

There is a rumor in our family that my grandfather was a fugitive who changed his name to escape justice. His given name was Frank, but he called himself Charles. One of his brothers, Willie, told my father my grandfather's real name was Frank. My father knew him only as "Charles." When still a child, my father told his father what Uncle Willie said. My dad said his father looked at him with a dead stare and said, "Boy, what did I tell you my name is?" My father answered, "You said your name is Charles." My grandfather responded, "Then that's my name. Don't ask me again." My father told me that story many times. When I began to do genealogical research, I confirmed my grandfather's name was in fact "Frank." His death certificate, however, gave his name as Charles. Why he changed his name will remain a mystery. He was the only one who could answer that question and he was very secretive. There is not a single picture of my grandfather because he did not allow pictures of himself to be taken. It may have been because he was superstitious about capturing one's image. Or he may have been guarding himself against a picture being used by law enforcement to identify him.

I never met my grandfather. He died eight years before I was born. According to both my father and his brother—my uncle Charles (his namesake)—my grandfather had some strange ways. He was very harsh and had a violent temper. Somehow, my father emerged from all this a decent man with a kind heart. He, too, was capable of anger. I was afraid of the consequences of disobeying him, but I was not afraid of him. He was good to me.

One of the moments I will remember forever was when, after I went to bed, he would come in to my room and put his hand on my forehead for just a few seconds. That small gesture communicated that he loved me. After ten years in foster care, the reassurance of my father's love made all the difference in the world.

CHAPTER 9

MY FATHER'S INFLUENCE

It is an understatement to say moving to live with my father changed my life. While I did not suddenly become the perfect child, the seething resentment fueling my rebellious behavior vanished, and I generally complied. He had rules about how far I could go from home without his permission. I was to be within earshot when he returned home from work. He did not want to have to call twice or have to look for me. I made sure he didn't. When the time came near for him to arrive home from work, I made sure I was no farther away than the basketball court across the street from our apartment. I went from roaming the streets of Chester to staying close to home. The petty thievery and delinquency stopped abruptly from the day I went to live with my father.

Within a few months of being with him, I earned the one and only instance of corporal punishment my father had to exercise. I remember it well and I am still amazed by the wisdom of this man with a sixth-grade education. I had a teacher in sixth grade who was a terror, literally. I was deathly afraid of the man. His name was Mr. Council. He was frighteningly mean with boys and very friendly with girls, particularly one. I remember her name, but I will not use it here. I told my father about him, and he listened but cautioned me to go to school. He promised to look into it. My father went to work, and I committed the cardinal sin of not going to school. I could not put myself through the torture of being in Mr. Council's presence. Even at that young age I noticed he had a particular affinity for one of my female classmates who was physically mature for sixth grade. The way he interacted with her gave me the creeps. Something was wrong.

Instead of sitting quietly at home, I acted out. It was a cry for help. I bounced my basketball and made every kind of noise I could. I was a ten-year-old who needed immediate relief and didn't know how to get it. I never left the house that day, but I certainly made an impression on the other tenants, and it was not a good one. When my father arrived home, he was met by Miss Shelby, the third-floor tenant, who told him it sounded like I was going to destroy the place. He was not happy.

I directly disobeyed him by not going to school and embarrassed him by acting out all day long. He was astoundingly calm about it. He must have sensed something was terribly wrong to cause me to behave as I did. On the other hand, I disobeyed him. This would be the first and only time he would "tear my behind all to pieces."

He let me know corporal punishment was coming. He sent me into a room where I was to wait. He came in and used a strap to carry out the sentence. It was the only time my father ever used physical punishment. I was not punched, kicked, marked, or bruised, but I did get the strap, and it was not fun. It reinforced the idea that education is important, and not taking it seriously would lead to unhappy consequences. I learned my lesson and went on to become academically successful.

In our world today, corporal punishment is frowned upon. In some states, it is outlawed altogether. Most parents know how to use corporal punishment without crossing the line into abuse. As a pastor, I caution parents not to use physical punishment out of anger and frustration. It should be about reinforcing a lesson and discipline. It should be rare, reserved for the most egregious behavior. By adolescence it should be out of the question. I was ten when my father gave me that whipping. It was the last time it happened.

However, my father did not ignore my complaints about Mr. Council. He told me years later he went to the school and demanded I be removed from Council's class.

When I went back to school the next day, I was transferred to the classroom of Mr. Charles Ballard. I will always remember Mr. Ballard as one of the greatest influences of my life because he was the first teacher to make me feel bright. He was the opposite of Council. He showed sincere interest in the well-being of his students, and he wanted us to learn.

During one class, each student had to read aloud. I read my portion, and Mr. Ballard stopped the classroom. He said, "Now I want you all to notice how Mr. Jackson did that. When he came to a word, he wasn't sure of, he sounded it out and then kept reading. He didn't go back and repeat what he already read. He maintained his place."

That lasted all of one minute, maybe two, but fifty-seven years later, I remember it as if it were yesterday. I did not think I did anything special, but that moment made a lasting impression on me. I cannot remember the name of the other two elementary schools I attended, but I remember Dewey-Mann Elementary and Mr. Ballard. I give Mr. Ballard a great deal of credit for helping change my perception of myself, and that is half the battle.

Mr. Council, the teacher who struck such terror in me, was later arrested, and found guilty of molesting the girl who garnered so much of his attention. Council was every bit the monster I feared him to be. My dad got me away from him.

The idea of being "smart" was reinforced when I graduated from sixth grade and based on standardized tests, was tracked into the top classes in predominantly white Pulaski Junior High School. This was 1963, when desegregation policies were being implemented. Only a handful of black students were in my classes. From that point forward, my classmates have always been predominantly Americans of European descent. I did very well when I wasn't clowning. I was barely edged out by Roberta Hertzog for the Latin Award before graduation in the 9th grade.

In hindsight, I believe socialization helped instill in me the conviction that people are just people. Most of us exaggerate the importance of race because we live in a culture that gives such emphasis to the concept.

Academic achievement helped me realize hard work gains you recognition and promotion no matter who you are. While most of us will encounter people who are against us for all kinds of reasons, no one can stop a determined individual from moving forward in life. The disgraced late President Richard Nixon said something I will never forget: "Life rewards determination." That is absolutely true, and he proved it.

Few politicians have been as lacking in charisma as Mr. Nixon. Few were written off as thoroughly as he was, after his "Checkers" speech. Yet his persistence landed him the presidency. His character deficits and paranoia were his undoing, but even after his scandalous fall from grace, he reinvented himself as a quiet senior statesman advising presidents behind the scenes. Determination is clearly a major factor in success.

My father's life was hard. He could have become bitter, angry, and irresponsible. That is how many people react when they feel life has dealt them a poor hand. He could have abandoned me as so many men have turned their backs on their children. Instead, he used his experiences to teach me life lessons. He was raising me in the tumultuous decade of the 1960s, when the country was in racial turmoil. Never once did my father tell me race would be a barrier to my success. He taught me the greatest obstacle to progress is oneself—laziness, dishonesty, and selfish disregard of others will prevent you from reaching your potential.

My father always said, "Son, what you make of yourself is up to you. Don't ever come back to me with excuses." This was a rather remarkable attitude for a man with a sixth-grade education who clawed his way through family dysfunction, racial hostility, a school for homeless, abandoned boys, and the Great Depression. His mother died when he was five years old, and Frank was no model of fatherhood.

My uncle Charles was three years older than my father. He had rickets as a child, which stunted his growth, and left him barely five feet tall as an adult. Yet he was a rebellious youngster and tough young man. As strict as my grandfather was, Uncle Charles constantly pushed the envelope. My father told me about the beatings inflicted on Charles. One time, Frank angrily picked up a brick to throw at him as he ran away. The brick hit Uncle Charles on the back of his shoe and knocked the heel off. Frank finally gave up. In 1926, when Charles was fourteen, Frank took him to a rooming house in Pittsburgh, paid two weeks rent and warned him not to come back. My father did not see his brother for five years.

Years later, when my father asked Frank about it, he said, "That was better than killing him." My father did not take that as a joke because Frank didn't mean it as one.

When Charles was in his eighties, I talked to him about his father. He had nothing good to say. He was filled with bitterness against him. I do not know if Charles ever forgave him. Frank died in 1944 in Philadelphia at the age of seventy-one. Charles was called to identify his body, and his signature is on the death certificate.

My uncle had a severe drinking problem. His only child, Charlotte, became a lifelong heroin addict. He almost spent the rest of his life in prison after shooting his girlfriend in their Baltimore apartment. He came home in a drunken stupor, accused her of stealing his money, and shot her four times. Miraculously she not only survived but refused to cooperate with prosecutors or testify against him. I visited Charles in his prison cell and talked to him about God. During that crisis, he asked Jesus to take over in his life. He quit drinking and began to live a stable life. I cannot help but speculate that his problems had their root in his unresolved issues with Frank. Even after surrendering his life to Jesus Christ, he remained bitter against his father.

William Jackson, my father, was raised by the same man, and somehow loved him. He was eleven when Charles was sent away. Shortly thereafter, my dad found himself estranged from his father and living on the streets. He was in the sixth grade and his class was reading aloud *The Adventures of Huckleberry Finn* by Mark Twain. The book reflects the culture of its time and has some racially charged language in it. According to my dad, they came to a passage referring to "nigger wench." There was a young white girl sitting in front of him who turned around and snickered. He then showed he was, indeed, Frank's son. Each child had an ink bottle on the desk for writing with a quill pen. He hit the girl with his ink bottle. When the teacher saw it, she marched back to his desk, and announced, "William Jackson, I am going to slap your face." When she raised her hand to hit him, he parried the blow and with one punch to her chest, knocked her to the floor. Neither the girl nor the teacher was seriously injured, or my father might have been arrested on the spot.

He was removed from the class and sent to the principal's office. I have no idea how, but they sent for my grandfather, and he showed up at the school. The principal explained what my father did, and that he would be suspended. My grandfather said to the principal, "I'm going to take this young man home and when he comes back, I guarantee you he will be a genuine good fellow." My father knew this meant he might be beaten to within an inch of his life, literally.

He begged the principal and my father to allow him to take an important test being given that day. The principal allowed the suspension to begin after the test was over. My father took the test, left the school, and did not return home for four or five years. He was nearly grown when he finally showed up again. He lived and slept in the streets at times. He lived for a time in Chester with a woman I called Aunt Isabel, although we were not related. She knew my grandmother's side of the family and took some interest in my father. He would stay with her at times. He remained close to Aunt Isabel and her daughter Harriet until their deaths. My grandfather never went looking for him, there or anywhere else.

He finally landed in a school for homeless boys and stayed there for a year or so. By that time, he was in his late teens, nearing adulthood. He showed up at my grandfather's shanty house in Philadelphia and found him sitting on the front stoop. When my father walked up, he was greeted with, "Hey there, young fella. You got any money?"

In spite of this horrid treatment, my dad loved my grandfather. He understood him.

Dad could have repeated his father's pattern. Instead, he transcended it. Though not perfect, he was in most ways a model father.

He was firm without being abusive. He taught me to demand the best from myself and expect the best from life. He always made clear I was first in his life. For example, he told me if I did well in school, he would give me a car when I was sixteen. That meant mainly A's, certainly nothing lower than a B. When I turned sixteen, my father couldn't afford to buy me a car, so he gave me his. In 1967, I was driving a black Catalina Pontiac. My father wasn't rich, but he made me feel like we were. I was a big man on campus. The only demand he made of the car was that I pick him up after work—a price I gladly paid.

The thing about my dad that most marked his character was he was a man of his word. If my father made me a promise, he would go through hell to fulfill it. I was celebrating class day with my friends as we were concluding our senior year in high school. We had been drinking early in the day even though I knew I had to pick up my dad. Being a know-it-all teenager, I figured I could suck on some breath mints, and he would be none the wiser.

I wasn't staggering drunk, but I was under the influence. Had I been stopped by a police officer; he probably would have smelled alcohol because my dad certainly did. I drove home, parked the car, and figured I'd gotten away with it. I went into the house with him, passed a few pleasantries and was about to head out again. Up to that point, he acted like everything was normal. Then he said, "So, you're going to do some more driving while you are drinking?" I will never forget that moment because I suddenly felt a crushing weight of guilt. I betrayed my father's trust. I did one of the most dangerous and irresponsible things you can do with a vehicle. I got behind the wheel under the influence of alcohol, endangered myself, my friends, my dad, and others. I disappointed the man to whom I owed so much.

I did not go out again that day. The following morning, I apologized to him, and handed him the keys to the car. He asked me why I was giving him the keys. I told him I didn't feel worthy to have the car anymore, and assumed he wanted it back. But Dad said, "I gave you the car. That means it's yours. I don't want it back. What I want is for you to use it in a responsible way. Don't ever drink and drive again."

That was my dad. He reinforced a lesson he taught me from the moment he picked me up on that corner and rescued me from the streets. He demonstrated honor, integrity, and the importance of keeping your word. It is a lesson I have carried with me all my life and have always sought to model.

CHAPTER 10

THE ROOTS OF A BLACK CONSERVATIVE

I have no delusions of grandeur. I am not the most successful person you will ever meet. I know people who are immensely wealthy. I am not, at least not so far. There is always hope in America. I know others who have achieved highly prominent roles in government or the corporate world. I've run unsuccessfully for elected office. I have not achieved everything I've set out to do, but my life is not over. I will continue to find new mountains to climb because I live in a nation of opportunity.

I also know, coming from my background—gang member, juvenile delinquent, raised in foster care, and later by a single father—my life has been remarkable. Things could have turned out very differently. Mine is one of millions of American success stories. I've served my country in the Marine Corps, graduated from top schools, practiced law, written three books, have a beautiful wife, a happy marriage, and three successful children. I am grateful to God for my life.

I know enough about world history and politics to know that while I was not born with the proverbial silver spoon in my mouth, I nonetheless entered the world with one gigantic advantage over 96 percent of the people on earth. I was born a citizen of the United States of America. I had personal disadvantages, but I also had the gigantic advantages of freedom, opportunity, and hope. For this and many other reasons, I love my country.

I am a proud conservative because I want to assure that every American child who comes behind me—regardless of skin color or circumstances of birth—has the same advantages. My conservative values come from my father. He voted Democrat his entire life because he felt a bond with Franklin Roosevelt. From his perspective, Roosevelt personally saved his life during the Depression. My father spent six months in a Civilian Conservation Corps ("CCC") camp at the age of twenty-one. He grew six inches and took on the body weight and frame of a man after years of scrounging for food and sleeping wherever he could. He worked, ate three meals a day, and got a good night's sleep every night. The camp was rough, but it beat the alternative.

My father voted for liberals, but he lived and thought like a conservative. He worked and was proud of it. He took responsibility for his life and expected me to do the same. He refused any hint of welfare. He wouldn't accept government food or help even though his income level might have justified it. He expected me to rise on my own merit and effort. He taught me nobody owed me anything and it was up to me to do him proud and make something of myself. He let me know life is filled with obstacles, and excuses for failure can always be found. On the other hand, if you are committed to making something of yourself, nothing and nobody can stop you.

What success I've experienced in life was not due to affirmative action or any government program. I do acknowledge the Civil Rights struggle and all who have contributed to helping America be true to the Declaration of Independence and the Constitution. No one can deny the efforts of heroes like Frederick Douglass, Booker T. Washington, George Washington Carver, and Rev. Dr. Martin Luther King. They not only helped open doors of opportunity for black Americans but helped change the hearts of fellow citizens who were indoctrinated with racial ideology.

Because of these and other brave souls, racism is no longer acceptable in mainstream American culture. However, civil rights laws cannot guarantee success. They can open doors, but each individual has to choose to walk through them. Opportunity does not bestow purpose and direction in life. It merely offers freedom to find and pursue one's purpose.

What made the difference for me was a loving father who sacrificed for me. He worked for thirty-three years at Sun Shipbuilding and Dry Dock Company. He labored in heat and cold, rain and snow, from dangerous high perches and deep, tight spaces. He earned a living welding, using both hands (he was ambidextrous) and contorting his whole body. He raised a son who would use his brain to earn a living. He was there for me every step of the way. He was enormously proud when I graduated from college and then Harvard Law School. He always told me, "Son, reach for the stars—because even if you don't make it to the stars, you may land on the moon. You'll certainly get a lot further than if you don't reach at all."

After graduating and beginning to practice law, I went to him once for advice on some decisions I faced about my professional career. He said, "Son, you need to talk to people who understand the world you have entered into. You have far surpassed what I know anything about." He was proud of that fact and proud of me. His impact on my life is immeasurable. He passed away in 2002, and I still miss him very much. My philosophy is a reflection of my father's practical wisdom and guidance. I left the Democrat Party and became a Republican because the latter is basically in agreement with me and William Jackson. The Democrat Party, for which my father voted all his life, left us a long time ago.

CHAPTER 11

FAKE REVOLUTIONARY

It is a miracle I made it out of Chester, Pennsylvania. Some of my friends died, and several went to jail. One lost his mind; another died of a cocaine-induced heart attack. Another did a long prison sentence for murder. One of my friends drowned swimming in a creek when he should have been in school. Another was stabbed to death at a party. Their lives and potential were cut short.

My relationships with these guys ended when I moved from foster care to my father's house. However, like most teenagers in the '60s, I dabbled with marijuana. Hard drugs like cocaine, heroin, and LSD scared me. I believe now the restraining hand of God kept me from getting swept up in the drug culture as so many did. I was never an addict. Still, I wish I never touched marijuana. It contributed nothing to my life. I am vehemently opposed to all drug abuse because I have seen the destructive impact it has on people's lives.

My first year in college was at Indiana University of Pennsylvania. I was sucked into the far-left culture of college youth. I assumed a radical persona but thank God I was never really committed to the cause. I had Mao's "Little Red Book," but never read it. I wore a black beret and black leather jacket, but that was the sum total of my association with the Black Panthers. I attended anti-ROTC

rallies and then went to ROTC class. My friends and I comman-
deered the university radio station, but we left when we got hungry.

My father instilled a desire in me to make a better life. So, peer
pressure and the desire for acceptance made me walk up to the line,
but I never crossed it into illegality. I wanted Dad to be proud, and
I knew campus radicalism was not the pathway to success. I did just
enough to be accepted, but never enough to be arrested.

My academic performance at Indiana State was unremarkable.
I did not return after the first year.

CHAPTER 12

MY HIGH SCHOOL
SWEETHEART

I met my future wife, Theodora Jordan, at Chester High School. I like to say she chased me, but the truth is the reverse. I saw her on the high school campus, but she resisted my charms at first. She had no idea how persistent I could be. My pursuit was probably just short of the legal definition of stalking. She thought I was conceited. I thought of it as self-confidence. I was, after all, driving a sleek, black Catalina Pontiac. I considered myself a big man on campus, but of course, it was a very small campus.

I was drawn to her. Toward the end of her senior year, she was having a class day at Hershey Park, about eighty miles from our hometown. With friends in tow, I drove to the park with one intention—finding her. I did. When she asked me what I was doing there, I said, "I came to see you." It was at that park I bought her a necklace with a charm inscribed, "I will always love you." She still has that necklace and shows it off from time to time.

Shortly after I met her, our high school burned down. We had to hold classes at a junior high school. Half the high school held classes in the morning, the other half in the afternoon. She and I had classes at the same time, so I started speaking to her on our borrowed campus. Finally, I asked if I could come by and see her. Once I started dropping by her house, I never stopped. Our visits continued through graduation and right into college. I fell deeply in love and knew she was the woman I wanted to marry. It is one of the best decisions of my life.

The summer after I graduated from high school I was talking to a friend of mine, hanging out in front of our apartment on Third and Yarnal Streets. We would be out all hours of the night trying to catch a summer breeze in the heat. On one of those nights, I told my friend "Wolf" I met the woman I was going to marry. He looked at me with shock, maybe because I was so young. He said, "Really?" And I said, "Yeah, she's the one."

I told my father the same thing. To my surprise, he was pleased with the girl I chose, because he knew her mother and family and respected them, particularly Floretta Jordan, my wife's mother. He told me, "She comes from a good family. She will make a good wife." I can't remember a time when my father was wrong about his assessment of people. Nonetheless, he had reservations about me considering marriage at such a young age. He made clear he did not want me to get married at that time because we were both too young. He was right to be concerned, but I was my daddy's son, and once my mind was made up, I could not be dissuaded.

In August 1970, I joined the United States Marine Corps. Several factors contributed to my decision. First, I was looking for a sense of direction in life and felt serving my country would help me find it. The Vietnam War was still raging, and I expected I would go. I just missed the draft as I recall, but I volunteered anyway. I also knew there was a GI Bill of Rights providing educational benefits, and I was committed to finishing my education at some point. Like most kids at that age, I had no real idea what I was getting myself into, but it turned out to be a decision I never regretted.

Before joining the Corps, I got a year of college under my belt. I went there determined to excel academically. That lasted about a week before I fell in with the party crowd. I did not fail out of school, but I certainly did not live up to my potential. I felt guilty about it because my father worked hard to scrape together funds to help me go to school. I was not going to waste his hard-earned money any further. I needed time to figure out what I really wanted to do.

I decided not to go back to school until I could pay my own way. The military allowed me to do that. Many people have asked me why I joined the Marine Corps. Of all the branches, I chose what most view as the toughest. I was all but guaranteed to see action in 'Nam. The explanation is simple. I believed in America, even then. Once I got away from the wanna-be radicals on campus, I got in touch with myself again.

At IUP, there were 10,000 students and only forty were black. That was 1969, still in the eye of the Civil Rights storm and the heated debate over the Vietnam War. IUP was a microcosm of the broader society, with the added problem of black students in an environment completely new to us, to the school, and our fellow students. It was a charged atmosphere, which forced the few black students to band together for the sake of security and survival. That gave the group an immense amount of cohesion and influence over us as individuals. I found myself outside the ROTC building protesting. I'm not sure whether we were protesting the War or ROTC on campus or both. I protested to fit in, but I went to class anyway because I wanted to pass the course. Some of my friends refused to go and failed. I wasn't prepared to be an academic martyr.

Once I got away from that environment, I was normal again. It was clear to me every American owes our country loyalty and service, and I was no exception. I chose the Marine Corps because I liked to challenge myself. I knew the Corps would be a test of my mental and physical toughness. I was confident I would measure up, but once I arrived at Parris Island and began training, I had my share of doubts.

My biggest problem was not the physical rigor, but adjusting to military discipline, taking orders, and having someone else in control of everything I did. That required a significant attitudinal change. I had to spend a few days in "motivation." That's where recalcitrant recruits were sent to "get your mind right." After a few days of moving dirt piles, cleaning rifles, and forced marches, I was fully persuaded. I was born-again green from that point on.

I came home from boot camp and married my high school sweetheart. The year 1970 was momentous.

PART II

BECOMING A CHRISTIAN AND A REPUBLICAN

After boot camp at Parris Island, advanced infantry training in Camp Lejeune and some time off, I received orders to go to Marine Corps Recruit Depot (MCRD) in San Diego for basic electronics school training. My in-laws frankly believed I would go to California and never send for my wife. By that time, we had our first child, and they believed a young man my age would not follow through to bring a wife and baby to the other side of the country.

They did not know William Jackson's son. I was young, but I was taught to be responsible, to be a man of my word. I told my wife and her parents I would go to California, find a place, and send for her. I told them I didn't know how long it would take, but I would get it done as soon as I could. Even though it was frowned upon by Marine Corps command for a married Marine Private First Class to live off base with his family, there were no regulations prohibiting it. I knew Command didn't like it, but I had given my word.

Within a month after arriving on base, I found a studio apartment on Grape Street, under the landing path for the San Diego Airport. I stocked the place with food and sent my wife an airline ticket to come to California. I cannot remember how I accomplished all that on an E-2's pay, but I saved the money and got it done. After all, I had been trained by my dad and the Corps to have a can-do attitude. This is one of the reasons I will never buy into the victim mindset promoted by the Left that has become so prevalent in the inner city. I believe human beings can do almost anything we set our minds to do. It may require discipline and sacrifice, but very few things are impossible in the sphere of human endeavor. I believe that was true even before I gave my life to Jesus Christ. My belief in that principle is now rooted in my faith, which makes it all the stronger.

My daughter asked me recently, "Did Mom think you were going to send for her?" I told her she would have to ask her mother, but I figured she knew me well enough to know if I said I was going to do something, I was going to do it. My wife's parents were a different story. When Theodora got that airline ticket and told them I had an apartment set up and she was headed for California, my stock went way up in their eyes, and I don't think they ever doubted me again.

I faced another daunting challenge after five months in beautiful San Diego. I was given orders to report to Twentynine Palms for radar technology training. I had to pack up our small family in an old '62 Ford Galaxy I purchased and make our way 200 miles into the desert to remote and austere Twentynine Palms. You could not imagine any more contrasting locations. San Diego was beautiful and bustling, while Twentynine Palms had one blinking traffic light at the main intersection of town. In fact, calling it a town is an exaggeration. My wife hated it. I was scheduled to finish training at the end of October 1971. She left at the end of September to go home until we got settled in our new duty station. Then I began the process all over again of finding an apartment. This time I had to furnish it, and I had no car. On weekends, I traveled all over the greater Boston area by bus to find things I needed, and then rented a truck to pick them up. I stocked the place with food and sent for my wife again. We got a little two-bedroom apartment at 224 Taffrail Road in the Houghs Neck section of Quincy, Massachusetts.

CHAPTER 13

BECOMING A MARINE RADAR TECH

I graduated third in my class from electronic school at the Marine Corps Recruit Depot (MCRD) in San Diego. We were given the privilege of choosing from several sets of available orders based on our class rank at graduation. There were two sets of orders in California, and at that time I wanted to stay in the Golden State to enjoy the beautiful weather. Much to my disappointment, I missed second place by a hair, and the next best orders from my point of view were to Naval Air Station South Weymouth, just outside Boston. I wanted the warmest place in the country. I was sent to one of the coldest. I now know things worked out exactly as God intended. I am grateful I did not stay in California. For a variety of reasons, that was not where I was supposed to be, not the least of which is it turned out to be one of the most liberal states in America. Living in California would have been frustrating for me once I became a Bible-believing Christian.

Ironically, as I developed a conservative conscience, Massachusetts turned out to be no better than California. In 1998 I escaped to Virginia, my ancestral home. This is not only the home of the great George Washington, "Father of His Country." This is also the home of Thomas Jefferson, chief draftsman of the Declaration of Independence; Patrick Henry, one of the greatest orators and spokesmen for liberty our country has ever produced; James Madison, father of the Constitution, and George Mason, father of the Bill of Rights.

Virginia is also an important part of my family history. I live not three hours from where my great-grandparents, Gabriel and Eliza Jackson, raised my grandfather and his siblings. My grandfather Frank was born in 1874 and my great-grandfather in 1798, the year before George Washington died. The Left has gained more and more influence here in Virginia as well, but this is where I plant my flag. I am in the fight to save this historic state that has contributed so much to the founding of our country.

This is why I and so many other Virginians were filled with hope when in November 2021, after a decade of dragging us into far left policies, Democrats lost all three constitutional offices and the House of Delegates. We elected Republicans Glenn Youngkin as governor, Winsome Sears as Lieutenant Governor, and Jason Miyares as attorney general. Winsome is the first black woman elected to statewide office in Virginia. Jason Miyares of Cuban ancestry is the first Hispanic elected statewide. All three are professed Christians. They love our country, believe in the Constitution, and the rule of law. Some thought the Commonwealth was on its way to becoming California—a one party state where leftist extremism is the norm. However, Democrats overplayed their hand. They told parents they had no say in what their children were being taught. School boards in league with the teacher union were indoctrinating children with critical race theory and transgender ideology without the parents' permission or knowledge. Parents responded at the ballot box. The lesson here is we must never give up. There is prevailing power in truth.

To return to the Marine Corps, my Military Occupational Specialty (MOS) was Air Radar Technician for the ANTPQ-10 radar, designed to help airplanes drop bombs from high altitudes. We were known as "air-wingers"—reputedly the least "high and tight" Marines in the Corps. While it is true we did not "blouse our boots" or starch our uniforms, we were still Marines and proud of it. However, most of us air-wingers were stationed on Navy air bases. There were a few Marines with lots of pilots and air support personnel. It was unquestionably less rigid than a typical Marine base would be.

Nonetheless, the pilots, mechanics, and technicians keeping us in the air knew their stuff and served our country well. I came to respect them highly.

As I said earlier, God had a plan. In that unlikely place, something happened that would change my life forever. My staff sergeant didn't particularly like me, probably for good reason. In basic training, I was full of youthful Marine Corps bravado, and I could be a little snide. I was not taking things seriously. I sometimes even laughed at the drill instructors' absurd screaming. After a few days in motivation, I had an epiphany and changed my attitude. The alternative was to be kicked out of the Corps, which was unthinkable. To go home having failed to get through boot camp would have been shameful. I could handle the physical demands and the emotional pressure. I could not handle quitting. I still can't.

In the loose, less-than-Marine-Corps "high and tight" environment at Naval Air Station South Weymouth, I reverted to some of my old ways. When orders came for someone with my radar technician MOS to go to Okinawa, my staff sergeant had an easy choice— send me. The Vietnam War was winding down, but Okinawa was the staging base, the last stop before Vietnam.

The radar I was trained to operate and repair, ANTPQ-10, was designed for combat. We were to deploy the radar in the bush, and from a concealed position give bombers coordinates so they could make accurate drops. This was to keep our aircraft beyond the reach of surface-to-air rockets. Today's satellite technology makes that system anachronistic, but it was cutting edge at the time. It could guide an aircraft at high altitudes in difficult weather and calculate the drop zone with unprecedented accuracy.

While the radar was considered lightweight, transportable by helicopter, it had three heavy modules that Marines had to sling. Because of that I wondered how effective it would be in the Vietnam jungle. Little did I know at the time I was training on it—it was used extensively in Vietnam from 1965 to 1971. Its most notable mission was the Battle of Khe Sanh in 1968. It apparently performed well, as did the Marines who were charged with operating it.

I was one of those Marines assigned to an Air Support Radar Team (ASRT). However, after the grueling Marine Corps boot camp in Parris Island, Advanced Infantry Training at Camp Lejeune, and radar electronics school at MCRD San Diego and Twentynine Palms, I never saw combat. Frankly, any youthful romantic notions I had about war were shattered by the treatment our soldiers and Marines received from fellow citizens when they returned to the United States. It was bad enough many came home with PTSD as well as physical wounds and disabilities. But they suffered abuse from fellow Americans on top of it.

When I got orders to Okinawa, I suspected I was on my way to 'Nam. I was preparing myself for a long separation from my family. I would have been gone a minimum of a year and was told I would not be allowed to take my wife and son.

Then something happened I attribute to divine intervention. There was another Marine on base with my exact MOS. We worked together, and although we were not close, I considered Terry Lazer a friend. In fact, I defended him at times from the ridicule he endured because he was a devout Christian.

There was a lot of down time on the base. If we weren't assembling and disassembling the radar or doing mock repairs, there was little to do. During those times, we played cards, talked smack to each other, and complained about the Corps. Every Marine does it. We often ridiculed the "hurry up and wait" culture, which required us to rush to get somewhere only to wait in line after arriving. Things would be so much better if we were in charge, or so we thought. I laugh when I look back on those days. Young Marines were like most young people. We knew it all. Why didn't they just turn things over to us?

Terry Laser was different. While the rest of us shared our profanity-laced wisdom, he would be off in a corner, engrossed in reading the Scriptures. He had a small, personal Bible with him all the time. He didn't curse, drink, or smoke. He was as even-tempered as any person I've ever met. He wasn't trying to prove how "gung-ho" he was. He quietly did his job without bravado or complaint.

In his own quiet way, he had an impact on me. He had something I did not, and I knew it. I saw in him a peace, a serene confidence I never saw before. I don't think I ever acknowledged it to him, but I liked and respected him. I would later realize God used him to get through to me. I remember telling my wife, "I look at this guy and I think to myself, *If I want to get my life together, I need to become a Christian.*" That is as far as it went at the time. I did not fully understand what it meant to be a Christian, but I knew I was not one. Nevertheless, another seed was planted in my heart, and I confirmed it with my own words.

When Terry found out our staff sergeant was planning to send me to Okinawa, he volunteered to take my place. I learned later he made the case to our squad leader that it made more sense for him to go. He was single and wanted the experience, whereas I would have to leave my family. He had the same MOS with the same experience. The Corps allowed volunteers first preference for orders, all things being equal. I am not sure that fully explains it because my sergeant would have much preferred to get rid of me than Terry. I was salty and tended to question things. Terry did not. He was a much more compliant Marine.

You would think I learned my lesson in boot camp after a few days in motivation. However, in the less-disciplined environment of an airbase, my true personality came to the surface. I was not openly defiant, but I had opinions and was not shy about making them known. I have often reflected how God wired me that way. It's fine for a preacher, talk show host, and political candidate. It doesn't work so well as a corporal in Uncle Sam's Marine Corps. In spite of all that, Terry shipped out to Okinawa, and I stayed there for the duration of my service.

Terry and I drew closer for the time he had remaining at Naval Air Station South Weymouth. Little did I know that once he departed, I would never talk to him again. After I was honorably discharged from the Corps, my wife and I decided to drive to Kentucky to visit my mother. On the way back, we planned to stop by Indiana University of Pennsylvania in Indiana, Pennsylvania—the birthplace and home of Jimmy Stewart. I spent my first year of college there. Terry Laser was from Johnstown, only thirty miles south. Knowing I was that close, I wanted to see Terry.

I knocked on the door, and his mother answered. After introducing myself, I asked to see Terry. I only vaguely remember what she looked like, but I have a vivid memory of the pain on her face and the tears in her eyes.

"Terry was killed," she told me. I was shocked. Terry was my age, only about twenty when I met him. Yet he was already gone. I was dumbfounded.

She said, "The Marine Corps has classified his death, so we don't know how he died." She revealed that after his duty in Okinawa, he was sent to Cherry Point, New Jersey. While there, something happened. I've always assumed it was a duty-related accident. During that time there the government experimented with drugs, and among my worst suspicions was Terry somehow got tapped for something like that and lost his life in the process. That's sheer speculation on my part. It remains a mystery. It is reasonable to conclude an accident during normal duty would not have been kept secret from his own mother.

Terry's death had a profound impact on me. I have always interpreted his kind action as a sacrifice for me that ended in the loss of his life. We had the same job. In all likelihood, my career would have followed the same path his took had I taken those orders to Okinawa. What happened to him likely would have happened to me.

Only after becoming a Christian could I see the hand of God had preserved me. Terry was ready for heaven. I was not. I look forward to seeing Terry in heaven and thanking him for what he did for me and my family. I do not claim to fully understand this story, but I do know Terry is one of the people God used to get me ready for heaven. Now I know I will meet him there, and I will always be grateful for the graciousness he showed me.

Terry was an American of European descent. Our racial difference never came up between us. It didn't matter to him, and the only feelings I remember having about him were admiration and gratitude. Reflecting on it, I realize this was one of those encounters in life that shaped my thinking. There are those who would have us believe we live in a country where Terry, as a young white man, would have said, "I would take those orders myself, but Jackson is black, I'm not taking orders for a black guy." That's not what happened. No such thing ever came to his mind. He identified with his

Christianity and his faith, not his ethnicity. He did not posture as if he was doing some heroic thing for the black guy. He just did it, without fanfare or self-congratulations. Yet his simple act of kindness cost him his life, and I will never forget him for that.

Three and a half years after learning of Terry's death, I surrendered my life to the Lord Jesus Christ. Then I understood Terry and what motivated him. It was the love of God. He was not "religious." He had a relationship with the Living God through His Son Jesus Christ. Although Terry was in heaven when it happened to me, a life-changing encounter with God brought me into the same relationship with Jesus. Terry was one of the people God used to bring me into that relationship, and I know I will see him again in eternity.

CHAPTER 14

LEAVING THE MARINE CORPS

I was honorably discharged from the Corps in 1973 with partial disability. As I explained earlier, the AN-TPQ 10 radar was a very heavy piece of equipment. It was designed to be mobile, but it had three heavy modules that had to be disconnected from the base and moved quickly. In that process I suffered a severe back injury which landed me in the hospital. The doctors found I suffered a crack in my L-5 vertebrae. I was in tremendous pain and stayed in the hospital several days.

I was being treated at the Naval Hospital in Charlestown, Massachusetts. I remember the doctors coming in to tell me I had two options. If I wanted to stay in the Corps, I had to have a spinal fusion for the crack in my vertebrae. They said it was a dangerous operation that could result in paralysis. The other option was a medical discharge. They wouldn't allow me to stay in the Corps without the operation. I was proud of my Marine Corps service, but I wasn't prepared to risk paralysis. I had a little more than a year left. I opted to take an honorable discharge with partial disability. I was told I would experience chronic pain or discomfort, but I could live a normal life. I was also told the symptoms would likely get worse as I got older. That has proved to be true. I was honorably discharged fifteen months early on February 21, 1973 at the rank of Corporal (E-4).

CHAPTER 15

RETURNING TO COLLEGE

When I drove away from Naval Air Station South Weymouth for the last time, I knew exactly what I wanted to do—become a lawyer. While at NASSW, I worked with what we disparagingly referred to as "weekend warriors." They were reservists, and I later came to respect their service. At the time however, we active-duty Marines thought the whole thing was a joke, like Boy Scout camp. "These aren't real Marines," we often said. Of course, "grunts" said the same thing about us as air-wingers. Grunts were combat Marines, and they were rightly proud of it.

Marine Reservists showed up one weekend a month for training, and we saw them as second-class Marines. As I saw reservists respond to the call, leave their civilian lives behind to do battle for our nation, I shed such juvenile notions. I respect every person who puts on a uniform for our country. Regardless what branch they join or whether they are reserve or active duty, they deserve our respect and thanks.

Those reservists changed my life. Some I met were studying law at Harvard Law School. In talking to them and listening to their plans, a light went on. I knew I wanted to be a lawyer and concentrated like a laser on achieving that objective.

When I was discharged, I was more focused than ever before in my life. The Marine Corps gave me the discipline and the time to figure out what I wanted to do. There was never a doubt in my mind I would go back to college. The problem was I had no goal, no purpose. I knew education was important. My father drilled that into me. Nonetheless, I allowed myself to be distracted during my first year at college. I think the reason was that I had no higher purpose. I was getting an education for the sake of getting an education. That was not enough to keep me focused and disciplined in the midst of college parties and campus protests.

By the time I left the Corps, I was a man on a mission. I was going back to college to finish my degree, attend law school, and become an attorney. I started reading everything I could get my hands on. I was particularly interested in philosophy because I thought it might prepare me for the law. I found myself gravitating toward Ayn Rand's libertarian novels. It would be nearly a decade before I realized those were the first stirrings of a conservative conscience. I had no coherent worldview at that time, but I was imbued with the racial awareness of the era.

I also read Plato and Aristotle, Rene Descartes, and existentialists such as Camus and Sartre. I enjoyed it so much I decided to be a philosophy major. It was the right decision because I excelled at it, and it offered courses in logic that sharpened my analytical skills. I thought it would be good preparation for law school and it probably was.

By the time I enrolled in the University of Massachusetts at Boston, my goal was to go to Harvard Law School. Known as Umass Boston, the urban campus was a new extension of Umass Amherst, which was Massachusetts' most prestigious public university. The Boston campus now has dorms for resident students, but when I attended, there were no dorms. Most students lived locally and commuted to campus. There were traditional students who had just graduated from high school, but many were like me, already out of high school for a few years.

My wife and I enrolled together. The tuition was affordable without borrowing. It was perfect for my wife and me. We had the GI Bill and other income from full and part-time work. We could go to college without burying ourselves in debt, but it meant double duty. I worked a part-time job as a salesman for RCA television repair contracts. In those days, people actually bought television repair insurance and I sold it. My full-time job was security guard on the third shift. I worked all night, then went home in the morning to take a brief nap. I left for school about 8 a.m. and returned in the afternoon to study. I took another brief nap and went to work at RCA. After that I would go to my security guard job. We lived that way for two years.

When I hear socialists argue how college should be guaranteed and tuition should be free, I remember the sacrifices my wife and I made to finish our education. It was tough, but we were proud of ourselves. It built character in us. I wonder what the future will be if we continue to spoil and weaken our young people with a sense of entitlement? Will they have the fortitude to weather their personal storms? Will they have the courage to face and overcome national crises?

The University of Massachusetts Boston was established in 1965, only eight years before my wife and I showed up on campus. It had a better reputation than might have been expected for a new school, but I learned the administration and faculty felt they had something to prove. As I asked questions about my law school prospects, I discovered the college pecking order.

Because this school had a reputable name, it wasn't at the bottom of the barrel; but because it was so new, it didn't carry the same weight as the main campus in Amherst. I remember asking whether any graduate was ever admitted to Harvard Law School. The first answer I heard was "no." That response was quickly amplified to suggest it would be a long time before any student from Umass Boston would be admitted to HLS. Then I heard rumors one Asian student graduated and went on to Harvard Law School, which encouraged me. If one student preceded me, I would be the second. Otherwise, I would be the first. Either way, I was going to Harvard Law School. I never doubted it.

That belief in my own ability was in large part the result of my father's influence, who made me feel special and expected me to do great things. The other major influence was the can-do spirit of the

United States Marine Corps. The Corps instilled in us that defeat was never an option. When I finally landed at HLS, professors told students we were there to learn how to think like a lawyer. Well, the Marine Corps instilled in us how to think and behave like a Marine. It was an immersion in the warrior code, with the goal of making Marines not only physically tough, but mentally tough. We were pushed to the limit, and if you didn't break, you got to call yourself a Marine. If you broke, you went home.

We were not taught merely to fight, but to win, and winning was a matter of the heart as much as the head. That is the attitude I brought to my studies when I returned to college. At Indiana University of Pennsylvania, I was a boy who frittered the first year of college away. I entered the University of Massachusetts at Boston as a man who knew what I wanted to accomplish for myself and my family, and I would not be denied.

I studied hard, took no summers off and finished up my final three years of college in only two years. With the exception of one or two Bs in my first semester, I became a straight-A student, graduated with a 3.9 average, Summa Cum Laude with a Phi Beta Kappa Key.

My wife and I expected to be given nothing. We worked for what we wanted. That is the way we were brought up, and how we lived. It was not extravagant, but it had dignity. That is the way almost all Americans thought until attitudes began to shift in the 1960s. In his inaugural address in 1961, John F. Kennedy admonished, "Ask not what your country can do for you—ask what you can do for your country." The mantra today is "Don't ask, but demand, that your country do for you." In fact, you don't even need to be a citizen to demand America do for you. Sixty-three percent (63%) of non-citizen immigrants, including illegals, receive some form of welfare assistance.[4]

Forcing tax-paying citizens to do for others what they can do for themselves is a travesty. Forcing us to subsidize illegal immigrants adds insult to injury. The Left justifies this as compassion and "social justice." It is in fact theft and gross immorality. It is no less immoral than robbing someone at the point of a gun.

CHAPTER 16

ADMISSION TO HARVARD LAW SCHOOL

START HERE

When the time came to submit my law school applications, I approached the professors I liked and expected they would be happy to write me letters of recommendation based on my achievements in their classes and the relationships we enjoyed. They gladly wrote the letters, but they also had a grave warning I have never forgotten.

I was told by more than one that the Law School Admissions Test (LSAT) was very difficult and doing well on this test was essential for admission to top law schools. That did not surprise me. What they said next did.

According to these professors, black people don't score well on standardized tests because the tests are "culturally biased." I was warned not to expect to do well on the LSAT and not to expect to get into a top law school. It was suggested I apply to Suffolk School of Law and New England School of Law, which had lower standards of admission. I am in no way disparaging those institutions. They have produced some fine lawyers. I went up against some of them in my law practice. The insult was personal to me, with a patina of compassion to hide its true import.

It did not matter how bright I was or how well I did academically. According to confirmed liberals in a very liberal college, there are certain intellectual challenges black people simply cannot over-come. That was my first encounter with the velvet-gloved racism of liberal condescension.

Far from dissuading me from my goal, I became that much more determined to do well. I never bought the myth of cultural bias in standardized tests. If that were true, Asians who come to America from very different cultures, speaking another language, would fare poorly in academic testing. Yet, they outscore Americans from all ethnic backgrounds.

I prepared for the LSAT on my own by taking practice tests and scoring myself on them. I replicated the test setting including time allowed in the actual test. It is not possible to study for the LSAT in the usual sense. It assumes a base of knowledge acquired through years of education and experience. It tests reading comprehension, analytical ability, and writing skills. I had the intellectual skills, but without practice, I might not have been psychologically prepared.

When I walked into the test, I knew what to expect and did very well. In fact, I was an early admission to Harvard, but also got into Columbia, the University of Michigan, the University of Chicago, NYU, and every other school to which I applied. Yale was consid-ered far harder to get into than Harvard because its class size was so much smaller. I was placed on a waiting list and later admitted to Yale as well. However, the first letter of acceptance to hit my mail-box was the one I most coveted—Harvard. I'll say more about that later.

I kept the acceptance letters not only as a testament to the achievement, but also as a reminder of how wrong my professors were. My beloved father taught me never to quit or accept from myself anything less than the best. The acceptances proved I listened to him, not hyper-racial liberal naysayers.

Something interesting happened while I waited to hear from law schools. My wife, son, and I lived in the Germantown neighbor-hood of Quincy, Massachusetts. It was populated mainly by the Irish, many of whom were transplants from South Boston, a notori-ous neighborhood made infamous during the busing crisis.

I arrived there in October 1971 and commuted back and forth to the base like a regular job, except I wore a Marine Corps uniform. During that time, racial tensions became high as a result of "forced busing." As a Marine, I was not politically aware at all, certainly not of the ideology and politics behind court-ordered busing. In addition, our son was not of school age, and we lived ten miles outside the city of Boston. The closest we got to the melee was watching it on the news.

Little did I know a decade later I would find myself in South Boston agreeing with its residents in opposing busing. At that time, I was a full-fledged conservative. It was obvious to me that transporting poor black children out of a poor black neighborhood and substandard schools to go to substandard schools in a poor white neighborhood might have made liberal elites feel good, but it would not improve education for any of those students. I was right. As one might imagine, the media attacked me viciously. That was when I first learned journalists were not neutral. They had a liberal perspective and an agenda to destroy anyone with whom they disagreed, particularly any black person.

I was accused of siding with racists. It is true that busing brought some ugly sentiment to the surface, and I did not want to encourage racial hostility. What I wanted was to see all children get a better education. The people of "Southie" wanted to see their own children get a better education. These proud Irish came to America in the mid-nineteenth century under the most horrendous circumstances. They faced signs declaring, "No Irish Need Apply." They were considered of less value than a slave because the life of a slave was an investment, but an Irishman was worthless. They were given the most dangerous jobs. They had no choice but to band together into a political force. It was a matter of survival. Having a judge living in a swanky suburban neighborhood order the massive intrusion of children into their enclave was poking a tiger.

I do not doubt some Southie residents had racist attitudes, but they also had a legitimate grievance. Why should their communities be targeted with a massive influx? The irony is Americans had a similar response to the influx of Irish escaping the potato famine.

That response is never virtuous, but it is how human beings react to what feels like an invasion.

The hostility and protest of South Boston residents should have been directed at Judge Arthur T. Garrity, the architect of the busing order who virtually took over Boston schools for a decade. His children and those of his neighbors were never affected. I found this as morally objectionable as the violence and racial hostility over the so-called "school integration." Despite all the disruption, protests, and sacrifice, education was not improved for the children of Boston.

■ ■ ■

Getting back to 1973, busing changed the atmosphere all over the Greater Boston area. I didn't notice until after my discharge from the Marine Corps. Perhaps wearing the uniform shielded me from it or perhaps busing engendered such racial tension that eventually the uniform wouldn't have protected me. I'll never know for sure. The first time I noticed the difference was while riding home on a crowded bus. A young white guy sitting beside me smiled and said, "You're a long way from home, aren't you?" I smiled back, and said, "No, I live right up the street." It was not until I got home when I realized what he was saying—I did not belong in that neighborhood.

I wrote that off as one jerk having a little fun. The neighborhood was at the top of a hill and the public library was at the bottom of the hill about three or four residential blocks from my house. I would go to the library to read and study when the apartment was a little too loud. Once, I was walking down the hill and the police drove up. I had a book bag with me. The officer who was driving rolled down his window and said, "We don't allow solicitors in this neighborhood." I told him I lived at 225 Taffrail Road, "right up the street." He looked at me without saying another word. That message was not lost on me because there was no smile to throw me off. It was *not* friendly.

My wife and I were too busy working, studying, and taking care of our son to think about it much. I liked the apartment, the neighborhood, and I was not afraid. That would soon change.

I have been a big boxing fan since early childhood. My dad introduced me to the sport and his passion for it. I gravitated to it, and even did some boxing training for a few years in my mid-to-late teens. He told me some great stories about Joe Louis and Sugar Ray Robinson. I told some of those stories to my son, and he shares the same passion.

The infamous Ali – Foreman fight, one of the biggest in boxing history, was scheduled to take place in Kinshasa, Zaire, on October 30, 1974. The fight was promoted as "The Rumble in the Jungle." Like many, I wanted to see whether George Foreman would finally shut Ali's big mouth. Millions of Americans were hoping to see the colorful champ humbled. It was shown live at the Hynes Convention Center in Boston. Somehow, I scraped together the money to go. It was not a wise investment, but I was twenty-two years old.

Ali shocked the world, knocking Foreman out in the eighth round. He was more than a big mouth. He was in fact one of the greatest fighters ever to climb into the ring. He won my respect that night. Foreman got "rope-a-doped." Ironically, that fight proved to be a major turning point for the better in the life of George Foreman, although I'm sure it did not feel that way on the evening he went down on the canvas. He later accepted Jesus Christ as his Lord and Savior and became a millionaire products promoter and entrepreneur. The famous George Foreman Grill made him a very wealthy celebrity.

I will never forget that fight or that night. It happened on a Tuesday. When I got home, my wife was sitting in the apartment frightened because bricks had been thrown through our windows. I sat awake all night with a shotgun on my lap. When day broke, my mind was made up. We were leaving. It finally dawned on me something had changed, and the environment was too hostile to have my wife and children living there.

That week, I found an apartment in a large building at 362 Rindge Avenue in Cambridge. Four days later, on Saturday morning, with the help of some of my Marine Corps buddies, we loaded up a U-Haul and moved out of Quincy.

This is part of the reason I find it laughable when I am accused of denying the reality of racism. I do not deny its reality. *I deny its authority over me.* I will not be controlled by what others think of me. I refuse to smear an entire group of people because a few act like fools. Americans of African descent have sought to escape stereotyping based on what one black person or one segment does. Yet many black people do to others—especially to people of European descent—exactly what they do not wish done to them. I refuse to do that. I treat every person as an individual and draw no conclusions until that person gives me reason. Whatever conclusions I draw are based on the behavior of one person, not prejudices about the ethnic group to which he or she belongs.

I believe most Americans want to see the vision of our Pledge of Allegiance fully realized—"one nation, under God, indivisible, with liberty and justice for all." The United States of America is the only nation whose citizens profess such a wonderful dream, and this is "the last best hope on earth" for seeing it realized.

CHAPTER 17

HARVARD LAW SCHOOL ADMISSION

I left Quincy in too big a hurry to have mail forwarded. I must have had it held for pick up. On November 19, 1974, I walked into the Quincy post office to pick up our mail. The only thing I remember was seeing the Harvard Law School return address on the envelope. It was thin, and on bonded stationery. It was either a letter of rejection or acceptance. This was a moment which had consumed my thinking for at least two years. This was what I worked for and hoped for. I had already determined that if I received a rejection letter, I would wait another year, strengthen my application, and reapply. My feet were glued to that spot as I opened the letter. At that point in my life, these were the most important words I had ever read:

Dear Mr. Jackson:

It gives me great pleasure to report that your application for admission to the Harvard Law School has been accepted. You have been given a place with the class beginning its work in September, 1975. Please accept my warmest congratulations.

I dropped to my knees with joy. I walked out of that post office on cloud nine. I did it! Little did I know the challenge was just beginning, and I still had a lot of growing to do.

Since the sixth grade, I was accustomed to being one of the smartest students in the classroom, a standout. I was disciplined about studying. Harvard Law School was a place where practically every student was a standout. No longer was I the first person with the answers. It was a bit of culture shock.

For the first time I realized family background matters. I met students who were going to be third-generation lawyers. It was not that they were inherently brighter or had more native intelligence. They were simply more conversant with the legal system and were enculturated with how lawyers think. My children have had that advantage, but I did not. None of my progeny chose law as a profession, but they are all analytical thinkers.

Studies have shown, children from poor and uneducated families hear one-third the vocabulary words as children with educated parents.[5] The children of lawyers probably hear more vocabulary words than they would like. My own children have remarked that my questions were often challenging, even a little intimidating. Today, they probably get a similar response from their friends and associations. My purpose was to make them think, rigorously and analytically. Without consciously setting about to do so, I was training them to think like lawyers.

During the early days of my law school years, we were told the goal of law school was just that, to train our minds to think like lawyers. The late Professor Milton Katz, who taught Torts to first-year students, encouraged us with the assurance we would all "get it" because we would not have been admitted had we not been bright enough to get it. "Some will get it sooner than others," he admonished, "but you will all get it." He was right, but for me there would be some serious distractions on the road to graduation.

CHAPTER 18

SPIRITUAL CRISIS AT HARVARD

I have told the story often of my dramatic conversion at Harvard, but I rarely tell of the preceding crisis. My expectations of Harvard were very high. I anticipated not only meeting the best and the brightest but being inspired. Undoubtedly, highly intelligent, gifted students were assembled on that small piece of real estate. Many had already proven themselves in professional life. The law would be their second career. I met scientists, doctors, business owners, former professors, Rhodes Scholars, and people from almost every heritage. Most of the students followed the traditional path of college to law school without any real-world experience. A few, like me, had already experienced adult responsibilities and first careers.

What shocked me was not any lack of talent, but a lack of integrity. I expected to meet a better quality of people. What I found instead was a smarter class of people but with all the same vices you would find in the poorest precincts of the country. I learned the stark reality that education does not produce good people. Harvard was really no different from the rest of the world. There were drug-dealing students who, to my knowledge, were never caught. Certain professors regularly got together with students to smoke pot and party. A few years after my graduation, some students were arrested for running a prostitution ring. The leader secretly videotaped students having sex. He used those tapes to blackmail female students to provide sexual favors for money. He was the Harvard Law School pimp.

Harvard was choosing students not based on moral character, but career potential. I've heard it said many times how Harvard does not make people successful. They choose people who will succeed and then Harvard gets credit for it. Success as they define it does not include integrity, honor, and uprightness. It was naive for me to have thought the people I would meet there would be decent. I had a vision of Harvard Law School as a place of virtue. It was a jolt to my psyche when I considered how many venal and immoral people would become the leaders of our society.

Mel Reynolds, who became a congressman from Chicago, was the first student I met when I visited the campus. It was an encounter I will never forget because his appearance was a contradiction. He was sitting on steps near the entrance as if he didn't have a care in the world. He was wearing little round glasses and a cowboy hat, shirt, and boots. He reminded me of Teddy Roosevelt, except that he was black.

Reynolds symbolized how I came to view Harvard Law School—intellectually brilliant and morally bankrupt. While serving in Congress, he was convicted of twelve counts of criminal sexual assault, sexual abuse, obstruction of justice, and solicitation of child pornography. In 1995, he was sentenced to five years in federal prison. Two years later, in 1997, he was convicted of sixteen counts of bank fraud, misuse of campaign funds, and lying to Federal Election Commission investigators. He spent eight and a half years in federal prison—a brilliant Harvard man with great potential destroyed by his own low character.

To be sure, most students at Harvard Law School were not the frightening characters I have described here. Nor am I implying I was a paragon of virtue. Nevertheless, the depravity I saw made me anxious about the future of our country if such people were to be its stewards. These were not Plato's philosopher kings or future enlightened statesman.

There were a few black students on the campus, and there was a social expectation that we would hang out together. Unlike most of them however, I was a family man who lived off campus. I had little time to "hang out." I still did more of that than I should have. In addition, I've always wanted to meet people with different backgrounds and learn about their experiences. As part of that effort, I ran for president of the John Marshall Club, named after the First Chief Justice of the Supreme Court. It was a prestigious legal club on campus. There were no other black members of the club as I recall. I joined, became known, and thought I had a good chance of becoming president. I made the mistake of telling some black students who I considered to be friends and thought they would be gratified I was trying to break new ground. This is where I learned how vicious some of my fellow students were.

On the day of the election, about three of these so-called friends showed up at the election meeting and did the "ghetto thing." They caricatured how they thought white students might expect black people to behave. They were loud, disruptive, and wore what we used to call "big apple" hats. They made clear they were there to "support" me. The truth was they were there to sabotage me and make sure I could not be elected as club president.

The message they communicated was, to elect Jackson would be to turn the Marshall Club into the "black ghetto club." It had the desired effect. I lost the election, and, needless to say, I was quite angry. I grew up in the ghetto and knew some very rough people, but I never saw such devious, backstabbing behavior. It was done either out of pure jealousy or to send a message to stay in my place. One would have expected that message to come from racist whites. Surprisingly, it came from racist black students. I later learned the most racist people I encountered were liberals—black and white— committed to keeping black people in line. That was another milestone toward my political, ideological, and spiritual awakening.

This group that blocked my election at the Marshall Club were revealed as mortal enemies. They always were, but I was previously unaware. The tension between us got so bad it began to look like it would get physical. I had to bring a friend and fellow Marine Corps veteran to join me on campus to let the group know if a physical confrontation was in the offing, they would not be facing me alone or if they managed to jump me, there would be retribution. The idea of fighting two Marines was enough to back them off and the threat subsided.

That was my introduction to the envy and utter evil possessed by some of my fellow students. It was profoundly disturbing. They had bigger vocabularies and more sophisticated ways to rob you, but they were no different in substance from what I saw growing up in the ghetto. It was less honorable because fights in the ghetto were straight up, mano a mano. This was vicious, conniving behavior from men considered to be the best and the brightest.

The incident also reinforced another valuable lesson. The touted racial and ethnic solidarity within the black community is a facade. Generally speaking, people look out for themselves. In fact, many will pat you on the back, call you brother, and drive the knife in as deep as they can. There is a virtual genocide of black-on-black crime, with thousands of young black men losing their lives every year at the hands of other young black men.

Jesus broke through the superficial nature of ethnic and family loyalty when He said, "Whoever does the will of My Father in heaven is My brother and sister and mother" (Matthew 12:50). Loyalty to principle is a much more reliable basis for trust than loyalty to an ethnicity or race. Principle, not race, is supposed to be what unites Americans. The sooner we embrace that truth, the more secure will be our national future.

CHAPTER 19

BECOMING A CHRISTIAN

There have been five major milestones affecting the trajectory of my life. These are in order of chronology, not importance. The first was my father taking me out of foster care. The second was joining the Marine Corps. The third was wedding Theodora, to whom I have been married fifty-two years as of September 11, 2022. The fourth was my admission to Harvard Law School. While the births of our children did not change my life trajectory, they were all very important and had a hand in changing me as a person. There are other events which loom large. Founding a church in 1980 was extremely important. Resigning from the Democrat Party to become a Republican was a life-changing step. Writing and publishing my first book was a breakthrough achievement. This book is my third. These milestones enriched my life tremendously.

Yet the greatest milestone of all is becoming a Christian. Surrendering my life to Jesus Christ as Lord and Savior is the best thing that ever happened to me. My conversion was dramatic and permanent. I have never wavered in forty-four years.

Looking back, I know God chased me from my childhood. When I was five or six years old, sitting in little Mt. Levi Baptist Church in Chester, Pennsylvania, I had my first spiritual experience. Pastor Leslie L. Sapp was preaching a sermon on Job. I was sitting at the end of the front row, and he was no more than ten feet away expounding vigorously.

Suddenly it made sense to me, as if a light was turned on. I understood and hung on his every word for the remainder of his message. The fact I have such a vivid memory of something that happened in my early childhood is supernatural. When nearly twenty years later I surrendered my life to Jesus Christ, I understood how the Holy Spirit touched me on that occasion. Perhaps it was to mark me for the future awaiting me, with the realization God has always been with me. I have never forgotten that moment.

When I was fourteen years old, out of the blue and without any logical context I can remember, I told my dad I wanted to be a preacher. I do not believe I ever made that statement any time before or after that. This was the second seemingly minor and momentary event indelibly inscribed on my heart. Although my conversion appeared sudden and dramatic, looking back I see stepping-pingstones along the way on a path guiding me to God.

I spent some time prior to law school in a spiritual search but had no epiphany and reached no conclusion. I was reading everything I could get my hands on, from Ayn Rand to books on Buddhism and even Satanism. Interestingly enough, I never read the Bible during this time.

This is a common mistake of Americans. We live in a culture steeped in Christian principles and values, but we are drawn to the exotic. Our culture is Christian. Most Americans still identify as Christians, and yet eastern religions and philosophies are much more interesting to us. I was no different. Americans should want to learn all we can about the faith that motivated the Pilgrims and animated the Founding Fathers. Sadly, there is a growing cultural hostility toward Christianity. That is something I am determined to address because the well-being and future of our nation depends upon it.

In 1976, during my second year of law school, I finally got around to reading the Bible. My father taught me to respect God, but he could not teach me to serve Him when I was younger because he wasn't. However, in 1975 my father had a profound conversion, went back to church, and accepted the call into the ministry. Once again, he was the key factor in changing the trajectory of my life.

I loved and admired my father immensely. He was my hero. From June to August 1976, my wife, son, and I stayed with him while I worked a summer law internship at Morgan, Lewis & Bockius in Philadelphia. At the time, I thought I would return to the Philadelphia area after graduation. I was impressed by the changes I saw in Dad. He had been a habitual drinker. Now he didn't drink at all. He had always used salty language, but now he didn't curse anymore. He was cynical about church and did not attend while he was raising me. Now he went to church every Sunday.

A short and seemingly trivial conversation with my dad shortly before leaving his apartment after the summer proved to be one of the most important conversations of my life. He told me, almost in an offhand remark, that for the first time in his life, he was reading the Bible from cover to cover. I don't recall being struck by that when he told me, but I remember thinking about it during the drive home. It was a thought I could not shake.

By the time we finished that six-hour drive, I was determined to do what my father was doing. I would read the Bible from cover to cover. My interest was not spiritual, but intellectual. I rationalized, as a Harvard intellectual, I should read the Bible as one of the great books. I later realized it was the Holy Spirit working on my heart. In September 1976, I started reading the Bible and within two months I began to come under conviction. I did not understand what was happening to me, but I could not ignore it or pretend it was nothing. It was powerful and undeniable.

In late October, I began to read the Psalms and was re-introduced to King David. I read about him in the historical books of the Bible, which are about his life and actions. However as I read the Psalms, I saw David's heart, and I was moved. Part of my thinking about Christianity was, church was boring and a place for women and children, not men. David, however, was a man's man who nevertheless spoke with passion about God. It was as if he knew God intimately, as his closest friend. Psalm 63 made an unforgettable impression on me:

O God, You are my God;
Early will I seek You;
My soul thirsts for You;
My flesh longs for You
In a dry and thirsty land
Where there is no water.
So I have looked for You in the sanctuary,
To see Your power and Your glory.
Because Your lovingkindness is better than life,
My lips shall praise You.
Thus I will bless You while I live;
I will lift up my hands in Your name.
My soul shall be satisfied as with marrow and fatness,
And my mouth shall praise You with joyful lips.
When I remember You on my bed,
I meditate on You in the night watches.
Because You have been my help,
Therefore in the shadow of Your wings I will rejoice.
My soul follows close behind You;
Your right hand upholds me. (Psalm 63:1–8)

The Bible, unlike any other book ever written, demands a decision. Do I believe it or cast it aside? There is no middle ground. I didn't have the answer. I wasn't going to a church or prayer meeting. I wasn't seeking spiritual counsel. I simply began to ask God if He was real, to show me. I prayed, *I want to know You the way David and these other people in the Bible knew You. If You are real, make Yourself known to me!*

Looking back, I know I was always being drawn by the Holy Spirit. Most of the time I was running away. It finally became my quest to determine once and for all whether God was real. I have heard others say they tried that, and it did not work. I tried it, and it worked. I remember sitting in the car outside the supermarket while my wife went in to pick up groceries. I had my law books with me so I could use the time to study. Suddenly it came to mind that I had in effect challenged God to make Himself real to me. I looked up from my Torts casebook and said in a loud voice, "Well, God, I'm waiting!"

I did not share this quest with my wife or friends. I didn't talk to my father about it. It was between me and God. I wanted no human intervention or input.

About a block or so from our apartment building was a ballpark. It had a cage at the top of a high set of bleachers, probably built for sports commentators. So deep was my hunger for a definitive answer to the question of God's existence that late at night I would occasionally drive to that park and climb to the top of those bleachers. I would sit in that cage, look up at the sky, and call on God at the top of my lungs: "If You're real, show me!"

One Saturday afternoon while hanging out with some fellow students, I had the first glimpse that my life was changing. It wasn't a formal party, but to be sure, we were not having a prayer meeting. There was a knock on the door, and I answered it. A young guy my age was standing there, and he was very troubled. I cannot explain why he came to that door. Perhaps he was accustomed to crying on the shoulders of his neighbors. All I know is he began to unload on me at the door that he was having problems. He did not strike me as mentally ill, just burdened with worry and probably depressed.

To my recollection, he never came inside. I listened to his story and found myself telling him I had been reading the Bible and it is of immense help to me. I asked him if he had a Bible. He said he didn't. I excitedly told him to go back to his apartment, which was one or two doors down, and I was going to go buy him a Bible because that would help him. I rushed to get my coat, got on an elevator, went to my car, and headed out into Boston's snowy streets to buy a Bible for this troubled young man.

As I drove, it suddenly hit me: I was in my car going to look for a Bible for somebody who needed help. My actions stunned me so much I actually stopped the car and thought, *What am I doing? I'm going out to buy someone a Bible?* It was a revelation, and I wasn't sure what it meant. I was acting in a way I never acted before, doing something I never did before. I found a Christian bookstore, purchased a Bible, and took it to him.

It was unprecedented behavior on my part and I thought this might indeed be from God. I remember muttering to myself, "Thank You, Jesus," but even that seemed odd and out of character, as if it was not coming from my mouth. It was clear something very powerful was happening to me, but I had not reached the permanent and dramatic change soon to come.

During that period leading up to my conversion, each day ended the same. When everything quieted down and my wife and son were in bed, I turned to the Bible sitting on the coffee table of our small living room. It was open to the page I was reading the night before. I was drawn to it. That Bible was a gift from my father. It is a family heirloom and the only Bible I had. I would plop my tired body on the couch and begin reading. It became my routine. The impact was extraordinary. Dad and the Bible he gave me were the final instruments of my surrender to Jesus Christ.

CHAPTER 20

"THE BOY'S GONE"

There is an old spiritual that says, "I woke up this mornin' with my mind stayed on Jesus."[6]

On the morning of December 22, 1976, I awoke in the presence of God. I felt like I was levitating six feet above the bed. For the first time in my life, I experienced the presence of God, and it was unmistakable. It was supernatural and powerful, as if He quietly entered my room during the night and was waiting for me to wake up. Over forty-six years later, at this writing, the moment is still fresh, powerful, and emotional. I awoke in the presence of Absolute Holiness, and Infinite Love. It was exhilarating and frightening, but the question of God's reality and existence was forever answered that morning. I have never doubted since, not for a second.

It was in a two-bedroom apartment at 362 Rindge Avenue in Cambridge, Massachusetts. My wife was sweeping our son's bedroom as I went to her and rested my hand gently on her shoulder. She looked at me sweetly as if she knew I was about to say something important. I said, "You know what?" She said, "What?" I said, *"I think I'm saved."* I will never forget that moment. Those were the most important words I ever spoke. When I expressed them verbally, it was as if they took on tangible reality. They not only came out of me, but they came upon me with great force. These were the

103

first words of a new life, spoken by a new man. The most important change in my life was happening, my destiny was taking a dramatic turn. My wife must have felt the weight of my confession, but she was not sure what it meant. Her mouth gaped, she dropped the broom she was using, and exclaimed, "What?"

I responded, "I don't know how to explain it, but God is doing something in my life. Where do you go to church? I'm going with you on Sunday." She took about three steps back and stared at me with shock and confusion on her face. She then said to my surprise, "You're not going with me."

People laugh now when I tell that story, but it was certainly not funny at the time. I should not have been surprised by wife's reaction. Up to that point, she saw no outward signs leading to this dramatic announcement. For her, it was out of the blue and disconcerting. She suspected I was experiencing a nervous breakdown. Once our families heard about this sudden and powerful change, they reached the consensus I had lost my mind. I learned later there was some discussion about having me committed. I doubt they could have succeeded had they tried and thank God they never did. I was quite lucid, but filled with a holy and unbridled zeal, which undoubtedly looked like a man unhinged. It was a 180-degree departure from what they knew about me. The day before I had been the worldly law student. The next day I was the overzealous evangelical Christian. Looking back, it must have been very difficult for my family to process.

My perspective was I found the true meaning of life, everyone needed to know, and I needed to tell them. As a new and immature Christian, I had no idea whether other professed Christians had the same experience and understood the urgency of telling others. At that point, as far as I was concerned, it was my sole responsibility to tell every human being on the face of the earth. There is a tremendous blessing to being saved outside any organized experience. I was unhampered by the restraints of tradition. I was not a Baptist, Methodist, Pentecostal, or Catholic. I was merely a follower of Jesus Christ. It was new and exciting.

The downside is most Christians have a traditional frame of reference, and when God moves outside their expected norms, it can be difficult to understand. Those operating outside the familiar boundaries can find it difficult to be accepted. My wife had been going to church fairly regularly, but I was not going at all. So, I asked her what church she was attending, because I wanted to go with her the following Sunday. She graciously declined to be part of any spectacle that might ensue around her newly minted husband. She was confused by the abrupt change.

On Sunday, December 26, 1976, I went alone to St. Paul A.M.E. in Cambridge, Massachusetts. Reverend Brandon was pastor at the time. When he gave the call to receive Jesus Christ as Savior, I bolted from the balcony to the altar. I cannot say I ran, but that is the image indelibly inscribed in my mind. I still see myself running, sprinting to the altar. I knew Jesus was my Savior, and I wanted everyone to know. To this day, it brings tears to my eyes to think about it. I laid at that altar for what seemed forever, weeping and wailing. All of the sin that held me in bondage was washed away. I'd come face to face with the Holy and Righteous God.

Literally, overnight, I went from cursing, drinking, and hanging out with my buddies to thinking and talking about Jesus. My wife and family thought Harvard Law School proved too much for me.

When I returned to law school that January, many of my fellow law students began to keep their distance. I was consumed with one idea: People are on their way to eternal damnation in hell, and Jesus is their only hope of salvation and heaven. I later understood how strange it must have looked for me to suddenly want to tell everyone about Jesus.

Yet, I was absolutely right even if my delivery and demeanor needed some refining. We are made by God to know Him, love Him, and serve Him. He has an eternal plan for humanity and for every human being. It is a perfect and glorious plan including the end of all sin, pain, and death and the creation of a world of perfect love, joy, peace, and prosperity. Sin has separated us from that plan. The good news is Jesus Christ has solved that problem for us by taking the penalty for our sins. He is the King of God's perfect kingdom and the only door through which we enter.

It was good news 2,000 years ago. It was good news in 1976. It is still good news today, and I will tell it at every opportunity until

my time on earth is done. In less than a year I preached my first
sermon and was licensed by the historic Ebenezer Baptist Church
in Boston to proclaim the gospel of Jesus Christ. I have been doing
it ever since.

I have never been a moderate person. My father saw that in me
before I saw it in myself. I remember him saying to one of his friends
about me when I was a teenager, "My son never does anything half-
way. When he goes, he goes all out." When I heard him say that, it
struck me as idle chatter. I did not realize my father understood me
better than I understood myself. Like most teenagers, I was not
doing a lot of introspection, but Dad took note of my personality.

He observed what I could not see in myself. When I was studying, I studied hard. When I played basketball, I played hard. When
I joined the military, I joined the toughest branch I knew—the
Marine Corps. When I decided to go to law school, I chose the
hardest school to get into. When I got saved, it was no casual matter of joining a church. I was consumed with the God who revealed
Himself to me, and I wanted everybody to know what I knew
because their lives depended on it.

As you can imagine, the change in my perspective and character was, to say the least, disorienting to my fellow students. When
I returned to law school after the Christmas break, walking down
the corridors was like the parting of the Red Sea. Fellow students
scattered to get away from me. They knew I was going to talk to
them about Jesus if I had the slightest opportunity. They were
right. Four decades later, Jesus is still my passion. He remains the
most important Person in my life and the most important subject
of conversation.

In time, I grew to understand decorum and appropriateness
of time, place, and methodology. At the time of my conversion
however, I was too full of youthful enthusiasm to consider how
others might perceive my behavior. If a student today were to do
what I did forty years ago, he would be accused of offending
people or worse.

Jesus said His name would be a stone of stumbling and a rock
of offense. It is amazing to me that people do not seem to be
offended by Islam, Buddhism, or Hinduism. Even socialism, which

is all the rage today among millennials, is accepted. We should all be offended by it, but many of our mainstream institutions applaud it. It should be called out for the insidious evil it is, and for its genocidal history. Marxism, socialism, and communism leave a trail of starvation, torture, and murder in their wake. This fact is greeted with a yawn or weak rationalizations, but too few are offended by it. Every American should be.

However, the name of Jesus is a different matter. It offends people. Indeed, institutions, signs, and symbols representing Jesus or Christianity are deemed offensive. Wearing crosses, displaying Bibles, or posting Scriptures are forbidden in schools, corporate offices, and even in the military. Years ago in the Boston area, one teacher was reprimanded for having Jesus written on the blackboard of his office. One servicewoman was court martialed for having a Bible verse stuck on her computer monitor.

You do not hear such complaints about public expressions of Islam. In fact, efforts are increasing to accommodate Islam at every turn. In the meantime, Christianity is often met with harsh objections against any accommodation whatsoever. On some college campuses, Christian groups cannot be recognized unless they agree that non-Christians can be officers. The reality is America has developed a virulent strain of anti-Christian bigotry. Over the last sixty years, the Judeo-Christian cultural consensus has been eroded by increasingly secular values and moral, spiritual, and cultural relativism.

Responding to my newfound Christian faith, some of my fellow students at Harvard Law said to me, "I'm a Christian too." My first thought was, *Why am I only hearing this now? Where were you? Were you part of a secret club? All this time I've been trying to find my way to God, and you never said a word to me until I openly professed my faith in Jesus Christ.*

There was a giant spiritual vacuum at Harvard Law School, and I gladly stepped into the breach. I was praying for people in the corridors before they knew what hit them. I still have that tendency today. If you meet me in public and ask for prayer, be prepared for me to pray on the spot, aloud. Every Christian should develop that practice. The results are amazing. Ten years after I graduated, one fellow student at Harvard wrote me a letter telling me the impact I had on his life by praying for him in a corridor. He told me it was on his heart for years to tell me my prayer launched him on a journey that led him to accept Jesus Christ as his Lord and Savior.

It took a little while for people to realize I hadn't lost my mind. And it also took me a little while to settle down and figure out the best way to approach people so they wouldn't think I was nuts.

In fact, I struggled with whether to stay in law school. I wasn't sure I was on the right path anymore. I went to see the law school dean, told him what happened in my life, and that I belonged at the divinity school and would be withdrawing from law school. For a week I did not attend classes. That was zeal without maturity and knowledge. God made clear to me I was making a huge mistake and should finish law school. I went back to see the dean, and he told me he took no action on my withdrawal. I returned to classes and graduated in May 1978.

CHAPTER 21

A PREACHER OF THE GOSPEL

For the first time since my years in foster care, I began attending church regularly. In fact, it would have been impossible to keep me out. After resisting for well over a decade, I finally wanted to go to church. God did a major work in my heart. It was truly miraculous, and I am still in awe of it. It was fascinating to experience old hymns from my foster home years coming back to me as if kept in a secret compartment of my memory waiting to be discovered. For the first three months after my conversion, I continued attending the church where I made my first public witness of salvation— St. Paul AME (African Methodist Episcopal Church). However, I was dedicated as a baby in Calvary Baptist Church in Chester. I also attended Shiloh Baptist and its two split-offs—Friendship Baptist under Rev. Michael Hayes, and Mt. Levi Baptist under Rev. Leslie L. Sapp. My background was Baptist. Over time, I felt led to go back to the church of my roots.

As a Christian I became active in any ministry I could. I was still faced with the enormous task of finishing Harvard Law School, but my newfound spiritual energy and drive needed an outlet. I did prison ministry with volunteers at St. Paul. I visited the sick and shut-ins wherever I could find them. Having been saved through such an overpowering, supernatural encounter with God, I had no problem believing He could heal the sick. I was excited to see it happen or even be the instrument of prayer God used to make it happen.

It might be fruitful here to clarify a misconception about Christianity. Many people believe you are born into Christianity through family. That is not true in the sense of natural birth. Being raised in a Christian home, attending church as a child, reading and memorizing Scriptures do not make you a Christian.

Jesus said in John 3:3, "unless one is born again, he cannot see the kingdom of God." The Greek language there means "born from above." You must have a heavenly rebirth. This puzzled Nicodemus, a Pharisee, to whom Jesus spoke these words. He wondered whether this meant returning to the womb and coming out again. Jesus made clear He was talking about a spiritual birth, not a physical one. That is what I mean when I speak of being a Christian. I was raised in a Christian foster home during the early years of my life, but I was not a Christian. I was even baptized at the age of nine, but I was not a Christian. I became a Christian on December 22, 1976 and confirmed it in a public confession four days later on December 26.

Because of my zeal to do ministry and a love for people instilled in me by the Holy Spirit, I found myself ministering to an elderly man I befriended through a married couple my wife and I knew. I went to the hospital to see him several times. He had many health problems. During one of those visits, he told me about his church and how much it meant to him. Something resonated with me, and I knew my wife and I were going to visit this church. That is how God led me to Ebenezer Baptist Church in Boston.

The first time we visited, the pastor was not there. An associate minister spoke. He mumbled through his message, and we did not understand him. However, he was not the pastor, and before we wrote the church off, we wanted to hear and meet the man leading the ministry. That is where I met my pastor and first spiritual mentor, the late Rev. Dr. Rafe Taylor. We returned the following Sunday, and he preached the message. He was spectacular, full of the Holy Spirit and fire. We never looked for another church.

Rev. Taylor was a bear of a man, only five feet eight inches tall, but he weighed about 250 pounds. He was built like a tank. He had a gravelly voice and a quick temper. He did not suffer fools gladly. He fought in the Korean War and was called to preach while in a POW camp. He was tough, but he was powerfully anointed and could preach the paint off the walls. I sat under Rev. Taylor until I was called to pastor my own church. During my years of training at Ebenezer, I took classes at Harvard Divinity School and the Weston School of Theology. I was still going to law school, but I was hungry for spiritual knowledge. Unfortunately, it was not to be found at Harvard Divinity School.

I was called into pastoral ministry less than three years after my conversion, a year and a half after law school. Once I was officially licensed to preach by the historic Ebenezer Baptist Church in Boston and then installed as a pastor, my wife and my in-laws settled into the realization that what they thought was a break with reality was in fact a break with my old life to answer the call into ministry.

CHAPTER 22

BECOMING A LEADER

Until I was called, I did not think of myself as a leader. If any such aspirations were in me, they were buried deep in my subconscious. While in the Marine Corps, I was offered the opportunity to go to Officer Candidates School. I turned it down because they were asking me to extend my enlistment two more years. I wanted to finish my education as soon as possible. That decision is one of my life's regrets. Becoming a Marine Corps officer would have been the honor of a lifetime. At that young age, I did not see myself as a leader and had no conception of what it meant to be one. I take solace in knowing if God's plan for me included becoming a Marine Corps officer, it would have happened. I still wish it had worked out that way.

Once I had my dramatic encounter with God, my perception of myself began to change. First, it is the responsibility of every Christian to lead others to Jesus Christ. Concern for what happens to others is intrinsic to Christianity. After surrendering my life to Him, I began to assess my life's impact on others rather than considering only what I was doing for myself.

Since my conversion, I have studied, thought, prayed about, and tried to better understand leadership. As a young convert and student, I only knew my life was no longer about myself, but about serving others. I have come to believe leadership is best defined as influencing people to fulfill God's plan for their lives and His kingdom. That involves helping people move from godlessness to discipleship and from living for oneself to living for Jesus.

I know now the impulse to lead has always been a part of my life. As a child, I formed a gang called the Eagles to defend our street. I was the point guard on a Biddy League Team called Lloyd Eyre. Mind you, I was no genius basketball player, but I landed on a team that chose me as the leader. During my first year in college, I was asked to speak at one of the many rallies on campus for various causes. After speaking, I was asked to lead a group of students, who followed me around for a time until I shooed them off. When I was in the Marine Corps, I became the Guard Arm carrier for one of my platoons. The Guard Arm carrier sets the pace for runs and marches while carrying the platoon flag, an extra weight and responsibility. I was comfortable and fulfilled in that role. Leadership has always been a part of my life, but I didn't realize it until God called me to that role. I had a lot to learn, and I am still learning.

CHAPTER 23

BECOMING POLITICAL

Becoming a Christian opened a whole new vista for me. Until that time, I was not politically active, although always opinionated. I remember expressing political opinions in high school, but I was not an activist. The closest I came to activism was one half-hearted attempt to join the Black Panthers at the height of their notoriety. I also attended rallies during my first year at college. There was not much depth of conviction about any of it. I mentioned earlier how I participated in an anti-ROTC rally and left the rally to go to ROTC class. That's how deep my commitment was. It was cool to be seen at the rally. However, I wasn't willing to fail the course. I was not a candidate for academic martyrdom.

That was my first year of college, and my political ideas were not informed. I was going with the flow. In fact, a coherent political philosophy did not take shape until I became a Christian. My faith gave me a lens through which to view the world and it dramatically altered my perspective.

Within a short time after my "Damascus Road experience," God began to show me the truth about America. We are a providential nation, His unique gift in human history. Our freedom can be sustained only through the stewardship of every citizen committed to guarding our liberty. When I put on a Marine Corps uniform to serve as an official sentinel of our country, it was out of a sense of duty. I was willing to give my life to defend America because that was the job. My faith transformed my patriotism from duty to love. I understood being born an American citizen is the equivalent of hitting the lottery, but not by luck. This is a conclusion I reached over thirty years ago, and it has strengthened and deepened throughout the years. We Americans are here by divine appointment.

And He has made from one blood every nation of men to dwell on all the face of the earth and has determined their preappointed times and the boundaries of their dwellings. (Acts 17:26)

I believe my destiny and the destiny of every American is inextricably bound to the destiny of our country. That truth percolated in my mind and heart a long time before I founded STAND: Staying True to America's National Destiny. My destiny is tied to my country. America's fulfillment of her destiny depends upon me and every other citizen embracing our civic responsibility as a free people.

Like most Americans of African descent, I was raised as a Democrat. My father was a Franklin Roosevelt Democrat who credited that president with saving his life in the Civilian Conservation Corps (CCC camps)—a public works project created during the Great Depression. My initial steps toward political engagement were as a Democrat because that was all I knew. I had no idea the Democrat Party was replacing Judeo-Christian values with moral relativism, identity politics, and the creation and perpetuation of victim classes.

After law school, I worked at Coopers & Lybrand (now PricewaterhouseCoopers) in their tax department. I didn't care for the job and was thrilled when I got appointed as deputy commissioner of banks. Shortly thereafter, I was elected to the Massachusetts Democrat State Committee, made up of the top leaders and activists.

As I got involved in the State Committee, I began to see major incongruities between my views as a Christian and the views of the Massachusetts Democrat Party. To that point I never heard of "gay rights." I certainly knew what the Bible teaches about homosexuality, and I took that seriously. My first slap in the face came when I ran for the State Committee seat only to find they had affirmative action seats set aside for blacks and "gays." The idea of special seats for black people made me uncomfortable. The idea of affirmative action for homosexuality was shocking. That was the beginning of the end of my relationship with the Democrat Party. I was elected to one of those affirmative action seats, but it was not going to last because my conscience haunted me.

Then I found out about their position on abortion, which was entirely incompatible with the scriptural mandate to "choose life, that you and your descendants may live" (Deuteronomy 30:19). It was the Democrat Party that forced me to begin comparing biblical truth to political ideology. Feelings of discomfort grew into a full-blown crisis of conscience. The Democrat platform could not be squared with my Christian convictions.

I could not support abortion and homosexuality. How then could I remain in the Democrat Party when one of its most influential leaders in Massachusetts was Barney Frank—a prominent "gay" activist? He was not officially out of the closet yet, but it was well known he was a homosexual. His public pronouncement took place while he was serving in Congress. I found it particularly abhorrent that he was supporting legislation in Massachusetts to lower the age of sexual consent. Seeing him operate gave me a sickening feeling. There was something disturbing about him, but I could not identify it. It didn't take long to find out what it was. He was a moral degenerate, and that proved out over the years of his political career.

For the first time in my life, I began to look at the Republican Party. This was a leap because the people in my circles had three things to say about Republicans. They are rich, racist, and could care less about the poor. However, as I examined the platform of the Republicans, I was surprised to find it made sense to me. Then, Ronald Reagan came on the scene. He spoke not only to my head, but to my heart.

I voted for Jimmy Carter when he ran the first time. He was a Christian and that excited me. He even taught Sunday school. Like many fellow believers of my generation, I lived to regret that vote. My motives were pure. However, by the time he ran for re-election, I was deeply disappointed with him. That was one of my early

lessons in practical Christianity. I learned that in politics, claiming
to be a Christian means nothing. I cannot say Jimmy Carter is not
a Christian. I would say if he is, he is not true to the faith. Any person who supports the killing of unborn babies or same-sex relationships is either deeply misguided or not a Christian at all.

Although Ronald Reagan was criticized for not going to church
enough, I believe Reagan was truly a Christian. I have my doubts
about Jimmy Carter, Bill Clinton, Barack Obama, and other Bible-
toting liberals. I became a Republican and voted for Ronald Reagan.
I have never looked back.

Like my spiritual conversion, my political conversion did not
happen overnight. I struggled with leaving the Democrat Party
mainly because I did not want to disappoint my dad, a confirmed
Roosevelt Democrat. It was just a given that all black folks are
Democrats. I was contemplating the betrayal of that orthodoxy, and
"betrayal" is exactly how many perceived any black person who
voted Republican. Ultimately, one consideration predominated.
What did God want me to do? I believe God wants to be involved
in every important decision in life. It should have been obvious, but
it is not easy to break with cultural norms, behaviors, and traditions
and face the rejection and hostility that comes with doing so.

As I was faced with a momentous decision, the Rev. James
McFarland from Tupelo, Mississippi, came up to Boston to do a
revival for Rev. Rafe Kelly at St. John Missionary Baptist Church
in Boston. Rev. Kelly was a mentor of mine, and I often attended
his services to support him. On this particular night, Rev. McFarland preached, "If you are going to follow Jesus, you've got to turn
around . . ." By the time he finished preaching, I knew exactly what
I had to do. I had to turn around. Shortly after hearing that message,
I resigned my position on the Democrat State Committee and left
the party forever. My wife followed me, and that was over forty years
ago. Not only have we never regretted that decision, but the godless
evolution of the Democrat Party has confirmed it again and again.

I was very nervous about telling my father, expecting him to be
offended. Instead, he was surprisingly accepting. "You're in a different world, son," he said. "You have to do what you think is best
for you." I later realized his reaction was based on his respect for

what I had achieved. He was a third-class welder. His son was an attorney and graduate of Harvard Law School. He concluded my status created options he never had or even considered. My relationship with my father was never affected. I can't say the same about other relationships. I learned the depth of the cult-like hold the Democrat Party has over most black Americans.

Getting saved had a profound effect on my perception of life. I began to see the hand of God working through my experiences, and my conclusions were very different from my previous thinking. It did not happen all at once, but immediately after my conversion an intellectual transformation began.

As a child of the '60s, I came of age during some of the most tumultuous times in our country's history. The Civil Rights Movement was at its zenith. The Vietnam War protests were raging. Race riots engulfed cities across the country.

Without Christ in my life, I probably would have been drawn into the chaos. Instead, my relationship with God caused me to relate to my country and fellow Americans with love instead of bitterness and resentment. The tenor of the times demanded all black people embrace a singular, monolithic identity. Being black was considered the very essence of one's identity—a victim of oppression and discrimination. After several years of soul searching, I concluded it is impossible to maintain two separate, core identities—one Christian and spiritual, the other racial. That is the definition of schizophrenia.

Jesus said the same thing in a different context. "No one can serve two masters; for either he will hate the one and love the other, or else he will be loyal to the one and despise the other" (Matthew 6:24).

Racial obsession is a merciless master. It brooks no competition. Understandably, it has long been a preoccupation of the black community. The very real history of racial oppression has embedded the issue deep in the subconscious mind of black Americans. This is not a view shared only by black activists. Even black conservatives who have consciously rejected liberal orthodoxy can easily default to racial thinking. The Left has thoroughly saturated the culture with the idea that all problems of black people are the result of slavery, racism, and discrimination. Cultural norms of thought and behavior can be as restricting as formal laws enforced by the state. However, Christians cannot be ruled by both the politics of race and the righteousness of God. It has to be one or the other.

Of course, we all maintain many identities. We are husbands and wives, fathers and mothers, and hold titles for a variety of family and professional roles we play. That does not change who we are at our core. If we never become any of the aforementioned, each of us is still a human being. A true understanding of ourselves and others cannot be found in complexion or national origin. We all come from God. That is the essence of our identity and what it means to be human. No genetic or physiological trait supersedes spiritual reality.

In 1980, God made me painfully aware of my own racially obsessive thinking. It was completely subconscious, but totally antithetical to the gospel of Jesus Christ. In some extemporaneous remarks not part of a sermon, I made a derogatory comment about interracial couples. After the service, an interracial couple approached me about it. They were hurt. Honestly, I never connected my remarks to the real people sitting in the pews, and I knew they were there. I was oblivious to my own prejudices and the impact of such thinking on others. When they pointed out what I said and the implications, it was a revelation. I apologized immediately, but more importantly, I went home that day and repented before God for using the pulpit to engage in racial demagoguery. I began that day to ask God to cleanse me of such thinking. For the first time I realized I was capable of harboring thought patterns in direct contradiction of the dictates of Christianity.

I also learned from that experience how even born-again believers can be captive to the predominant cultural influences and not know it. God transforms us only in the areas of our lives we submit to Him. Nowhere in the Bible does God justify separation or discrimination based on race.

The only separation Jesus justifies is separation from the world's ungodly values. The only hostility Christians should nurture is against Satan and his spiritual forces of evil. People—no matter how corrupt or depraved—can be redeemed, just as I have been. Race is among the most absurd justifications for hatred that human beings ever devised.

I did not realize it at the time, but my spiritual transformation was causing a political metamorphosis. The incident I've described triggered some serious soul searching. On one level in the black community, "white people" were our neighbors, our merchants and friends. I had a couple of fights with white guys, but race was not the issue. I had fights with black guys too.

On the other hand, there was a subliminal divide which did not show up in regular conversation. There were "us" and there were "them." They were against us, and for that reason, we were against them. You would never know it watching most black-white interactions, but it was there.

As a Christian, still young in the faith, I began to ask myself whether my attitudes about race were consistent with Christianity. They weren't. Eventually I got around to asking myself the ultimate litmus test question: "How would I feel if one of my daughters wanted to marry a white guy?" I do not remember raising the same question about my son. There was again an unspoken acceptance of men crossing the color line that did not apply to women. It is something akin I suppose to white silence as male slave masters regularly availed themselves of black women, but the thought of a white female with a slave was unthinkable.

Realizing I thought like a racist was not a proud moment, but it was an important one. I knew such prejudice is incompatible with Christian truth. It didn't happen immediately, but I learned to care only about Christian character, not the color of a person's skin. Race should be irrelevant to marriage and all human interactions. Unfortunately, the Left is dragging the country in the opposite direction. Race is becoming the only relevant factor.

After my racial epiphany, a coherent non-racial, biblical worldview began to take shape. Over a short time, I shed the racial thinking of the '60s and began to look at the world through spiritual eyes instead of the eyes of a black man. In other words, it became my quest to see the world the way Jesus sees it.

PART III

THE CONSTITUTION, LIMITED GOVERNMENT, AND AMERICAN PROSPERITY

No government in history has ever been the trustworthy friend of the people, including the government of the United States. Governments have provided law enforcement, order, essential services, and even income to the disabled, elderly, and poor. Yet because their ultimate tool is force, they are mechanisms of power that historically devolve into governing by tyranny and subjugation. Until America was founded, governments were created to conquer and rule. The idea of government serving rather than ruling the people is the unique contribution of the American experiment. It was a groundbreaking idea, indeed revolutionary. The world watched skeptically, believing it would never work. It was at best a doubtful proposition that "the people," inheriting rights and freedom from God, could govern as sovereign by electing fellow citizens to represent and serve them.

Most men who have found themselves with power over a nation have asked, "What must I do to secure my position and power in perpetuity?" The Founding Fathers asked a different question: "What must we do to secure the liberty of our fellow citizens in perpetuity?" They had the humility and self-awareness to know even they were subject to the corruptions of the human heart. They were unwilling to trust themselves with absolute power, but instead created a form of government limiting the power of every individual who exercises its authority. They were all too familiar with what can happen when any person or group controls the life and destiny of an entire nation. What they wanted was for every individual to control his or her own destiny. What they did not want was another King George or an American equivalent.

They devised a system which, as far as humanly possible, would eliminate the possibility of robbing the people of their liberty. They wanted to limit the ability of government to exercise arbitrary control over the lives of its citizens.

Thomas Jefferson said, "A government big enough to supply you with everything you need, is a government big enough to take away everything that you have." Some scholars suggest this is only a paraphrase of what he actually said. Nonetheless, it expresses a sentiment common among our Founders.

He also noted, "The natural progress of things is for liberty to yield, and government to gain ground." That is why our Founding Fathers devised checks and balances to ensure that neither the executive, legislative, nor judicial branch would have absolute power. Each branch would have the ability to check the power of the others.

Barack Obama has complained the U.S. Constitution is a "charter of negative liberties"—but that is exactly how it was designed. The Founders wanted government to be limited to only those powers explicitly outlined in our Constitution, not to become a giant octopus with its tentacles controlling every dimension of life.

The proper role of government is to protect the inherent rights of every human being. What makes our American republic exceptional is it is established on the "self-evident" truth that freedom and rights come from the Providence of God—not the beneficence of government or any man-made institution. Our rights are inherent in who we are as human beings. They are not the dispensation of enlightened rulers. Since they derive from no human source, no human institution has the authority to arbitrarily take them away. This is the foundational principle of our nation.

The Preamble to the Constitution says its purpose is to "secure"—not create— "the blessings of liberty:"

We the People of the United States, in Order to form a more perfect Union, establish Justice, insure domestic Tranquility, provide for the common defense, promote the general Welfare, and secure the Blessings of Liberty to ourselves and our Posterity, do ordain and establish this Constitution for the United States of America.[7]

Our Founding Fathers understood fully that no person, no matter how virtuous, is capable of exercising absolute power over the lives of other human beings. When tried, no matter how reputedly brilliant the leader—Hitler, Mao Tse-Tung, Lenin, Stalin, Fidel Castro, Hugo Chavez, Hafez al-Assad, Pol Pot—the result is always tyranny and human slaughter.

The road to totalitarianism within a free society begins with surrendering more and more liberty and giving more and more power to government to meet the crisis. That is how freedom is lost. One day, the government controls everything and everyone.

While I was writing this book, the world was struck with the COVID-19 pandemic. President Trump issued guidelines based on recommendations from the Centers for Disease Control. We were asked to use "social distancing" to slow the spread of this highly contagious disease. The CDC also recommended people not gather in groups of more than ten. Most people were willing to comply with requests by our government and the president.

Then governors and mayors began to issue "orders" going far beyond the CDC guidelines with threats of arrest, fines, and imprisonment. Churches were closed, but abortion clinics and strip clubs left open. These orders included requirements to stay at home unless you went outdoors for certain authorized purposes. In some jurisdictions, you might need "papers" from your employer to prove you had the right to be outside your own home. One father was arrested at a park with his wife and daughter. One pastor was arrested for having church services. The mayor of New York threatened to permanently close churches or synagogues daring to meet after being "told not to."

The pandemic is a sober reminder of how fragile freedom can be.

CHAPTER 24

A GROWING THREAT

One of my motivations for writing this book is my deep love of liberty. It is my conviction that of all Americans, the most passionate about freedom should be those whose ancestors were once enslaved. Hence the title—*Sweet Land of Liberty—Reflections of a Patriot Descended from Slaves*.

It is profoundly disturbing to me so many of our citizens have been seduced by Leftist ideologies which are nothing more than glorified slavery. Progressivism, rooted in Marxism, socialism, and communism, requires higher and higher levels of state power to create the "social justice" and "equality." No government bureaucracy ever restrains itself or rejects the growth of its budget or the breadth of its power. American bureaucrats and politicians are no exception. The social service industry created to end poverty only serves to perpetuate it. No bureaucracy makes itself obsolete. As the bureaucracy grows, along with the taxes it takes to support its ever-increasing jurisdiction, liberty shrinks.

We have seen this from the implementation of the "Great Society" programs of Lyndon Johnson to Barack Obama's "hope and change" to Joe Biden's vaccine and transgender mandates. From the creation of new cabinet agencies to the appointment of czars,

Americans should be alarmed that government and the politicians who run it have an insatiable hunger for more and more power over the lives of ordinary citizens. In the eyes of Marxist-inspired politicos, the citizens are not people. They are ignorant masses who lack the liberal elite's insight and wisdom. We see this with the "deep state" politicians and bureaucrats who worked with big tech and the mainstream media who tried to silence seventy-five million people who cast lawful votes for Donald Trump in 2020. Donald Trump was elected President in 2016, and government forces including the intelligence agencies ceaselessly undermined his administration including impeaching him twice.

Abraham Lincoln presided over our country during a time when it was torn apart. He led through four years of bloody civil war in which Americans killed Americans by the hundreds of thousands. He observed, "America will never be destroyed from the outside. If we falter and lose our freedoms, it will be because we destroyed ourselves."

The greatest danger to the future of our country is the false ideologies poisoning the minds and hearts of many citizens. The Left has embraced and promoted these toxic ideas antithetical to our constitutional republic.

CHAPTER 25

COLLECTIVISM OVER INDIVIDUALISM

In the philosophy of Karl Marx, the individual does not matter. Life is not about the quest of each person to realize his or her God-given potential. Life is instead about class struggle between the privileged wealthy and the working poor. When Marx developed his theory, the only two classes of people in Europe were the rich and the poor. The poor were frozen in place with no hope of a better life. Europe was dominated by monarchies, which doled out land and wealth to keep its elites loyal and subservient.

America has confronted Marxism with a new reality—upward mobility for all. The class warfare of socialism and communism is difficult to sell in a country where income levels of individuals and families can move dramatically higher over the course of a lifetime and career. In America, more than in any other nation in history, it is possible to be born into poverty and then become wealthy. All but 3 percent of the top 20 percent of income earners worked their way into that bracket.

Most Americans do not envy or hate the rich. They want to be rich, and they believe with hard work and what George Washington called "the propitious smiles of heaven," it is entirely possible. Americans have seen friends, classmates, and neighbors who start from nowhere become highly successful. They have heard a thousand Horatio Alger stories. They have seen the American Dream come true before their very eyes in small and big ways. They have watched the first member of the family graduate from college. They have seen small businesses grow into industry giants. They have been born in poverty and grown into affluence. Upward mobility is deeply embedded in the American psyche.

One would think Marxists would give up on America as hopelessly wedded to free enterprise and the American dream. However, they are undeterred. Nothing stops them from the pursuit of power. When it comes to America, a more creative strategy is necessary to obtain buy-in for the Marxist vision. It requires no small amount of lying and deception.

One has to pay very close attention to notice the steady encroachment on our rights and freedoms engineered by Leftist forces. It is always in the name of helping people. Mark Levin calls this approach "soft tyranny." Just as in Marxism, the strength of progressivism comes from creating a sense of grievance and entitlement. Any deprivation is the result of social injustice that must be corrected because everyone has a "right" to what others have earned.

The free market guarantees opportunity. The socialist state guarantees everything—except freedom, of course. They say everyone has a right to healthcare, college education, housing, food, a cell phone, and a guaranteed income to pay for their every want. Children are guaranteed security by their parents with the expectation they will one day be independent. When adults are treated like children, they become de facto slaves. How many parents have uttered the words, "because I said so." When adults receive everything at the hands of government bureaucrats, they may never hear those words, but the underlying rule is the same: "Do as you are told without question because we say so." If you want to continue to get the subsidies, you will comply. That is the level of control socialist welfare policies produce.

Under Obamacare, the state "mandated" everyone to have health insurance or pay a penalty. Insurance would be provided for everyone who could not afford it. The nature of the available plans would be dictated by government, not the free market. If you wanted or tried to get more or less than required by law, you would pay a penalty. It was a bold power grab to take control of the entire health insurance industry, 1/6th of the American economy. Some Democrats admitted this was only the first step toward single-payer health care, leaving the U.S. government as the sole healthcare provider.

In 2017, President Trump signed into law the Tax Cuts and Jobs Act, which repealed the mandate's penalty, but still left much of Obamacare intact.

Given the government's track record running things, this is a nightmare scenario. Bureaucracies are not capable of operating efficiently and effectively, because they don't have to. They do not function under free market pressure of competition. Their continued existence does not depend upon generating a profit, controlling costs, or beating out a competitor.

Every governmental failure to solve a problem is the justification for higher taxes and more government intrusion into the personal lives of the American people. The only reason why the problem is not solved is that government needs more money and power to get the job done. When government has absolute power and control over everything, it will be able to solve all those intractable human problems and create utopia. That attitude is the very definition of communism, totalitarianism and dictatorship. Every communist system calls itself a democracy. I shudder every time a progressive claims to be acting to protect our "democracy." They mean something very different from Abraham Lincoln's formulation of a government "of the people, by the people, for the people." What they mean is a government of the Leftist elites, by the Leftist elites, for the Leftist elites. To be clear, Leftist equals progressive equals Marxist, equals socialist equals communist.

When government goes to the extreme of requiring all Americans to purchase a product—no matter what that product is—the doctrine of limited and enumerated powers has become a dead letter. We have gone from a government designed to serve the people and do our will to a government commanding the people to do its will. No matter how attractive and fair Democrats make socialism sound, Americans should remember Marxism always ends at the point of a gun.

Americans should never cast a vote for a presidential candidate unless he or she has an unwavering commitment to individual liberty and free enterprise. Those ideas are foundational to our constitutional republic.

Free enterprise is not perfect. It is, however, the most free and fair system known to man because it diffuses economic power by allowing individuals to make their own economic decisions. Each person may decide what to purchase and where. He or she may also determine what goods and services to sell. We make these choices based on personal values and private goals, not government coercion.

If socialists are able to control the thoughts, speech, behavior, and economic destiny of individual lives, we become a nation of slaves - impoverished, oppressed and silenced. That is the fulfillment of Lord Acton's solemn warning, "power tends to corrupt and absolute power corrupts absolutely."[8]

Freedom is the natural state of mankind under God. We were created to be free, but freedom is not inevitable. It is fragile, and it must be guarded with vigilance.

CHAPTER 26

THE POWER OF THE INDIVIDUAL

America is the most prosperous, innovative, technologically advanced nation the world has ever seen. Our unparalleled success is not the result of superior genes or intellect. It is due to the superior values and principles of our culture and society. In the politically correct world of moral and cultural relativists, it is offensive to say our nation has certain qualities superior to others. The Left would much rather falsely attribute our success to exploitation, racism, and imperialism. Yet people from every ethnic and racial background have succeeded in America in every era of our nation's history. Even during slavery, there were free black landowners who amassed wealth. What made this possible is the most enduring principle of our founding—liberty. Even during the two and a half centuries of enslavement of former Africans in America, the idea of each individual created by God with inherent freedoms and rights spoke to the American conscience.

Freedom is why almost anything is possible for almost anybody in our country. We invent, create, try, fail, win, lose, and start all over again because we are free.

Government didn't create automobiles, airplanes, telephones, televisions, computers, cell phones, the internet, or social media. These are just the infinitesimal tip of the iceberg. The inventions and ideas, too numerous to list, came from individuals who dared to dream big and risk everything. That same story unfolds again and again all over this country creating breakthrough innovations.

Conservatives believe in individuals, not racial or identity groups. Conservatives believe if you are competent and capable, you deserve every opportunity that comes your way; and if you are undisciplined and lazy, you get what you deserve—no matter what identity group you claim.

Conservatives believe in the potential of every individual. The Founding Fathers believed this too. They understood that people rooted and grounded in the Judeo-Christian culture do not need government to dictate its version of virtue. Virtuous citizens would exercise self-restraint based on human conscience and faith in their Creator, reinforced in churches and synagogues all over the land.

Our Constitutional Republic secures the God-given freedom intrinsic to our humanity. Liberty is not due to the beneficence of government but to the grace of God. It is a gift we must never surrender at any price.

PART IV

RACISM IN AMERICA

More than 156 years after slavery ended in America, we discuss race as if the enslavement of black people ended yesterday, or never. It has been nearly sixty years since Jim Crow segregation was outlawed, but those on the Left would have us believe real or imagined "micro-aggressions" are the equivalent of Klan-enforced racial stratification. Indeed, the cry of racial injustice is heard as loudly as it was when discrimination was open and undeniable.

Now that mistreatment on the basis of race has been all but eliminated from the legal and cultural landscape, why do accusations of white supremacy and white privilege fly so freely? Racial injustice is ultimately a moral issue, but it has been so thoroughly politicized that it serves the interests of the Democrat Party and its machine to keep the issue alive. A racial grievance industry exploits the history of our country by creating new ways of accusing America of racism. If they cannot prove it as a current fact, they can conjure up "implied bias" and "systemic racism." Every racial disparity in employment, education, income, and incarceration is explained by the racist nature of America.

Thomas Sowell in his book *Discrimination and Disparities* argues persuasively that it is unrealistic to expect all people to be repre-sented in every area of life in numbers equal to their proportion of the population. He surveys the entire world to prove most disparities have nothing to do with discrimination. The self-selection of individuals and the impact of cultural, geographic, and demographic factors at a given point in time are more determinative of social outcomes than any invisible and undefinable social injustice.

Politicizing race has necessitated the myth of America as a white supremacist nation. The false and poisonous propaganda of the Left says the evil of racism is characteristic of white people only. It is impossible, they say, for "people of color" to be racist because racism is a matter of power. Since blacks and other minorities have no power, they cannot be racist. Tell that to the truck driver nearly beaten to death by black assailants during the Rodney King riots in Los Angeles.

Racism is not a matter of power, but a matter of the heart. A politically powerless person filled with racial hatred only needs a gun, knife, brick, stick, or a few equally hateful friends to exercise power over another person. The skin color of the attacker does not matter. All people are capable of prejudice. When an American of African ancestry blames all Americans of European ancestry for whatever deprivation he feels, he is just as racist as the Nazi who blames Jews for the plight of Germany. Having political power and control of the state certainly gives a racist group the ability to implement racist policies. However, a relatively powerless group could harbor similar hatred and stereotypes that they would gladly implement given the chance.

In May 2020, Lori Lightfoot, the black lesbian mayor of Chicago, announced that she would no longer take interviews from white reporters, only from "reporters of color." That is racist to the core and undoubtedly unconstitutional for a public official. Racist animosity is a sickness of the human heart; it is not a moral deficiency unique to a particular group of people.

Before we go any further, let us take a moment to examine the vocabulary of race. The concept of white people is itself racist. Leftists divide the world between white people and people of color. First, all people have color. Even albinos, who have an unusual skin condition, have color. People of lighter complexions whose ancestors come from Europe are not white. Recently, I saw a young man doing a commercial on television. While making his pitch, the name of the product was juxtaposed beside him in white lettering. The contrast made clear he was not white at all, but a light tan. He is, after all is said and done, "a person of color."

These categories are not meant to be descriptive because they are highly inaccurate. They are intended to create an us-against-them mentality. The concept of people of color is so broad as to be meaningless. It does not define a homogenous group. Yet it purports to create commonality between, for example, the child growing up in the rainforests of the Amazon with the child growing up in the streets of Chicago. It would be silly and laughable if it were not so pernicious.

Likewise, *white people* is a meaningless term. It was concocted for the same reason as *people of color*—to create an us-against-them mentality among Europeans during the slave era. It defines everyone else in the world in contrast to Europeans. Settlers arriving in the New World from different parts of Europe had no more in common than the two children I cited earlier.

There is a long history of wars, conquest, and enslavement to prove it. Those divisions continued after they arrived in this country. They stayed to themselves and their own kind. Italians did not mix with Irish immigrants. Germans stayed to themselves, creating their own communities. Settlers from England had nothing but disdain for the Irish. There was even division within those ethnic groups. Northern Italians despised southern Italians. The Irish despised the Scots Irish. They had different histories and different cultures. The experiences and perspectives and cultures of the Polish and the French are as different as two groups of people can be.

Lumping the entire population of mankind into two groups— white people and people of color—is a racist idea worthy of Adolph Hitler. Both concepts were created by racists. The concept of "whiteness" was created during slavery to keep Europeans—no matter how desperate or ignorant—from ever believing they had anything in common with slaves. Mere whiteness became a badge of superiority. Likewise, the concept of people of color is a modern invention intended to portray descendants of Europe as oppressors.

This stereotyping is at the root of slavery and genocide. To say white people are racists is no better than saying black people are lazy or Irish people are drunkards or Polish people are stupid. It denies the uniqueness of each individual and dehumanizes an entire group. The stereotyping of the modern Left is even more insidious because it claims all people with lighter skin, regardless their diverse ethnic backgrounds and experiences, share a common destiny or more to the point, a common depravity.

Racism is simply an expression of group hostilities existing since the beginning of history. People have subjugated, enslaved, and killed each other based on kin, clan, tribe, geographic competition, religion, and the culture of conquest on every populated land mass. America did not invent human exploitation, nor is it America's "original sin." Humans have original sin. Nations do not. All nations have division, wars, and conquest in their history. America indeed has racism in its history, but so does every country, particularly if you broaden the definition to include any national attempt to justify exploiting another group. The oppressed have usually shared the same demographic and ethnic background as their oppressors. Therefore, to take the irrational leap from acknowledging racism in our national story to accusing our country of being racist and white supremacist is the intellectual equivalent of saying Greece is now a nation of conquest because of Phillip of Macedonia and Alexander the Great. It would be an absurd claim even though it has some historical basis.

The civil rights activists of today are doing the equivalent of smearing all Greeks with the violent legacy of Alexander. They have become creative at insinuating racism and making it ubiquitous especially where no tangible evidence exists. Since they no longer have much in the way of overt racism to justify their existence, they are inventing racism where there is none to be found.

In 2020, major news organizations began capitalizing White and Black as descriptor words, the better to focus relentlessly on race. "A White cop shot a Black suspect." Somehow, when it was the other way around, race often did not get mentioned.

Recently, a movement began in the NBA to do away with the word "owner" to describe those who purchase NBA teams. The word "owner" is racist we are told because it implies ownership of the black players. Far Left commentators have implied owners' managing their teams as they see fit is the equivalent of slavery. An institution that ended 150 years ago is now likened to professional basketball, which pays tens of millions of dollars to players, not to mention the fame and adulation heaped upon them. What is really happening is players are using race as leverage to gain power and influence beyond what they can obtain by simply playing the sport.

A professional basketball team is, after all, a business. It is part of the entertainment industry. Each team has owners as do other businesses. The players, although highly paid and globally celebrated, are still employees. Ownership of the business in no way implies ownership of the players as slaves, but this is the paradigm we are now supposed to accept. The language used in describing most businesses cannot be used here because the players are "woke." This is just another in the long, sad saga of racial exploiters keeping the issue alive for their own political and economic gain. Many black activists have become professional extortionists, exploiting the past for personal profit.

Jesse Jackson, Al Sharpton, Harry Belafonte, Maxine Waters, Stacey Abrams, the Congressional Black Caucus, and many others promote fear and obsession with race that has no basis in reality. They stoke the flames of racial division at every opportunity. They teach black and other minority youth to look for someone to blame for their failures.

They have come to the defense of murderers like O. J. Simpson and Stanley Tookie Williams—founder of the Crips street gang. They have defended a liar like Tawana Brawley, who falsely accused police officers of racially and physically abusing her.

When white Duke lacrosse players were falsely accused of sexually assaulting a black girl, the race baiters were quick to hurl accusations of racism. Jesse Jackson condemned the lacrosse players, but never apologized after they were exonerated.

What I call ROS (Racial Obsession Syndrome) is a sickness serving only the interest of the elites who benefit from it. They have good jobs, well-funded organizations, and high profiles. They do nothing for the people they claim to serve. Today's "civil rights leaders" are an anachronism, a throwback to a bygone era—without the benign intent. They are not about advancing civil rights, but rather enhancing their own influence, notoriety, and bank accounts.

Allegations of racism, discrimination, and social injustice are far more lucrative for the Rainbow Coalition and the NAACP than addressing social pathologies, morality, family breakdown, and personal responsibility.

Since so-called civil rights leaders are obsessed with race, they cannot address other causes of poverty and crime in the inner city. About 94 percent of black murder victims are killed by black people—but the "civil rights" establishment doesn't want to address this. They also won't address the gangs and crime prevalent in the black community, or the absence of fathers or the epidemic of out of wedlock births. They certainly do not address the death cult of abortion which affects the black community more than any other group in America.

In fact, a civil rights activist actually admitted to me, "We can't address these issues because it lets white people off the hook." Yet they have no problem letting the small percentage of black criminals off the hook while law-abiding citizens sleep on the floor of their homes to avoid being killed as collateral damage in drive-by shootings. Many of the victims are innocent children at play or sleeping in their beds. Anyone who can ignore this or talk it away as I have heard some try to do is not concerned about black lives or any lives. They are driven by a far-left political agenda, not true compassion for people.

Ask the relatives of Derrion Albert. On September 24, 2009, Albert, a sixteen-year-old black honor student at Fengler High School in Chicago, walked into the middle of a fight between two rival black gangs. He was knocked to the ground by a blow to the head with a railroad tie. Then he was punched, kicked, and stomped to death.

In his case and others like it, there was a deafening silence from some of the biggest mouths in America. The so-called civil rights leaders were mute. Had this been a white gang attacking a black student—or a black criminal with a long rap sheet killed by white police officers—there would have been protests and riots. But because Derrion's murder didn't fit the racial narrative, black "leaders" were silent.

The leading cause of death among black males ages eighteen to twenty-four is homicide by other black males. Absentee fathers, abortion, drug use, gangs, and crime have had a far greater impact on the black community than ethereal "systemic racism."

One of my missions in life is to help black Americans awaken to the fact the Democrat Party, to which they have been loyal for the last sixty years, is destroying them. They have been told by "civil rights leaders" that government is always the answer. We are a nation of individuals, but Leftists don't look at us that way. The black community, to them, is a faceless group of victims, and they are their saviors.

The Left has created a bogeyman—the "white man." They tell black Christians to ignore their biblical beliefs and vote for their racial saviors. They are warned that if they don't, the white man, especially a conservative white man, will get them.

Democrats continue to move to the extreme Left. The black community, especially Christians—the most reliable group of black voters—is fundamentally conservative. Blacks in California overwhelmingly supported Proposition 8 to define marriage as only the union of a man and a woman. Nearly 40 percent of abortions are performed on black women. Most blacks oppose it, and most Democrats support it.

Most black parents support choice in education to get their children out of failing schools. Most Democrats are sycophants to teachers' unions, which are busy pushing a Marxist agenda of sexual perversion and anti-American propaganda. Given the disparity between the values of a far-left Democrat Party and the black electorate, the Left must craft a way to keep blacks voting for an entity vehemently opposed to their values. The Democrat strategy is to overwhelm those values with fear—fear of the white racist bogeyman. These so-called civil rights leaders and liberal members of the Congressional Black Caucus have sold out the values of the black community for personal, political, and financial gain.

The Democrat Party has become functionally Marxist: atheist, anti-church, anti-Christian, anti-Constitution, anti-family, anti-American, and anti-democratic. The Southern Poverty Law Center, the ACLU, Planned Parenthood, NARAL, LGBTQ activists, pornographers, and militant atheists are undermining the Judeo-Christian values of our country. This political coalition poses an existential threat to the nation's future. Their only hope of guaranteeing the black community stays with them is to use racial demagoguery to manipulate and control black voters.

CHAPTER 27

OFF THE PLANTATION

It is time for Americans to realize the formerly "liberal" and now "progressive" political class is the most racist people group in our country. They treat black people and other ethnic minorities like objects to be possessed rather than human beings to be respected and served. Their racism is palpable in how they treat black conservatives and Republicans who dare challenge their orthodoxy. Like slave masters, they cannot abide anyone who wants to escape their control. The flaw, as they see it, is not in the slave masters or their ideology but in the "slave" who would dare break free.

This sense of superiority and condescension has actually been documented in at least two studies. According to *Yale Insights*, a Yale/Princeton study entitled "Self-Presentation in Interracial Settings: The Competence Downshift by White Liberals" showed "that liberal individuals were less likely to use words that would make them appear highly competent when the person they were addressing was presumed to be black rather than white."

The study further concluded, "Democratic candidates used fewer competence-related words in speeches delivered to mostly minority audiences than they did in speeches delivered to mostly white audiences."[9]

Americans of African descent are not people the Left respects as independent thinkers to be persuaded and won, but pawns to be controlled and manipulated. When blacks do not agree with liberal political aims, they are targeted for destruction. They only like the "good" ones—those who meet liberal, paternalistic standards. They have no use for those who reject their views. It is a supreme political irony that the people who are always demanding tolerance are thoroughly intolerant of anyone who thinks outside the boundaries of their intellectual plantation.

This liberal attitude toward racial minorities is cloaked in compassion, but it is the equivalent of a master/slave relationship. When escaped slaves were caught, they were lashed into submission by their masters. This was intended as a warning not only to that particular slave but to the entire stable of black servants. The message was clear: stay in your place or face dire consequences. The escaped slave was a threat to the entire framework of bondage. The master reasoned that since slaves are well-cared-for, they should be grateful and happy for the security they are provided. It is after all the way of life they were assigned by God or fate, and slaves only want to escape if they are infected with lies and sedition. What if one slave's desire for freedom inspires others? What if the misguided notion spreads that slaves should be free to think for themselves, decide for themselves, and, heaven forbid, perceive themselves as human beings equal to others? Such ideas could bring the whole artificial edifice crashing down. The nightmare of it all caving in on their heads kept the planter class awake at night. So, it is for the elite liberal class today. That is the only explanation for the aggressive and hateful response against black conservatives, particularly those who have a platform that could reach and influence others.

Slavery is a perfect metaphor for the relationship of black Americans to their Leftist masters today. Liberals' absolute commitment to maintaining their status of superiority over their black beneficiaries has distorted reality for them beyond all recognition. Most of them actually believe they are helping black people, even though their so-called "help" perpetuates black dependence.

The denunciation of Tom, lead character in *Uncle Tom's Cabin* by Harriet Beecher Stowe is a case in point. Uncle Tom is a model of Christian courage. The Left has turned him into a symbol of black sellout. His crime was refusal to hate his vicious slave master—Simon Legree. When two female slaves escaped, Tom refused to give any information on their whereabouts although he encouraged them in their escape. Legree beat Tom to death because he would not talk, but Tom did not fight back because he was concerned about the man's soul. He did not want Simon to go to hell. Tom wanted him instead to experience the love that might open his heart to God.

This good-hearted and courageous fictional character has become the scourge of the liberal Left. One of the worst insults that can be leveled at a black man is to call him an "Uncle Tom." Many do it ignorantly, having never read the book. For Leftist elites who have read it, the truth does not matter. The only thing that matters is maintaining a stronghold on black minds, so they think as they ought and vote as they ought. People like me are anathema because we will not make "white people" or anyone else an object of our hate. Dr. King said, "No man can make me stoop low enough to hate him." We will not make racism the catch-all for failure based upon choices individuals make. We are free, and we know it. Victimhood is incompatible with freedom. The left seethes at this rebellion, and viciously attacks those who reject the culture of their psychological plantation.

Consider the attacks on Herman Cain when he was alive. He was the child of a poor Southern family. He studied hard, became a mathematician and a successful businessman. His candidacy for U.S. president resonated with the American people because he was not a politician. He spoke the language of common sense which every American could understand. He was intelligent, successful, and well-spoken. The mainstream media, the Democrat Party and other forces of the Left despised him. His very existence was an affront to them because he was a successful black businessman who refused to yield his freedom of thought and action to the class of elite Leftists who saw themselves as his superiors and benefactors.

I, too, have been the recipient of this kind of backlash. I have been called an "Uncle Tom," an "Oreo" (black on the outside, white on the inside), a "sellout," "braindead," and "traitor" to my race. I have been the target of intimidation and death threats. As I write this book, the FBI is investigating a threat made on my life. Like Herman Cain, my black conservative contemporaries and so many others who have gone before us, I refuse to be silenced. The future of the black community is at stake, and I am determined to make sure they are free. The future of America is at stake, and I refuse to surrender my country to the suicide of tribalism.

All black conservatives who dare speak up face the same opprobrium. The black community is being exploited and manipulated by people who make a living stirring racial hatred and division with no plan for solving the problems. Al Sharpton's budget became public knowledge because of back taxes he owed. He brings in millions of dollars a year to an organization that is nothing more than a vehicle for Sharpton's self-aggrandizement and hunger for fame and power.

Today's ersatz civil rights leaders have no incentive to solve problems because real progress would leave them out in the cold. Their organizations would have no reason to exist. The Democrat Party would lose an essential constituency.

Because the Left believes themselves to represent "social justice," their condescension and racist stereotypes must be ignored. After all, we know where their hearts are. We all know they mean well, right? Here are just a few of many examples:

- "A few years ago, this guy [Barack Obama] would have been getting us coffee." (Bill Clinton to Ted Kennedy during the 2008 presidential campaign)
- "Is you their black-haired answer-mammy who be smart? Does they like how you shine their shoes Condoleezza? Or the way you wash and park the whitey's cars?" (Leftist radio talk show host Neil Rogers talking about Condoleezza Rice)
- "Blacks and Hispanics were too busy eating watermelons and tacos to read the fine print on their insurance policies." (Mike Wallace during a *60 Minutes* segment on insurance fraud)
- "Hymietown" was the anti-Semitic slur Jesse Jackson used to describe New York City during his 1984 Presidential campaign.

- Joe Biden once described Barack Obama this way: "I mean, you got the first mainstream African-American who is articulate and bright and clean and a nice-looking guy . . ."
- If Biden were a conservative, he would have been smeared as a racist and run out of Washington, D.C. But because he is a liberal Democrat, the media went into full defense mode, and it all was swept under the rug. He went on to become Obama's vice president and won the black vote overwhelmingly in 2020 to become president.
- Former Democrat Senate Leader Harry Reid made a similar remark. He said Obama had a chance to win because he's "light skinned" and didn't speak "negro dialect." Reid's career wasn't affected in the least.
- The level of hypocrisy is stunning. Leftists are constantly accusing conservatives of being racist, and yet I have never known a conservative with the kind of backward thinking of these so-called progressives.
- Trent Lott lost his position as Senate majority leader because remarks he made at Strom Thurmond's 100th birthday party were interpreted as endorsing Thurmond's former segregationist views. Lott's comments were intended to flatter the old man by telling the crowd the country would have been better off had Thurmond been elected in 1948. Thurmond had long since renounced segregationist views and from all reports was well thought of by his black constituents. Nor did anyone seriously believe Lott was saying segregation was good for America and should have continued. He apologized for his "poor choice of words." He regretted he wrongly conveyed an embrace of the "discarded policies of the past." When you are a conservative, there is no redemption from the smear of being deemed "racist" by liberal elites.
- Rep. Nancy Pelosi of California, who rose from House Democratic leader to House Speaker and holds that role as I write, said: "He can apologize all he wants. It doesn't remove the sentiments that escaped his mouth that day at the party." Lott resigned his leadership role and was driven from office, never to run again.

- Rep. Steve King of Iowa was stripped of his House committee assignments because of comments he made about the values of "Western civilization" that were interpreted as racially tinged. Neither Lott nor King said anything approaching the explicitly and personally racist comments of Biden or Reid, but the Republicans' careers were irreparably damaged.
- One of the reasons Leftists get away with such hypocrisy is the mainstream media are the propaganda arm of the Democrat Party. Miscreants can easily redeem themselves by proclaiming their "record." That record amounts to nothing more than being a Democrat. That alone inoculates white Democrats from racist comments while their Department of Propaganda—the mainstream media—goes into full defense mode to protect their political masters.
- Columnist Maureen Dowd attacked George W. Bush for appointing white men to the Supreme Court, calling it a "disgrace." California Sen. Barbara Boxer trotted out the NAACP to oppose the National Black Chamber of Commerce opposition to Cap and Trade environmental legislation. What Cap and Trade has to do with racism and discrimination, only Barbara Boxer and the NAACP know.
- Rhode Island Sen. Sheldon Whitehouse said opponents of Obamacare were "white Aryan support groups." Nancy Pelosi accused Americans showing up at town hall meetings to protest the healthcare takeover of being Nazis and racists.
- Harry Reid accused opponents of Obamacare of being the same as those who opposed ending slavery.

Liberal elites are the very definition of racists. They do not see minorities as individuals, but as part of a faceless group of victims. From their viewpoint, it is their paternalistic duty to protect these helpless creatures. Biden, Reid, and their cohorts give us a clear picture of how liberals view black Americans: none too bright, not very clean, jive talkers, in danger of being returned to their natural condition as slaves. These are the people whose policies have engineered entrenched ghettos, persistent poverty, poor education, breakdown of the family, and inner city crime and violence. Democrat machine politics rules in these communities. They have trapped black children in substandard schools and refuse to allow parents to escape through school choice. They ignore thousands of young black men dying in the streets of our cities each year. They make police their scapegoats for the very circumstances their policies created. This is a tragedy, and the puppet masters behind it must be exposed for who and what they are.

CHAPTER 28

OBAMA'S MISSED OPPORTUNITY

I always believed America would elect a black president. Most Americans of African descent did not believe it, but that political milestone was crossed in 2008 and is in our rearview mirror. Indeed, in January 2021, the first black woman—also Asian and Jamaican apparently—was sworn in as vice president of the United States. Leaving aside serious questions raised about the 2020 election, I am grateful to be a citizen of a nation that elects people who do not belong to the majority demographic. That said, had it been up to me, I would have chosen different leaders than Barack Obama and Kamala Harris. I did not vote for either.

I am opposed to almost every policy the former president espoused and implemented. He is enthusiastically pro-abortion. He sought to force upon public schools the radical LGBTQ agenda, including instantaneous recognition of a child's newly chosen gender. No questions should be allowed, and no psychiatric or medical opinion should be sought. He viewed the free market as an evil to be tolerated, not a blessing to be celebrated. As president, he operated from a decidedly racial worldview. Every time the most powerful man in the world and his wife acted like victims of racial injustice, I cringed.

Among every demographic group, there are people in America with racial animus. That is the reality of human sinfulness and imperfection. However, as a general proposition, Americans have rejected racism as unjust and unacceptable. That is why a black man was elected president. In fact, there were many Americans of European ancestry who were determined to see it happen. Some thought it would advance the cause of racial harmony and American unity. They were sorely disappointed.

Everything I came to know about Barack Obama suggested his political background was Marxist. His spiritual mentors such as Frank Marshall Davis, Bill Ayers, and Jeremiah Wright were all hard Leftists. I still believe Obama is at core a Marxist. American Marxism has substituted racial conflict for class warfare. That is why race has become the mantra of the Left and the Democrat Party. It was pure fantasy to think President Obama could lead us to a new era of racial harmony. That would have been inconsistent with his worldview. It was a missed opportunity of historic proportions. Instead of a major step forward, his presidency represented a giant step backward because he and the media cast all political opposition to him as racist. That served only to divide us and heighten racial tension rather than bring healing. By defaulting to a racial explanation of the political resistance he faced, Obama exacerbated the problem.

The White House "beer summit" between Henry Louis Gates and a Cambridge, Massachusetts, police officer underscored Obama's racial obsession. The officer was called to the home of Harvard Prof. Gates because a neighbor thought someone appeared to be trying to break in. It was dark and probably impossible to see the race of the suspected robber or that it was the professor, who misplaced his key. However, Gates, a thorough racialist, jumped to the conclusion he was a victim of racism. Obama, his personal friend, was all too happy to take the leap with him. Before learning all the facts, he condemned the police officer as having behaved "stupidly." Then, he hosted both men at the White House for the "beer summit." This was just a cover-your-backside exercise, in my view. The officer did nothing wrong. He was called by a neighbor about an apparent break-in and was just doing his job. Little did he know the suspect happened to own the house and was a very prominent black Harvard professor with access to the White House.

We are at a moment in American history where our future depends upon coming together and putting the racial past behind us. Obama was intrinsically incapable of doing that because he comes to the table with the predisposition that America is systemically racist and "white people" are the problem. Jesus said, "A house divided against itself cannot stand." Based on the narrative of the mainstream media, entertainment industry, higher education and the government school system and their ideological wellspring—the Democrat Party—America's future is bleak. They would have us believe our country is hopelessly racist, a nation founded and sustained by white supremacy.

They are teaching any student who sets foot in college and increasingly, every child sent by their parents to public school, America is as racist today as during the days of slavery and Jim Crow. Every bit of logic, common sense, and human observation rebels against the proposition. How can anyone believe something so preposterous?

The Left has a warped perception of reality. Their perspective is that racism is not just a personal intent to discriminate or hurt people on the basis of skin color. It is "systemic." There is an implied or unconscious bias in every American of European ancestry. These people are imbued with "privilege" and prone to "micro-aggressions." Conscious awareness has nothing to do with it. A problem that can't be identified except in the imagination of the person who sees it is a problem without a solution. A problem whose causation can't be measured is a problem for which there can be no resolution.

It does not help when the Left resorts to empty constructs such as referring to slavery as America's "original sin." Rather than illuminating the pathway to redress, it gives religious fervor to the idea that America, particularly our white citizens, are spiritually, culturally, perhaps even genetically predisposed to racial hatred and oppression of "people of color." They were created evil. The Nation of Islam has gone so far as to make the claim explicit. White people are monsters created in a laboratory, according to Louis Farrakhan, whose insane ravings were taught to him by the cult's founder, Elijah Mohammed.

The Black Lives Matter cult mainstreamed these extremist views. White Americans were expected to fall on their knees and grovel at the feet of black activists. Coca-Cola actually asked employees to diminish their "whiteness." These employees must spend their lives groveling and apologizing for the things done by their ancestors. They must also do penitence for their own racism, even if they have explicitly renounced it. They are still guilty.

Barack and his wife, Michelle, are much too smooth to express their true political extremism. Nonetheless, based on their history and conduct, before, during and after the White House years, they are racial radicals. They have no affection or interest in the United States except as a Petri dish for their Marxist experiments.

As a Christian, I was always disturbed that Obama claimed to be one, but even more disturbed so many Christians were willing to accept him as such. I have never given credence to his profession of faith. I believe he chose Christianity as a politically convenient label and joined Jeremiah Wright's church in Chicago because it fit his political views. I put Barack Obama in the same category as Jeremiah Wright, his spiritual father. Mr. Wright is a confirmed Leftist who perverts Christianity to match his politics. Barack Obama absorbed the man's teaching and influence for twenty years. He did not spend two decades listening to a leader with whom he disagreed. He and his wife supported the church financially and asked Wright to preside over their wedding and dedicate their children. Obama is a disciple of Jeremiah Wright, but he could not afford to have the country know that. When the time came, he severed the relationship with the same political pragmatism that led him to join the church in the first place.

It cannot be denied the former president is politically gifted. He was a kind of political Rorschach test allowing people to see in him what they wanted to see. For example, Barack Obama was always in favor of same-sex marriage. His record makes that clear. Homosexual activists knew this, which is why they supported him. He lied at Saddleback Church when he declared his belief that marriage is a union between one man and one woman. His own campaign website at the time said he was for overturning the federal Defense of Marriage Act, but he was not asked about that. After his presidency, his top advisors admitted he was lying about marriage. It was a political calculation.

He was a well-packaged product sold to the American people. His promise of "fundamentally transforming the United States of America" was one of the truest expressions of his intent. His America is not one of Judeo-Christian values, but of Marxism and cultural relativism. His vision is not "one nation under God" but one nation under a race-and-gender-obsessed elite.

While he was rewarding his long-time allies, the black community, which propelled him to office with unprecedented turnout, languished with nothing to show but feeling good about having elected the first black president. Barack Obama had other priorities. He did more than any president in history to advance the radical homosexual agenda. He is the first president who, "after much soul searching" and "wrestling with it," publicly came out in support of same-sex marriage. He appointed Supreme Court justices who imposed it on our society in a 5–4 ruling (*Obergefell v. Hodges, 2015*) in spite of thirty states having amended their constitutions to define marriage as a union between one man and one woman and many others strengthening their marriage statutes.

By Supreme Court decree, same-sex marriage is as fundamental as due process of law, freedom of speech, or religious liberty. In defiance of human history and a majority of the American people saying they did not want it, Barack Obama and the Supreme Court exercised authoritarianism worthy of a communist dictator.

That is Obama's most lasting legacy. It is not what anyone would have anticipated to be the signature achievement of the first black president of the United States. Having led this controversial change, he celebrated by lighting the exterior of the White House in rainbow colors—the misappropriated symbol of the LGBTQ movement. For Bible-believing Christians, this was an affront to our faith, our families, and to God. The rainbow is a sacred symbol of God's mercy, not a sexual symbol of homosexual and transgender desires.

Obama was a mediocre president on economic policies, an appeaser on foreign policy, and a divider on domestic policy. He touted Islam as a great religion and talked frequently about what it has done for the world. On the other hand, he denigrated Christianity and American culture both at home and abroad. He famously declared in Turkey during one of his earliest foreign policy speeches that America is not a Christian nation. He lectured Christians not to get on our high horse, but to remember the Crusades.

The media, of course, love him. As Geraldo Riviera once said, "he is too cool for school." Unfortunately, cool is a disposition, not a policy. It's a style, not an achievement. Answering questions, he is good at speaking slowly, measuring his every word, careful to say little or nothing. He is a master of the Harvard drawl, which is used to buy time to gather one's thoughts. In sum, he was and is an attractive package concealing a poison pill.

Barack Obama left behind a shameful legacy of denigrating America, marginalizing Christianity, and dividing us racially. He promoted an aggressive wave of sexual confusion and perversion which many, I among them, believe will one day introduce pedophilia as a legitimate sexual orientation protected against "discrimination." He should go down as one of the worst presidents in history, in the class of James Buchanan, who some historians believe was secretly homosexual.

Obama could have waited to get the facts before he accused the Cambridge police officer—but he didn't. He could have prosecuted the baton-wielding New Black Panthers when they were charged with intimidating voters in Philadelphia—but he didn't. He could have put on his big boy pants and recognized many Americans had legitimate philosophical and ideological differences with him that had nothing to do with race—but he didn't.

Far from being the post-racial president the media painted him to be, he was in fact obsessed with race. This was his great missed opportunity. He could have gone down in history as the president who brought the nation together. With a white mother and an African father, he could have been the incarnation of racial reconciliation. He could have ushered in an era of racial harmony. He did just the opposite.

Barack Obama was unqualified to be president, not because he was not bright enough or energetic enough. He was more cerebral than most presidents and used his power vigorously. He was unqualified because he lacked a fundamental understanding of what America is all about.

In his book *The Audacity of Hope*, Obama quoted his former pastor Jeremiah Wright, admiringly. Wright said, "white folks greed runs a world in need." Candidate Obama spoke of "typical white people" like his grandmother being inherently racist. Candidate Obama repeatedly accused his opponents of fearing him because he does not look like the presidents on our currency. One need not look like George Washington to govern with wisdom and integrity. Obama could have learned a great deal from those "dead white men" he so disdained, but he was convinced they had nothing to teach him. He never grew from being a far-left community organizer at his core, and he left our country the worse for it.

The presidency is the pinnacle of American politics. The person who holds that office should expect to endure incoming political missiles, not paintballs. That has been true from the founding of our republic, and it has nothing to do with race. Anyone who does not understand that is neither politically nor emotionally qualified to be president. It is not an office for the weak or the whiner. Only the strong need apply. Barack Obama was a divisive whiner when the country needed a unifying champion.

Baby Jackson was about four months old and being held up by hands behind him for this picture. The hands were probably his father's who had custody of him after his mother and father's marriage ended.

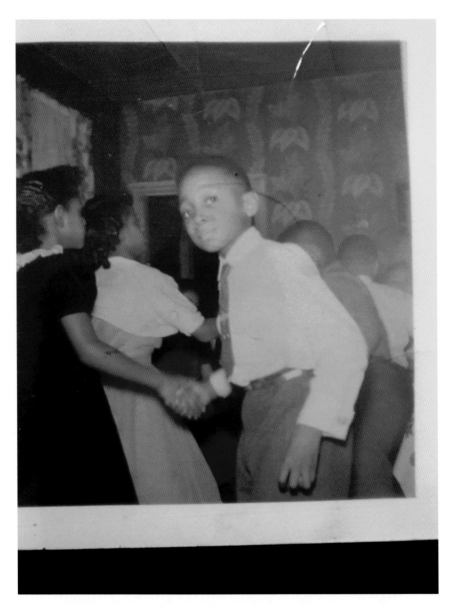

Birthday Boy. This was a birthday party for pre-adolescent Earl at about eight or nine years old. It was held in the home of Rebecca and Wille Molet, his foster parents.

Foster home—226 Pennell Street, Chester, Pennsylvania. This is the house Earl Jackson lived in from fourteen months to ten years old.

Marine Corps Private. This picture was taken at Camp Lejeune during Advanced Infantry Training after boot camp at Paris Island, probably in late October 1970.

1st Platoon, Camp Lejeune infantry training. Jackson is in the third row, 6th from the left.

Radar Technician School graduation class at Marine Corps base, Twenty-Nine Palms, California.

The man who changed E.W.'s life, his father William Jackson (February 16, 1915–June 20, 2002).

E.W.'s mother—Virginia Showell Jackson. Ninety-two years old in 2022.

Grandmother—Mabel Ross Jackson (March 26, 1885 – August 8, 1919). Married to E.W.'s grandfather Charles ("Frank") Jackson. He preferred to be called Frank because his brother's name was Charles. He was born in Orange County, Virginia, on July 4, 1874, and died in Philadelphia, Pennsylvania, on May 23, 1944. Bishop Jackson never met his grandparents on either side because they were all deceased before he was born. Mabel's father was Israel Ross, mother was Jasie Kirk Ross of Ohio.

Holding Rebecca Nicol Jackson, elder daughter at Women's Lying-In Hospital. He was in the finishing days of his final year at Harvard Law School when she was born on March 29, 1978.

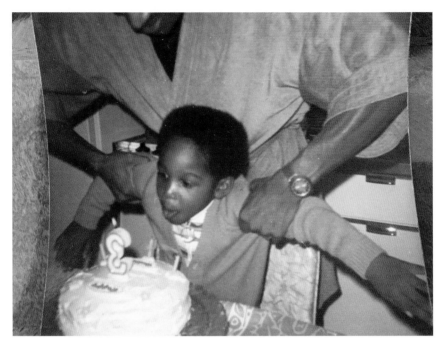

Lifting Earl Jackson Jr. high enough to blow out the candles on his third birthday cake.

Daddy's on the floor with his two girls, Rebecca—two years old—on the left and Jaquelyn ("Jaqui")—a few months old—on the right. They are successful women today.

Some of The Called Church family in fellowship, 2021.

E.W. and Theodora celebrating their 51st wedding anniversary at their favorite hotel.

Sacred Moment. Praying at the Wailing Wall in Jerusalem, April 2017.

The Jackson clan in 2016 enjoying some leisure time at Top Golf. From left to right is my son, Earl Jr., Rebecca, Bethany (Earl's wife), Theodora, Jaquelyn, and Earl Sr. Since then, Byron (Jaqui's husband) and Journie (their daughter) have been added to the family.

The legacy continues with granddaughter Journie Jackson Simmons (born March 8, 2022). Daughter of Byron and Jaquelyn.

CHAPTER 29

BLACK MESSIAH

I grew up in the inner city. We called it the ghetto. That world came close to swallowing me, but I escaped. The American dream is not a myth. It is the promise of our country to all of us. However, for the child who grows up in an impoverished, single-female-headed household, the Left says the dream is a cruel deception. When a child is fed such a steady diet of hopelessness, his God-given destiny is thwarted. The streets become an outlet for despair.

His measure of manhood is to join a vicious gang or to exploit multiple "baby mommas" who have children he neither sees nor feeds. Coming of age means going to prison, and coming out more hardened than when you went in. The utter tragedy is each of these young men has gifts, talents, and abilities that could help his family, his community, and his country. Instead, he is persuaded, often by highly successful black Americans, racism has doomed him to failure and there is nothing he can do about it. He is taught the lie that the American dream is a racist nightmare.

Your best friend was shot dead in a drive-by shooting. The school you attend is not accredited, and everybody you respect dropped out anyway. The guys wearing the most expensive shoes and driving the coolest cars are drug dealers, hustlers, or thieves.

The few kids you know who actually take school seriously and want to go to college are ridiculed for trying to be white.

While Leftists do everything in their power to perpetrate these problems, there are black Americans who want to solve them. We are not interested in wringing our hands over racism and pointing to "white people" as the cause of all woes afflicting black people. Some of us have reached the point of exasperation. We reject the tired bromides of traditional black leaders who have failed miserably for more than sixty years.

Their answers always boil down to two things: We need to spend more money on everything, and we need to have a nonstop conversation about race. We need to spend more on housing and more on education. We need to spend trillions in reparations. Black people need to speak more stridently and bitterly about being victims of systemic racism and oppression, and white people need to speak more apologetically about being oppressors. It is a never-ending cycle leading to more distrust, suspicion and division.

Progressives are long on demagoguery and short on progress. What they really offer is a repackaged Marxism based on race instead of class. If anyone thinks the inner cities of our nation have problems now, socialism would make the current condition of the black community look like utopia. Marxism and socialism are not an answer. They are a formula for unprecedented misery. Socialism turns everyone into a slave, except the government master, who serves up shortages, starvation, re-education camps, torture, and mass murder. That is the Left's history, and we should not be fooled by the naive claims that American socialists will do it differently. History has proved them wrong time and again, but their insatiable hunger for power overrides the lessons of history.

Barack Obama had the opportunity to do for the black community as much or more than any other American leader. He did worse than nothing. The Proverb says, "Where there is no vision, the people perish." Obama had no vision for the black community because his vision for the country was more of the policies eroding the inner cities, namely government dependence and control. What the black community needs is exactly what the government cannot provide: strong families, entrepreneurs, quality education, vigorous law enforcement to keep the streets safe, and spiritual renewal to change hearts and minds. Except for enhanced policing, government is incapable of producing the desired results. Therefore, these vital needs were alien to Obama, who yet was virtually worshipped as a messiah.

Hymns were written in his honor. Artists portrayed him as a descending divinity. Children were taught to march to the cadence of his name. Women swooned and fainted in his presence at campaign events.

Once he was elected president, the infatuation only deepened. He had a level of popularity and goodwill within the black community that could have been transformative. He could have gone into the inner cities and talked to gang bangers and drug dealers, and they would have listened. He could have encouraged young fathers who have abandoned their children to take responsibility, and some would have listened and heeded his call. He could have told those headed for a career in crime to stop destroying their lives and start building a life. He could have told them to stop blaming the police for their own bad choices. No doubt some, perhaps many, would listen to the great Barack Obama.

He once boasted he had "a pen and a phone." He could have used those tools to call forth billions of dollars of private investment in the inner city. This would have been hard work and there would have been resistance, but if anyone could do it, he could have. As the first black president in American history, his refusal to take visionary action to move the inner city from poverty to prosperity makes him an utter disappointment and failure.

CHAPTER 30

AFFIRMATIVE ACTION

While we can always debate how Dr. King would have evolved had he lived, his concept of liberation for black Americans was to end segregation and discrimination. He saw Americans of African ancestry as wholly capable of competing in a free economy if given the chance to do so. When Martin Luther King was leading the Civil Rights Movement, the concept of affirmative action had not yet been conceived.

As always, ideas designed to solve social problems bring with them unintended consequences. This is particularly true when their implementation requires governmental enforcement. Affirmative action was introduced by President John F. Kennedy in 1961 with Executive Order 10925. It required that government employers "not discriminate against any employee or applicant for employment because of race, creed, color, or national origin" and that they "take affirmative action . . ."[10]

In the years to come, affirmative action would come to include numerical quotas, race norming in testing and lowering standards for members of groups deemed "disadvantaged." It was conceived as a redress for the allegedly continuing legacy of slavery and Jim Crow having unfairly kept black Americans behind. In theory the heirs of slaves were supposed to be the beneficiaries, but the concept has been expanded to include illegal aliens, homosexuals, transgenders and women, especially if they are lesbians or women of "color."

The idea may have been well-intentioned, but it was a misguided attempt to guarantee black representation in all spheres of the economy and professional life. Over the years it has faced the inevitable and the unspoken stigma of not having to meet the same standards as others. This put a cloud over every black doctor, lawyer, engineer, and other professional. It subverted the ultimate goal—respect. Title and position can be granted by edict, but respect must be earned.

The story of Navy diver Carl Brashear is a case in point. He grew up in the segregated South, joined the Navy, and went on to become the most celebrated diver in naval history. The movie of his story does not sugarcoat the dehumanizing discrimination he endured. Yet it inspires us because Brashear did not define himself by the people who opposed him, but by the obstacles he overcame. He earned respect by striving to be the best, no matter the cost. He won a place among the most determined and courageous men ever to wear a Navy uniform. This honor was not given to him because he was black, but because he earned it, in spite of vehement opposition. Affirmative action cannot bestow respect, but it can rob a person of it.

The very whiff of special treatment caused even black Americans to express doubt about black professionals' ability, preferring the Jewish lawyer or the white doctor. It is not fair that black aspirants who meet the highest standards have their achievements clouded by the stigma of being an "affirmative action baby." Who would choose to be operated on by a mediocre surgeon or be represented in court by a mediocre lawyer and have one's taxes prepared by a mediocre accountant? Who would want to board a plane flown by a mediocre pilot? We all want competence and excellence. Fairness and equality are great political concepts, but on the operating table, we want skill.

Dr. King addressed the issue when he said:

If it falls your lot to be a street sweeper, sweep streets like Michelangelo painted pictures, like Shakespeare wrote poetry, like Beethoven composed music; sweep streets so well that all the hosts of Heaven and earth will have to pause to say, "Here lived a great street sweeper, who swept his job well."[11]

Dr. King envisioned a meritocracy where people are recognized and rewarded for their achievements regardless their skin color. He was not looking for a special dispensation for victims of past wrongs. He knew the only way of healing the racial divide is love, reconciliation, and community, not resentment and payback.

Affirmative action may have opened doors of opportunity for a few, but it has also perpetuated the myth that blacks are intellectually inferior. As long as any group of people is held to a lower standard than others, they will be plagued with the question of whether they earned their position, or it was given to them.

There is also a political side to affirmative action. It provides another way of solidifying the loyalty of black voters. Leftists do not care about any stigma if the program serves their political interests.

We want America to be an opportunity society. We need policies which unify, not divide. We want to create mutual respect among our citizens, not resentment. Most Americans would support a kind of "affirmative action" to identify bright and hardworking kids who need help finding opportunities for which they are qualified.

Children of all backgrounds face the disadvantage of poverty and uneducated parents who have never experienced college or professional life. When I was ready for college, even though academically gifted, I had no one in my family to guide me through the maze of college rankings, scholarships, and professional opportunities. No one in my family ever attended college, let alone graduated. I was feeling my way through, and some "affirmative action" to show me how the system worked and how to choose the best college for my background and abilities would have been enormously helpful.

I did not need race norming of my test results or lowered standards of admission. I did not need someone to treat me like a victim in need of rescue. What I needed was a guide, a mentor who looked at me as an individual, not as a representative of a demographic group.

What I needed was someone who appreciated my gifts and abilities and could help me explore my options and the pros and cons of the choices before me. America is indeed a land of opportunity, but if you do not know what those opportunities are, you certainly won't know how to seize them.

African people and their American descendants are capable of academic achievement, mathematical and scientific genius, writing beautiful prose and poetry, designing and constructing great buildings, running large organizations, and providing creative and compassionate leadership. Nothing in science, history, or the sins and circumstances of our fore-parents suggests otherwise. Infantilizing black people or other minorities deprives them of their destiny and the rest of us of their contributions. In an increasingly hostile world, with Vladimir Putin's Russia and Communist China breathing down our national necks, we need to tap the full potential of every American.

My children grew up very differently than their mom and dad. They had two parents with five degrees between them—two bachelor's degrees, two master's and one Juris Doctor. Our children had in-house help for figuring out college. They were in a privileged position as compared to a white kid from a single-parent home with a mom who didn't finish high school. My children were in no way disadvantaged, although Leftists want us to believe they were.

America will never truly be one nation as long as the myth is perpetuated that because of the past, every black citizen is oppressed, and every white person is an oppressor. Many Americans I know who grew up in poverty or had alcoholic and abusive parents or had no dad in the home are puzzled and angered by the notion they are beneficiaries of "white privilege" and "white supremacy." What George W. Bush called the "soft bigotry of low expectations" is really the hard bigotry of political manipulation.

I graduated Summa Cum Laude from the University of Massachusetts at Boston with a Phi Beta Kappa Key and then went to Harvard Law School. That was not the result of affirmative action, but discipline, sacrifice, and hard work. My wife and I worked while attending school full time. At various times she worked for South Shore Bank in Quincy, Houghton Mifflin Publishing, and the

Harvard School of Education Library. With the "systemic racism" we are told is pervasive in America, it is a marvel she was ever hired for one of those jobs, let alone all three. This was in the early '70s, during the racially charged busing controversy in Boston. Might it be that she was well educated and better qualified than other candidates who sought those positions?

During those years, I worked every evening as an RCA television contract salesman and all night as a security guard. I arrived home in the morning, got a few hours of sleep and went off to class. I did my homework on weekends and while working on my all-night security job. My wife did hers in the evening after putting our son to bed.

I am grateful to live in a country that made it possible for us to do what we did. We asked no one's permission. It required no political favors. We made up our minds we wanted more out of life and set about achieving it. This is pure Americana, and it if sounds unrealistic to the twenty-first-century ear, that is a testament to our cultural degeneration. Americans once believed in hard work and sacrifice to accomplish goals in life. We neither asked for nor wanted handouts. We relied on ourselves, our families, and Almighty God to get us through.

Today, we live in a victim entitlement society. A large segment of the population is trying to figure out what they are owed and how to collect it. We were once a nation of people too proud to accept from others what we could do for ourselves. If we do not arrest this trend soon, we will become a weak people willing to trade our freedom for whatever subsistence existence we are offered, either by our own government or some foreign power.

Identity politics requires playing the victim. Black people are the victims of "white" people. Women are the victims of men. Homosexuals and now transgenders are the victims of "straights" and "cis-genders." Muslims are the victims of American "Islamophobes." In this warped view of life, almost everyone is the victim of someone. "Old white men" are the sole exception, being strictly victimizers. It is psychologically and emotionally unhealthy to base one's identity on the idea that others are in control of your destiny. Our society is riddled with this pathology. It is a fatal affliction that will destroy our country if we are not set free from it.

I was taught by my dad not to make excuses. I was never told to blame the "white man" or anyone else. My father taught me the only way to grow and make progress is to take responsibility for one's own life and decisions. He made it crystal clear: excuses were unacceptable to him and should be to me as well. What I make of my life would be entirely up to me, not others. I was not taught to think this way by the Republican Party or some other political or social entity. I was taught to think this way by a proud black American—my dad.

He demanded I be brutally honest with myself, not for self-condemnation, but for self-correction. For example, basketball was my favorite sport growing up, and I thought I was a pretty good player. Most kids who like the game probably think they could be the next Michael Jordan. As I played with other boys, it slowly dawned on me I was better than some but could not compete with guys who were gifted with height and superior athletic ability. I loved sports, but my gifts tended toward the academic. I was the student who helped other basketball players with their math assignments. My father encouraged me not to sulk over the fact I was unlikely to start for our high school team. I never made the team, but I could make the most of what God gave me.

It is the nature of life to face resistance. Our dreams and ambitions do not get handed to us on a silver platter. The first resistance we face is our own fallibility and limitations. Yet in an American culture increasingly dominated by the idea of victimization, people are predisposed to blame someone else. We are encouraged by the new cultural "wokeness" to believe it is always someone else's fault. Social injustices—racism, sexism, and a variety of forms of "otherness"—are what damage and destroy our lives and the lives of those around us. The individual member of the designated victim group has nothing to do with it. He or she is an innocent bystander.

That is the big lie infecting America like a deadly cancer. Is there injustice? Of course. Are there people who hurt or discriminate against others because of irrational hatred and prejudice? Yes. Such people are the exception, not the rule. The biggest obstacle to progress we face in life, especially in America, is ourselves. The prejudices of others can be overcome. However, if we lack discipline and determination, all the governmental and social programs in the world won't change the outcome. If our character is predisposed toward wrong, evil, and hurting others, our landing in prison is not the fault of "systemic racism." It is the fault of the person who commits the crimes.

If we overcome the obstacles within ourselves, we will conquer those presented by others. People may oppose you because they don't like your personality, your family, where you come from, or your political beliefs. Some may seek to obstruct you because they do not like your race or ethnicity. These realities are excuses for failure, but they cannot cause you to fail. The real cause is you. However, failure need not be permanent. It is an experience we all face in life. How we respond is what matters.

When I arrived at Harvard Law School, I found some of my fellow students had the advantage of coming from homes where dad or mom or both were lawyers. In some cases, they were the third or fourth generation in their family to choose law as a profession. They were thoroughly familiar with the culture and vocabulary of the law. It was all new to me. My father had a sixth-grade education and was reluctant to advise me because as he put it, "Son, you have entered a whole new world that I know nothing about." I could not spend one second sulking about life being unfair. People are inherently different in their backgrounds, personalities, gifts, and abilities.

We must take life as we find it. The poor black kid who grows up in the ghetto of Chester, Pennsylvania, is worlds ahead of the poor untouchable kid who grows up in the slums of New Delhi, India. Inequality of circumstances is unavoidable. Thank God we live in a country where there is the opportunity to overcome every disadvantage and exploit every gift and ability we have. You can whine or you can win, but you can't do both. If you are whining, you are not winning; you are losing. If you're going to win, you have to get on with it.

My performance during my first year at law school was average because I fell in with a party crowd satisfied to get the gentlemen's B or C. It was not because I was black or because I come from a poor background with uneducated parents. It was because I was unwilling to say no to the negative influences around me. I bought into the false idea that my biggest success was already achieved—getting into Harvard Law School.

Anybody legitimately admitted to Harvard Law School has the intellectual ability to do the work. At least, this was true of all my classmates. I did not encounter any dummies. For one of these very bright people to fail required considerable effort, but a handful of students managed it. As I recall, a couple of them were black. Perhaps they were not prepared for the pressure and rigor of law school, but the more likely reason is they just didn't do the work.

I coasted my first year. During my second year I underwent a dramatic Christian conversion and struggled to figure out if law school was where I belonged. I rarely went to class, but still managed to pass all my courses by studying on my own.

I have no doubt I could have made law review, but I did not apply the first year and was distracted the second. It was not until the third year that I came into my own. It wasn't racism, cultural bias, or the proverbial "white man" preventing me from excelling. It was my own lack of focus.

Of course, it would have been helpful to have a mentor walk me through the process and guide me around the pitfalls, but there is no guarantee I would have listened. Furthermore, I wasn't the only student who could have used that kind of assistance. Some of my classmates came from far more difficult backgrounds than my own. In the end, I did what I needed to do to finish. I can only take credit for my success if I am willing to take responsibility for my shortcomings and failures.

God has given me the gifts of a sound mind and robust health. Others less endowed manage to build meaningful and successful lives. Aside from the severely mentally and physically handicapped, none of us has any excuse.

It helps to have a stable, loving family. This is one of the great tragedies of the policies intended to "help" the black community. Since the implementation of the 1960s Great Society programs, the black family has been decimated. Black individuals are, of course, capable of transcending the culture and circumstances around them. However, it adds to their obstacles when government policy incentivizes the breakdown of the family. Giving a single mother more money for more children when there is no man in the house, encourages welfare babies and scofflaw men.

I was blessed to have a wonderful father. While he had two unsuccessful marriages, my wife and I were blessed to celebrate our 52nd wedding anniversary on September 11, 2022. She has been by my side through thick and thin. I have a very small number of loyal and faithful friends who have been there for me as well. None of us achieves without the love and support of others, but those who love us cannot do our work. They cannot be our discipline. They cannot be the inner spark driving us on when the situation is dark. Even God will not force us to act if we are set on complacency.

While I was running for the U.S. Senate in Virginia in 2011, I held a community meeting in Richmond. Some of the people in that room were convicted felons. We had a wide-ranging discussion about solving the problems faced by the black community in the inner city of Richmond and throughout Virginia. One of the people attending was a recently released felon who faced some very hard times. During a discussion about prison and criminal justice reform, he said, "I always hear that the black people in prison don't belong there, but I didn't meet anybody in prison who didn't belong there, including me." A small fraction of people are wrongly convicted and they deserve corrective justice. Nonetheless, most of the people in prison have done things to land themselves there. The convict at my meeting spoke with authority when he said reform should focus on helping those people who really want to be helped, not pretending they all are victims of an unjust and racist criminal justice system.

Police are not walking the streets picking on black people randomly. If they are, I am the luckiest black man in the world that the lot has never fallen on me. I am gratified for the level of success I have achieved, and I expect to do more before I leave this earth. It has nothing to do with the color of my skin. It has to do with vision, purpose, and action toward one's goals in life.

An affirmative action program that reduces every person to nothing more than a member of a victim class only perpetuates the stereotypes we need to eradicate. It puts a stigma on the very people it is supposed to help. It fosters a sense of entitlement of the supposed victims and creates resentment rather than respect in those accused of being victimizers by virtue of their skin color. It is not justice to ask those who have not wronged others to pay the price for what previous generations did. People are not equal in heritage, gifts, or abilities. Life is not fair in the circumstances into which we are born. If we were to spend each generation trying to undo every harm done by every prior generation, the whole of humanity would be plunged into perpetual civil war.

CHAPTER 31

RETHINKING AMERICAN SLAVERY

The Left points to slavery as proof America is a racist nation, permeated with white supremacy and white privilege. One of the goals of this book, indeed of my life, is to restore a deep sense of love and gratitude for the blessing of being an American. Slavery is one of the issues the Left has used to indoctrinate many of our people, especially the young, to hate America. It is used to justify Marxist ideas for vast schemes of wealth redistribution such as reparations and radical notions of "social justice" such as defunding or dismantling police. "Slavery," we are told dramatically, "is America's original sin."

The first time slavery is mentioned in the Bible is in Leviticus. It prohibits slavery between Jews for indebtedness.

> "And if one of your brethren who dwells by you becomes poor, and sells himself to you, you shall not compel him to serve as a slave. As a hired servant and a sojourner he shall be with you, and shall serve you until the Year of Jubilee." (Leviticus 25:39–40)

The Code of Hammurabi, which dates back to 1754 BC, set the penalty at death for stealing a slave. This is written evidence of slavery dating back nearly 4,000 years. There is not a single continent or inhabited island on earth where slavery has not existed in some form. It is a human reality having nothing to do with race in our modern sense of the word.

The Arab slave trade was a booming business 700 years before Europeans started the Transatlantic slave trade. Scholars estimate the Arabs sold over twenty million slaves including five million Africans. Arabs also enslaved over a million Europeans captured by the Barbary pirates who were vassals of the Ottoman Empire. They captured and enslaved men and women from shoreline villages in Portugal, Spain, Italy, Ireland, Iceland, the Netherlands, France, and England. Until the need arose to justify the African slave trade and isolate African slaves from the moral sensibilities of Europeans, slavery was not a racial issue. Race is merely one in a long list of rationalizations for why certain people were subjugated. Religion, history, culture, geography, and tribe have all been cited to normalize ownership of human beings.

The British used slurs such as "barbarous," "filthy," "lazy," backward," and "animals" to justify subjugating the Irish.

Gerald of Wales expressed typical British views: "This is a filthy people, wallowing in vice. They indulge in incest, for example in marrying—or rather debauching—the wives of their dead brothers."[12]

Archbishop Anselm accused the Irish, saying, "men exchange wives as publicly and freely [as] horses."[13]

Objective knowledge of history is so scarce these days it is easy for the Left to slander America over slavery. Either out of ignorance or because it serves their Marxist agenda, the Left does not acknowledge the worldwide context into which America was born. The seventeenth-century world was a brutal place. Conquest and slavery were the norm, not the exception.

Yet from the moment slavery arrived on this continent, decent people fought against it. The earliest abolitionists were Christians. They were compelling and uncompromising in their denunciation of slavery as evil and contrary to God's Word.

Our country is never given credit for the fact that many Americans, at risk of their own lives, worked to remove it from our society.

The disagreement was so sharp the issue had to be left unresolved in order to hold the thirteen colonies together to fight Britain in the Revolutionary War.

Thomas Jefferson and other signers wanted language in the Declaration denouncing slavery. Benjamin Franklin, for example, called slavery "an atrocious debasement of human nature . . . a source of serious evils."[14]

John Jay said, "To contend for our own liberty and to deny that blessing to others, involves an inconsistency not to be excused."[15] John Adams opposed slavery all his life, calling it "a foul contagion in the human Character"[16] and "an evil of Colossal Magnitude."[17]

Even George Washington, denounced for owning slaves, came to disdain the institution he inherited. He said, "There is not a man living who wishes more sincerely that I do, to see a plan adopted for the abolition of [slavery]."[18]

The first draft of the Declaration of Independence included an explicit denunciation of slavery, but Georgia and South Carolina were opposed. Still, the statement "all men are created equal" condemned slavery without saying it explicitly. That was as far as they could go and still keep the colonies unified.

The Declaration states, "We hold these truths to be self-evident, that all men are created equal, that they are endowed by their Creator with certain inalienable Rights, that among these are Life, Liberty and the pursuit of Happiness."[19]

It has been reported that when slaves heard those words, they assumed it applied to them.

It was naive, but entirely understandable—they thought those words would bring about their immediate freedom. Historic cultural change does not happen quickly or easily. It would take nearly another century for Americans of African descent to be freed and another century to experience the promise. Yet it happened, and Americans like me are the beneficiaries.

The Founding Fathers could not possibly have understood the far-reaching significance of those words. Yet we must acknowledge the prophetic power of the Declaration, which sets forth the unique and providential nature of our country. I never cease to be amazed at how the Left condemns and dismisses the Founding Fathers.

What these great men accomplished is unprecedented in human history. Yet they are relegated to the level of racial criminals because of the times in which they lived and the world into which they were born. We treat them worse than the common criminal of today, whose sentences for crimes are tempered by consideration of "underlying causes." The American Founders cannot be defined merely as slave owners. That is one aspect of their multi-dimensional lives and character. Their contribution to humanity's well-being is immense, almost immeasurable.

Viewed through the lens of Marxist ideology, we can be made to look like a country of racists and bigots. In the middle of the eighteenth century, monarchs, warlords, and brutal dictators ruled.

Out of the brutality of that world, America was born. It was a bloody context, but our Founders sought to elevate us. They had a vision of a nation in which every citizen is free to use our God-given abilities to pursue happiness as we understand it.

Most Americans have not been taught how revolutionary this was, particularly in those times. It is still revolutionary, but we now take it for granted. What if there were a nation whose political leaders answer to the citizens, not the other way around? What if there were a nation in which the people are sovereign, and the government serves at their pleasure? Could such a thing even be possible? Yes, and we call that impossible thing the United States of America. It was nothing short of miraculous in 1776. Two and half centuries ago we made a dramatic break with accepted norms. Most of the world thought of it as a quixotic adventure led by a few iconoclasts who would ultimately submit to King George as obedient British subjects or be hanged for treason.

The French were reluctant initially to come to the colonists' aid because they considered the cause hopeless. The world agreed. But the nation created by ragtag colonists would quickly rise to dwarf the mother country and become its chief benefactor and protector. The Founding Fathers achieved a remarkable feat and created a nation of unparalleled greatness.

This is the nation into which I was born. I am the great-grandson of slaves, but I was not born into slavery. I am a full citizen of the most free and prosperous nation in the history of the world. My ancestors endured the Middle Passage, the captivity, humiliation, and violence of slavery. However, the Left would take history out of its context and act as if my ancestors' lives and mine would have been peaches and cream had it not been for the European slave traders. As mentioned, slavery existed in Africa and the Middle East 700 years before Europeans discovered the "peculiar institution."

Slavery is evil, but America did not invent it. It is not our "original sin." It existed all over the world for thousands of years before the first African slave landed on the American continent. It still exists in many parts of the world, but America is the greatest enemy of the evil of buying and selling human beings.

I am grateful to live in a nation of freedom. I am proud that my country overcame the scourge of slavery. I am inspired that 150 years after slavery ended, descendants of slaves are billionaires and lead Fortune 500 companies. This evolution should give every American an immense sense of pride and hope for the future of our country.

CHAPTER 32

DR. MARTIN LUTHER KING'S AMERICAN DREAM

The Civil Rights Movement was a uniquely American phenomenon. It was not a battle between blacks and whites, but a struggle between good and evil, freedom and slavery. The fight was brutal and bloody. However, as much as the Left would have us believe otherwise, the history of our country proves good wins out over evil. Freedom prevails over tyranny.

The lesson of the Civil Rights Movement lost in the machinations of politics is that Dr. King and his followers were not aliens from a distant planet or foreigners from a different country. They did not arise in a cultural vacuum. They were not conjured up in an isolated laboratory of social experimentation. They were Americans, steeped in the tradition of American rights and freedoms, educated in American schools and colleges, and knowledgeable about American institutions and systems. Most of all, they were confident enough in the fundamental decency of the American people that they pursued a strategy of winning hearts and minds rather than inciting violence, hatred, and revolution.

I first began paying attention to the speeches and writings of Dr. Martin Luther King after I became a Christian. What started as curiosity became admiration. I grew to see him as an American prophet raised by God to awaken our national conscience. His messages inspired my faith and confirmed my patriotism. There are many for whom the accomplishments of Dr. King are diminished because of what we have learned about his private life. I judge him with the same standard I apply to the Founding Fathers and all Americans who have come after them. Jesus Christ is the only perfect individual who ever walked the face of the earth.

The Founding Fathers and Dr. King were flawed human beings as are we all. The question is whether they fulfilled the purpose for which they were put on this earth. God used Rev. King to destroy the yoke of racial injustice that bound us all, victims and victimizers. His most powerful statement, perhaps the most quoted of his many eloquent expressions, is we should not be judged by the color of our skin, but by the content of our character.

The Civil Rights Movement at its best was an effort to free every individual to be all that God intended. The racial categorizing of the Left has merely substituted one set of limitations for another. The ideological impulse of the Democrat Party to control people has not changed. Joe Biden in 2020 said if any black person did not vote for him, "you ain't black." That is slavery-like control draped in a veneer of racial solidarity. That solidarity often takes on resentment, bitterness, and hatred against those who dare think for themselves.

Dr. King wasn't calling for a revolution; he was, like Frederick Douglass before him, calling on America to live out the *true meaning of its creed*. He spoke healing to the hearts of all people. The so-called civil rights leaders of today have betrayed his legacy.

When Reverend Dr. Martin Luther King Jr. ascended the platform at the Lincoln Memorial on August 28, 1963, he pricked the conscience of the nation. It was one of the most unifying speeches ever given, very different from the divisive tone struck by today's activists and so-called civil rights leaders.

Martin Luther King's movement was for freedom, not racial control, for unity, not division. He articulated his vision in an inimitable way. History will never forget what he said on the National Mall in Washington on August 28, 1963:

"In a sense we've come to our nation's capital to cash a check. When the architects of our republic wrote the magnificent words of the Constitution and the Declaration of Independence, they were signing a promissory note to which every American was to fall heir. This note was a promise that all men, yes, black men as well as white men, would be guaranteed the unalienable rights of life, liberty and the pursuit of happiness."[20]

No one can say with certainty where King would have landed on the ideological scale had he lived to old age. The pressure would have been great for him to succumb to Leftist indoctrination. That influence was evident when he spoke against the Vietnam War but never acknowledged the dangers and evil of communism, still a grave threat to our country today.

Yet much of Dr. King's intonements had a decidedly traditional and conservative ring. In one speech, cited earlier, he talked about the importance of personal excellence. This was more in line with the thinking of Booker T. Washington than W.E.B. Du Bois, who ultimately became a communist. The black community in America still faces the same choice as when Washington and Du Bois were feuding. Is true progress to be found in a collectivist approach? Or is the progress of the black community to be found in individual excellence and achievement?

Collectivism has failed miserably except in creating a political machine to keep liberal politicians in power. Ghettoes, poverty, failing schools, violence, drug dealing, addiction, family breakdown, and pervasive gang lawlessness persist. The Democrats who run these cities have no plan to end this dystopian nightmare. In fact, they exploit it as proof of "systemic racism," which absolves them of responsibility to solve these problems.

There will be no community-wide progress until it is a cultural norm for each individual to study hard, work hard, shun crime, and take personal responsibility to build a better life. That is how I escaped the ghetto of Chester, Pennsylvania, and how my wife's family escaped the projects. That formula will work for anyone who puts it to work, regardless of race. That is the promise of America, and the promise is real.

CHAPTER 33

CRITICAL RACE THEORY (CRT)

I will refer to this concept from time to time in the book. As a matter of substance, it does not deserve any attention. In my view, it is a racist black cult of pseudo-scholars pretending to have some brilliant breakthrough in understanding racism not only in America, but worldwide. It is responsible for many of the flawed racial concepts already discussed. It was pioneered by several scholars including Derrick Bell, who taught at Harvard Law School during my time there. I did not know him and never took his course. He later became a mentor of Barack Obama while he was at Harvard Law.

CRT is not a scholarly treatment of race, although it purports to be. It is a branch of Marxist thought and therefore far from original. Like Marxism, it views the world in terms of class struggle, refashioned as racial conflict between white people and the rest of humanity. Everything is to be viewed through this lens, which is why it is akin to a cult. Unlike some cults, it has no singular leader, though it has many who aspire to that role. I need not name them. My goal is to see to it their entire system of thought is soundly rejected by the American people from all backgrounds. It must be seen for the sophistry and racial demagoguery it is. Our colleges, universities, and public schools must be purged of it. It is spreading like a cancer through our institutions, and it will require a spiritual awakening as the chemotherapy needed to kill the cancer and discredit it once and for all.

Thomas Sowell gives an excellent treatment to its fallacies in his book, *Intellectuals and Society*. Mark Levine, in *American Marxism*, gives an updated exposition in light of the widespread controversy CRT has created in the aftermath of the 2020 race riots. I recommend both books for those who want a thorough understanding of this insidious movement, which began at least thirty years ago in ivory towers and has now found its way into every nook and cranny of our society.

CHAPTER 34

THE NEED FOR NATIONAL UNITY

I do not deny the problems our country has had with race. However, for every instance of racism, there are ten examples of goodwill and decency among Americans. Obsessing over the issue of race serves only to divide us and exaggerate the problem instead of solving it. Slavery in America ended over 157 years ago. Jim Crow segregation ended more than half a century ago. Studying the past to learn from it is one thing. Exploiting the past for political leverage and emotional manipulation is very different. It is time to let go of the bitterness of the past and embrace the promise of the future.

The challenges we face as a nation are daunting. The rise of Communist China as a global force is a reality every American must face. The future of our country demands unity. But there is political power to be had through racial division, at the expense of our nation's future. If fear mongering, race-baiting, and demagoguery is what it takes to keep black voters casting Democrat ballots, the Left will continue to spew it, to the detriment, decline, and ultimate destruction of our nation.

The liberal media, black elected officials, and self-anointed "civil rights" leaders like Jesse Jackson and Al Sharpton are all too happy to fan the flames of division. They incite our own citizens to hate their country. While the black community languishes in inner city ghettoes, these self-appointed elites are doing very well in America. Given the racial despair they promote, one can only conclude they are so extraordinarily talented as to transcend racial injustice. They live in mansions, send their children to the best schools, run non-profit organizations with budgets of millions of dollars a year, and collect top fees for their speeches and services. Their own success undermines the claim black people cannot make it in America.

These phony leaders, including most black elected officials, are more insidious than the Ku Klux Klan. The Klan is an overt enemy you can spot from a mile away. It is far more difficult when those who claim to be "friends" abort your babies, keep your children locked in failing schools, and perpetuate family breakdown, gangs, violence, drug dealing, and poverty. How do you deal with those who claim to be your advocates, but tell you that your destiny is beyond your control? How do you relate to self-appointed champions, who tell you that the lack of advancement for generation after generation is someone else's fault? You don't deal with them. You don't relate to them. You turn away from them toward those who offer a true pathway to a better future instead hopelessness and despair.

These self-appointed messiahs scream at the forces of racism holding you down but offer no way out. Why would they? Maintaining enclaves of poverty strengthens their political machine and keeps them and their allies in power. This is one of the greatest travesties in the history of black America. Any leader who offers a way out is labeled an Uncle Tom or sellout. In the meantime, the bodies of young black men as well as innocent women and children drop like flies, from skyrocketing murder rates in the black community. The bodies of aborted black children are thrown into garbage like leftovers and make up nearly 40 percent of American children murdered by abortion.[21]

To distract from that horror, black residents are told to keep their eyes on ethereal concepts like "implied" or "unconscious" bias, "systemic racism" and "micro-aggressions." Pay no attention to the fact that death by police is a fraction of a percent of the young black men murdered by other young black men in America's cities. Alas, the data do not matter when it comes to exploiting emotional issues for political gain.

This con game being played on the black community offends and angers me. It is part of my personal life mission to wake up black Americans to the truth and set them free from the psychological deception and bondage in which Democrats and the Left hold them captive. Black business leaders, ministers, writers, and commentators—along with conservatives of every color who are tired of being labeled "racist" for their beliefs—must fight back against the hypocrisy of liberal racism. The focus of black progress must become helping the individual rise, not the fantasy of collective black progress through reparations or some other government program.

"We take offense at the idea that we must think like liberals say minorities are supposed to think," said Harry Alford, president and CEO for the National Black Chamber of Commerce. "We will think for ourselves as individual Americans, not as members of a designated victim group. We will not stay in our place."

The black leadership of the twenty-first century must offer a vision of a better future instead of obsessing over past injustices. For the good of our country and every citizen, regardless of color, it is time to stop perpetuating division and start creating the unity upon which we can build a prosperous future for all.

Keeping before us the vision of "one nation under God, indivisible" is the only way to overcome the challenges ahead. We will never have unity if we allow the Left to balkanize us by race, gender, and economic status. We are Americans. Some of us are of European descent, some of African descent, some of Hispanic heritage, some of Asian descent, and some of our ancestors are indigenous to this continent. Americans are from everywhere.

We can all draw strength from our backgrounds and the triumphs of our ancestors. However, we must live for the present and the future, not the past. Our nation has made mistakes just as we as individuals have made mistakes. We are an imperfect nation because we are all imperfect people.

However, in the same way imperfect individuals overcome their errors and go on to do extraordinary things, so can a nation. Indeed, no nation has been as successful at rising above the inherent sinfulness of human beings to create an oasis of freedom, opportunity, and hope. No other nation has raised the standard of living for its citizens to the American level which is unmatched anywhere else in the world. No nation has come close to creating a meritocracy attracting people from all over the world who believe that here, their God-given talents and hard work will be rewarded. This is the hope the Statue of Liberty represents, and Americans have every reason to be grateful and proud. Those who have given their lives in defense of that hope have not done so in vain. It has been worth every sacrifice made and every drop of blood shed.

My ancestors came to this continent as slaves, but I am proud to be an American. Even though slavery as an institution is a universal human phenomenon and Africans were being sold into slavery hundreds of years before the first African slave came to America, the Left condemns our country as if we invented the institution. Virginia U.S. Senator Tim Kaine said exactly that, perhaps out of sheer ignorance, but more likely as demagoguery to fan the flames of racial resentment and division.[22]

There was never a moment in our history when slavery was not a painful and contentious issue. Yes, this evil came to our continent and our forefathers allowed it, but the people of this continent were never comfortable with it. Part of the greatness of this country is our unwillingness to be at ease with evil. Slavery was debated, resisted, fought over, and ultimately precipitated a Civil War costing over 600,000 American lives. One hundred and fifty-five years later you would be hard pressed to find an American who does not wish slavery never existed in America.

Thomas Jefferson, who is often criticized as a prominent slave owner, was clearly conflicted over it. During the Missouri Compromise debate, he wrote, ". . . we have the *wolf* by the *ear*, and we can neither hold him nor safely let him go. Justice is in one scale, and self-preservation in the other."[23]

He was admitting that slavery was inherently unjust - quite an admission for a prominent political figure who actually owned slaves. He went even further. Jefferson believed God would hold the nation accountable for what he understood to be an inexcusable evil.

> "The whole commerce between master and slave is a perpetual exercise of the most boisterous passions, the most unremitting despotism on the one part, and degrading submissions on the other. . . .
>
> "And can the liberties of a nation be thought secure when we have removed their only firm basis, a conviction that these liberties are of the gift of God? That they are not to be violated but with his wrath? Indeed, I tremble for my country when I reflect that God is just: That his justice cannot sleep for ever . . . ."[24]

We can choose if we wish to find every fault in our country, our Founding Fathers, and others who have gone before us. We can hold them to a standard of perfection we could never meet ourselves. That is what the Left does continually. They do not consider that their arrogant, condescending self-righteousness is far more contemptible than any character flaws in those who established the most just nation in the history of mankind. I will be forever grateful to God for giving me the privilege of being born an American. The Founders were inspired to pursue freedom for the American people rather than power for themselves, and every one of us owes them a debt of gratitude. I will never apologize for my patriotism, nor should any American.

My ancestors were tough enough to have endured what I perhaps could not have. I have never been an indentured servant, a slave, or been denied my humanity. I realize there are some black people and other minorities who would not say the same. Have I experienced racism? Of course, I have. However, it has been such an insignificant part of my life experience it would be insane to make that my focus. That is what the Left resents about people like me. We are not obsessed with being victims or looking at the past as if we are as bound as the slaves who lived two centuries ago. We are free Americans. We are full heirs to the land of the free and the home of the brave. Every American, regardless of skin color, should embrace that reality and look to the future ahead of you, your children, grandchildren and all who will come after you. That is what I do and what I urge every American to do, especially descendants of those who were once in bondage. I am a patriot descended from slaves, but I live in this sweet land of liberty, and I love it.

PART V

THE PRO-LIFE CONSCIENCE OF AN AMERICAN

The most fundamental right we have been given by God is the right to life. Abortion is an abhorrent assault on this right and should offend every American. Life is the first inalienable right, for without life, no other rights matter.

I did not always understand this. As a young man I thought nothing of it. Abortion was a mere academic issue. I never found myself in a position where it mattered. We were young when my wife and I had our first child. I was not a Christian. She was a Christian, but far from devout. Had she been, she would not have married me, then a heathen by biblical standards. Yet we never discussed or considered abortion.

On the other hand, had you asked me where I stood on the issue, before becoming a Christian, I might have considered it a matter of personal privacy or "choice."

After I became a Christian, it was not an issue I thought about. I was twenty-one years old when the Supreme Court handed down *Roe v. Wade*. I studied it in college and concluded the Court's analysis was specious. They completely made up the three-trimester standard. *In utero* babies do not grow in distinct time segments. Their development is a continuum that does not lend itself to separate stages, some when life may be snuffed out versus others when restrictions are acceptable. Science and experience are exposing the utter foolishness of these arbitrary demarcations.

Even while I studied the *Roe* decision, I had no epiphany. It was not until about ten years after *Roe v. Wade* when the gravity of the issue was brought home to me. A pro-life activist asked to meet with me. I was running a radio station in Boston and practicing law out of an office at the station. My schedule was extremely busy because I was practicing law, running a radio station and pastoring a church. Yet I agreed to meet with this person. That was undoubtedly the leading of the Holy Spirit. I cannot remember who it was, only that he spoke truth and awakened my pro-life conscience.

It is not politically expedient for the Left to admit what they really believe. Too many Americans would find it deeply offensive. As a political movement, progressives do not believe rights come from God. They believe rights are delegated by state power. Those with the power to pressure, bully, threaten, or force the state to yield to their demands can create rights out of thin air. The concept of fundamental rights given by God is replaced by fake rights engineered by political pressure. That is what abortion is. When the Supreme Court issued the *Roe* ruling in 1973, they were not announcing the discovery of a right heretofore hidden from us. Rather they were saying, "You win. We surrender." They surrendered to the cultural voices of radical feminism and the murderous and lucrative abortion industry.

Nine justices in black robes cannot change the truth that life begins at conception, and it is a supreme moral evil to destroy that life. Science has proven we are nascent human beings as we are developing in our mother's womb. We are in different form just as a baby is different from an adult. Unable to speak, understand, or act at will, an infant is no less human than I am. You are not today what you were at three months old, or three years old, or three minutes old, but you have been human every step of the way.

The abortion propagandists try to draw an arbitrary line between living inside the mother and outside. Once born, they tell us, there is a substantive difference because the child can live on its own. That is specious. The child is still completely dependent upon other humans for survival. Left to her own devices, a baby girl would be dead within hours. Indeed, pro-abortionists now argue a child born alive after an intended abortion has no more right to live than a child still in its mother's uterus. That makes clear a conscience hardened to the child in utero does not change after the child is born.

President Obama has made this argument throughout his career, and even blocked The Born Alive Infant Protection Act when he was an Illinois state senator. The bill provided for protection for a child born alive as a result of an intended abortion. Obama's view was and continues to be that if you allow a child born of a botched abortion to live, you are frustrating the will of the mother. This attitude lays bare the moral truth that abortion is the murder of a living child, and pro-abortion forces do not care. For them, whether the child is inside or outside the womb is morally irrelevant.

God has a purpose for every human being and each human life is sacred. The Bible makes very clear God knew us before we were conceived:

"Before I formed you in the womb I knew you . . ." (Jeremiah 1:5)

. . . You covered me in my mother's womb. (Psalm 139:13)

More than 62 million innocent children have been killed since 1973 when *Roe v. Wade* made abortion legal in America. That is the total number of people residing in Arkansas, Colorado, Idaho, Iowa, Kansas, Louisiana, Minnesota, Mississippi, Missouri, Montana, Nebraska, New Mexico, North Dakota, Oklahoma, Oregon, South Dakota, Utah, and Wyoming. This is a genocidal tragedy.

Even more disturbing is the fact taxpayers have been forced to fund these horrible acts of violence, mostly through the largest abortion vendor, Planned Parenthood. Some pro-lifers call it Murder, Inc. and it receives an estimated $500 million a year from taxpayers. That is state financed murder. Yet Planned Parenthood doesn't need the money. They have been known to raise $400 million more than they spend. They spend millions on political campaigns. Yet they demand taxpayers finance their bloody enterprise.

Planned Parenthood clinics are using the hundreds of millions of dollars extracted from taxpayers each year to exploit young girls. They have been caught on video encouraging pregnant minors to lie about their age and violating state sexual abuse reporting laws.[25]

Planned Parenthood and the media have tried to change the culture of America to one which praises abortion and the women who choose it. The Left has become a cult of death, but half of Americans refuse to join the cult. They have made the killing of an unborn child a cause célèbre. During the 2010 Super Bowl, an ad featuring football player Tim Tebow and his mother was considered controversial because it celebrated her decision to carry her pregnancy with him to term, even though doctors suggested she not.[26] The ad celebrated life, and pro-abortion groups were livid! On MTV's 2010 "No Easy Decision," a focus group of teenagers who had abortions were praised by Dr. Drew Pinsky as being "brave."

It is not brave to murder a baby. It is brave to carry a child for nine months and then to lovingly nurture it for life—or to give it a loving, adoptive home. Abortion is cowardly, not courageous. It is a solution to satisfy the selfish desires of those involved, often the man who doesn't want the responsibility of being a father. Sometimes parents pressure a daughter to kill her child, believing wrongly this will free her to live out her dreams. The aftermath of killing one's own child is a nightmare, a lifetime of trying to suppress the guilt and numb the pain.

Barack Obama once said, "I got two daughters. I am going to teach them first about values and morals, but if they make a mistake, I don't want them punished with a baby." Is that what his daughters are to him and Michelle—punishment?

Ninety-two percent of abortions are done for convenience.[27] Twenty-four percent of women who have abortions are doing it for the second time.[28]

Comedienne Martha Plimpton bragged at a Seattle pro-abortion rally how she had her best abortion in Seattle:

"Notice I said 'first' . . . and I don't want Seattle—I don't want you guys to feel insecure—it was my best one."[29]

When a crowd cheers as a woman brags about killing her own babies—her own flesh and blood—that is the depth of depravity. Our society gets worked up over the killing and torture of animals, but hundreds of thousands of unborn babies are tortured and killed every year in the United States.

I could have been one of those murdered babies. I was born into a broken home. My mother and my father were splitting up at the time I was born. What if Planned Parenthood had convinced my mother to end my life? Cynics will say I would not have known the difference. I do now. Furthermore, I believe aborted children are in heaven and will one day bear witness against those who killed them. Abortionists and those who supported them will be shocked to see the many children they murdered standing before them declaring they felt great pain as their innocent lives were snuffed out.

Martha Plimpton and her proud abortion cohorts had better think about that. Moreover, those who vote for politicians who support and celebrate this sin will also answer to God. They may not have wielded the knife or injected saline, but by electing pro-abortion politicians, they legalize the instruments of death in the hands of those who carry out the slaughter.

All those pro-life activists who have never given up the fight to save the lives of the innocents were rewarded for their steadfastness in an unexpected legal victory. On June 24, 2022, the Supreme Court handed down their decision on Dobbs v. Jackson Women's Health Organization, which overturned Roe v. Wade. This court ruling was a vindication of the pro-life view that there is no federal constitutional right to kill an unborn baby. It is now a matter for governors and state legislators, which is where the debate belongs. It is my earnest hope America will be a nation which affirms life, and we now enter a new stage of the quest for that ultimate end. If there is a principle to be gleaned from Dobbs, it is we should never give up on truth and righteousness. We should never give up on our ability to impact the world for good. God is long suffering, but history bends to His will.

CHAPTER 35

THE RACIST ROOTS OF ABORTION

Abortion is analogous to slavery and Jim Crow laws. Part of the rationale of slavery was black people weren't real persons. Some even argued they didn't have a soul. In most states, killing a slave was not deemed murder, because slaves were property, not persons.

That is precisely how unborn babies are treated. The legal system has decided a whole class of people—unborn children—are not human. As such they have no right to life. The child is the property of the woman who carries it. Since it resides in her body, she may dispose of it as she sees fit. It has no soul and therefore no rights that we human beings must respect. Like the slave was an invisible non-person, the unborn child is today.

Our nation eventually awakened to the undeniable evil and horror of slavery. We came to realize people of African descent simply have darker skin than people of European heritage. Aside from that, they are no different. They too are created in the image of God, with gifts, talents, abilities, intelligence, and creativity by which they may care for themselves and contribute to the community. Can any less can be said of the pre-born child?

Margaret Sanger, founder of Planned Parenthood, had a godless worldview. She believed some people are indeed unworthy of life.

Among those, in her twisted mind, were blacks and other minorities, as well as what she classed as the "feeble minded." She began a eugenics movement in an intentional effort to eliminate these undesirables, which she called "human weeds."[30] Sanger once said, "We do not want the word to go out that we want to exterminate the Negro population." Her record would suggest that is precisely what she wanted to do, and the fact so-called civil rights leaders take Planned Parenthood blood money is a gross betrayal of the black community. Her eugenics movement was difficult to sell in the age of Hitler, but she repackaged it under the far more marketable name of "Planned Parenthood." It is in fact "planned death."

As a result of Sanger's successful co-opting of black leaders, a disproportionate number of abortions are performed on black women. Planned Parenthood clinics are strategically located in minority neighborhoods. Black women make up only about 6 percent of the American population, yet over 38 percent of abortions are performed on them.[31] Almost 80 percent of Planned Parenthood clinics are in minority neighborhoods. The black community would probably be twice the population it is now were it not for legal abortion in America.

Martin Luther King Jr. said, "injustice anywhere is a threat to justice everywhere."[32] When human beings reject God and His morality, there is no limit to the depths of darkness into which they can sink. The fact our highest court sanctioned the mass slaughter of unborn babies is so egregious it defies understanding by the rational mind.

We will not be a nation of true justice until we stop the murder of the innocent. One would think doing this to minority children in disproportionate numbers would strike the conscience of liberals, who are obsessed with racial disparities of any kind. Apparently, the killing of unborn black babies at three times their proportion to the population is the one exception to the "racial justice" principles Leftists swear by. The blood of these innocents cries out from the ground for justice. Only God addresses the injustices of the past. Our job is to persuade the American people to reject abortion and choose life.

On June 24, 2022, there was a major victory in the quest to stop the slaughter of innocent babies in the womb. The Supreme Court in the 6–3 decision in *Dobbs v. Jackson Women's Health Organization*, took the historic step of overturning *Roe v. Wade* (1973). The Court declared what has always been true. There never was a constitutional right to abortion. It was a bad law written by justices who were more interested in advancing their social agenda than in upholding the Constitution.

With *Dobbs*, every pro-life American has been vindicated. *Roe v. Wade* may be likened to the 1896 *Plessy v. Ferguson* decision which upheld racial segregation under the "separate but equal" doctrine. That case was overturned by *Brown vs. Board of Education* in 1954 which declared Plessy to be a bad law because legal separation was inherently unequal, indeed its purpose was to enshrine inequality as a legal and social reality.

Chief Justice Roger B. Taney declared in *Dred Scott v. Sandford* (1857), which foreshadowed *Plessy*, Americans of African descent were "so far inferior, that they had no rights which the white man was bound to respect."[33]

Roe v. Wade said essentially the same thing about an unborn child deserving no rights which adults are bound to respect. Now, just as *Dred Scott* and *Plessy* have been recognized as violative of constitutional principle, so has *Roe v. Wade*. Unfortunately, it has not gone as far as those corrective racial cases.

While pro-abortion forces responded with paroxysms of outrage and threats of violence, abortion has not been outlawed. Unborn children have not been declared persons worthy of equal protection under the law. The Supreme Court has simply said there is no federal constitutional right to kill an unborn child. States may regulate it as they wish. That is where the new battles lines are drawn. In the meantime, some corporations have jumped on the pro-death bandwagon promising to provide transportation and financial assistance to any woman who wishes to travel to a pro-abortion state where Planned Parenthood will gleefully kill her child.

The battle will continue until abortion is outlawed in America except for ectopic pregnancies and other very rare circumstances which involve a real threat of death for the mother. Even in these circumstances, many women have chosen to deliver their babies and both mother and child have survived. There is no such thing as the "pro-choice" movement because the only choice they support is abortion. They advocate it, push it, and make plenty of money off it.

Perhaps the most stunning response to the overturning of *Roe v. Wade* is the accusation by many on the Left that *Dobbs* was a racist decision. It is a prelude to banning interracial marriage. The racial demagoguery and fear mongering is their default for manipulating black voters. In this case, the claim is egregiously preposterous since abortions are disproportionately performed on black women. Twenty million black babies have been aborted since 1973. Extrapolating, those children would have had at least one child, the black population would probably be close to eighty million instead of the forty million it is today.

One day, and that day is not far off, black Americans are going to awaken to the fact a genocide has been perpetrated against their community with many of their political leaders and even some of their ministers complicit in ethnic cleansing on a massive scale.

CHAPTER 36

THE BLOODY REALITY
OF ABORTION

Even the pro-life movement and its activists are reluctant to expose the depraved reality of abortion. However, if we are to end this barbaric practice, we must see it in all its bloody horror. Abortion is the torture of an innocent, defenseless human being. Doctors inject saline solution into babies in utero to burn them alive. Or, in so-called "late-term" or "partial-birth" abortions, a child whose head has emerged is stabbed in the back of the skull and his or her brains are sucked out.

These human beings are treated like pests to be crushed and discarded. I used to think such images would prick the conscience of those who commit such acts. Most who work for Planned Parenthood and the abortion mills of our country have a calloused conscience. It is there but covered by scar tissue built up over the years. Thankfully, some miraculously rediscover their moral compass. Most apparently remain hard-hearted and go to their graves drenched in the blood of the innocent.

Relaxed laws and concerns about protecting women's "choice" resulted in the horror of Dr. Kermit Gosnell's Philadelphia abortion clinic, where living, viable babies were murdered, and women died after botched procedures. Yet, these stories were glossed over or ignored by the mainstream media. Most of so-called journalists are part of the cult of secular atheism, for which abortion is a blood sacrament. Unborn children are placed on the alter of sacrifice to the idol of selfishness.

In spite of the many horror stories of abortion, it is portrayed as a mere health care choice. That is supremely disingenuous. Abortion in fact puts a woman's health at risk.

Doctors take the Hippocratic oath to "do no harm." Abortion is a blatant violation of that oath. It is time for America to break free of the death cult of Planned Parenthood and the abortion industry and become a nation honoring life at every stage.

We are losing millions of babies whose lives could have meaning and purpose. They could contribute to our families and experience life's joys. Yes, life also has its sorrows, but it is still worth living. I was born to a broken home and raised in foster care, but God had a plan. It is the height of arrogance for fallible human beings to determine which child should live and which should be snuffed out. We are made in the image and likeness of Almighty God. Only He can see the end from the beginning.

Everything about my life suggested I would be dead by now or languishing in prison for some heinous crime. My deceased uncle shot a woman four times and almost spent the rest of his life in prison. A younger relative who I will not name spent years in prison for armed robbery. Some of my childhood friends suffered similar outcomes. Yet for every child born into circumstances like my own who ends up succumbing to the downward forces of life, countless others rise above those obstacles to do extraordinary things. Who are we as human beings to determine which child is unworthy of life?

I want my country to save babies, not kill them. Thanks be to God that *Roe v. Wade* has been overturned, but that has not put an end to abortions in our country. In ancient biblical days, pagans offered their babies alive on an altar of fire to assure their own good fortune. Even the Israelites at times acted no different from their pagan neighbors, as the Bible attests. Abortion is a similar sin. Those who commit it are likewise deceived into believing it will make their lives better. Sowing the seeds of death will never bring a better life. It is the unjust taking of a human life. No amount of spin from the

Left can change that. There is no justice in the abortion industry—not for the murdered babies, not for the mothers who are scarred physically and emotionally, and not for those who profit from the deaths of the innocent.

America was founded on Judeo-Christian moral principles, and God will one day call us to account:

> "I call heaven and earth as witnesses today against you, that I have set before you life and death, blessing and cursing; therefore choose life, that both you and your descendants may live." (Deuteronomy 30:19)

It is time for America to choose life.

PART VI

HOMOSEXUALITY AND ITS ASSAULT ON AMERICAN VALUES

We are facing an insidious and deadly attack on our traditional, Judeo-Christian values by the homosexual movement, which is trying to transform America into something our Founders never intended, the Constitution does not support, the people do not want, and God will never bless.

When American culture normalizes homosexuality and trans-genderism, it is—as Daniel Patrick Moynihan put it—"defining deviancy down." We should have compassion for those who are trapped in these perverse compulsions and lifestyles. They should not be harassed, bullied, or beaten up. They are morally and psychologically confused human beings who need our prayers, not hatred. However, homosexuality is still sin.

The Bible makes crystal clear this behavior is condemned by God. Yet, in our politically correct society, there is a price to be paid for saying this. Many Christians are unwilling to pay that price. Others posture as Christians and use their pseudo-Christianity to legitimize what can never be made right in the sight of God. For example, former president Barack Obama, who claims to be Christian, told the Human Rights Campaign homosexuality is something to be "admired." That view cannot be squared with Christianity. Homosexuality is not something to be admired. It is not about "identity" but unhealthy and immoral behavior. It calls for repentance, not pride.

I am well aware this view will be characterized by some, especially the mainstream media, as bigotry and hate speech. They should be reminded that for most of human history, homosexuality has been condemned as perversion. This has been the Muslim, Jewish, and Christian understanding. This remained the predominant view in our country until the 1960s, when homosexual activists began to attack traditional morality.

With cooperation from the media, educational system, the entertainment industry, and even corporate America, they have managed to subvert thousands of years of human history and the most basic understanding of marriage, morality, and human sexuality. They have disconnected sexuality from the Judeo-Christian roots which one guided us. This postmodern morality is thinly veiled anti-Christian, anti-Jewish bigotry.

Any statement opposing homosexual behavior, no matter how lovingly stated, is condemned as "anti-gay" bigotry. In actuality, it is the homosexual activists who are anti-Christian bigots, but they are lauded for it. Characterizing conservatives in general as bigots and extremists is the default position of the liberal media. Not only do they fail to criticize the virulent hatred of the Left toward Bible-believing Christians, they feed that hatred. The cultural nihilists have infected our culture with a militant rejection of God and the Bible.

They deny the reality of God and absolute truth, not to mention the science of biology. The Democrat Party has repeatedly expressed disdain for the Christian faith. In the aftermath of any mass shooting or other national tragedy, when Christians offer sincere "thoughts and prayers," the Left ridicules them.

Devin Patrick Kelley killed twenty-six people and wounded another twenty at First Baptist Church in Sutherland Springs, Texas on November 5, 2017. As Christians across America offered "thoughts and prayers" on behalf of the victims and their families, MSNBC commentator Joy Reid mocked those expressions of empathy and support. She sarcastically said, "Remember when Jesus of Nazareth came upon thousands of hungry people, and rather than feeding them, thought and prayed?"[34] What Reid and her Leftist colleagues in their collective ignorance fail to understand is Jesus prayed before taking action in that situation and every other. Prayer was a central part of His life.

America is culturally a Christian nation, established by Christians and those influenced by Christianity if not official members of a church. The Left wishes it to be otherwise. In their Marxist mindset, they see Christianity as the problem. What Democrats are after is the power to fundamentally transform this nation. They have said so. They are deathly afraid of Christians showing up at the polls or running for office to block their pathway to power. They are right to be concerned, but they are blind to the true source of our power—prayer. They ridicule the concept, but they are going to find out we will ". . . overcome them, because He who is in you is greater than he who is in the world" (1 John 4:4).

Anti-Christian bigotry is driven largely by the homosexual activist movement, which seeks to criminalize biblical morality. That is because Bible-believing churches are the biggest obstacle to normalizing sexual perversion and deviancy and enforcing its mandatory acceptance. Most Christians do not understand just how much we are hated, but homosexual activists are clear in their minds, we are the enemy. Chai Feldblum, lesbian lawyer/activist and former commissioner of the Obama administration's Equal Employment Opportunity Commission, said:

> There can be a conflict between religious liberty and sexual liberty, but in almost all cases the sexual liberty should win because that's the only way that the dignity of gay people can be affirmed in any realistic manner.[35]

The Bible describes homosexuality as an abomination to God. It is not only a sin against God's moral order; it is a sin against God's natural order. Sin is a consuming force with a never-ending appetite for destruction. It destroys individuals and whole societies. It never gets enough. Americans be warned: homosexual activists will never stop pushing the envelope.

They began with "gay rights." That became same-sex marriage. Then they began pushing transgenderism. Now we have children subjected in school to homosexual and transgender propaganda, some of which is pornographic.

We are told we must believe two men or two women are just as effective as parents as a man and woman. Every credible sociological study debunks that idea. The idea that gender is a mere "social construct" is pure foolishness to most Americans. It defies science, biology, genetics, and common sense.

Because of the insatiable depravity of those who give themselves to it, there will always be new demands. Already articles are appearing suggesting pedophilia should be understood as a mere sexual "orientation." Cambridge, Massachusetts, has codified multiple partners as a legitimate expression of conjugal relations, i.e., marriage. It was not long ago the suggestion of injecting prepubescent children with hormones and preparing to surgically altar genitalia and breasts would have been considered madness. Entertaining elementary school children with drag queen strippers would have been considered a crime. Bringing these practices into public schools would have been unthinkable. Even now, for anyone who has refused induction into today's politically correct culture, all of this sounds insane. Indeed, for normal people, this is nothing short of child abuse that should garner fines and imprisonment, and the removal of children from parents who allow it.

Collective approval does not alter the nature of evil. The homosexual movement and the sexual revolution it has inspired are evil. It undermines the moral values of our society and corrupts our children. It is rebellion against Almighty God and a curse on this nation. As one who loves this country, I cannot be silent while this vile sexual sin eats away at the foundation of our civilization.

Nowhere is this more evident than in the push for same sex "marriage." Marriage between one man and one woman, as God intended it, is one of the bedrock principles of our nation and any successful culture. Yet, the homosexual community has changed that definition. As a result of the very loud and persistent work by Hollywood and other Leftist political activists, marriage is no longer a sacred covenant. LGBTQ individuals are no longer seen as lost souls in need of help. They are now victims of oppression. This movement's underlying principle says the Bible is a lie and

Christians are religious fanatics who use our faith to discriminate against so called "gay" people.

The Left refuses to acknowledge the truth that Judeo-Christian morality existed thousands of years before there was an LGBTQ movement, and the biblical view of marriage was not invented to irritate them. We believe marriage is the gift of God and He, not human beings, defined it from the beginning.

Jesus affirmed this truth:

> "Have you not read that He who made them at the beginning 'made them male and female'... 'For this reason a man shall leave his father and mother and be joined to his wife, and the two shall become one flesh'?" (Matthew 19:4–5)

In large measure, LGBTQ activists have succeeded by stealing the moral mantle of the black civil rights struggle. They have analogized homosexuality, transgenderism and the whole host of gender identities to being black. Equating the neutral physiological characteristic of skin color with the morally charged issue of human sexual behavior is one of the many absurdities of political correctness. The Left has managed to indoctrinate many to see sexual "preference" or "orientation" as the equivalent of race. Nothing could be more spurious, but when everyone agrees the emperor is wearing a beautiful garment, no one dares point out he is embarrassingly naked.

Human history is replete with instances of people who are different being mistreated, whether for physical deformity, mental illness, or sexual deviation from the norm. This is wrong. I do not believe homosexuals should be persecuted or homosexual behavior in private between consenting adults should be punished as a crime. However, we must resist forced acceptance of what we know to be wrong. And when it comes to corrupting or molesting children, it is a criminal matter whether the predator is homosexual or heterosexual.

People who are different are often targeted by bullies, and there's nothing wrong with a general policy of prohibiting bullying of any kind, especially in schools. But there is no justification for equating homosexuality and transgenderism with the black struggle for freedom and dignity. Here in America, homosexuals have faced nothing akin to slavery or the Jim Crow discrimination against black citizens.

Being black is an outward physical characteristic that cannot be hidden. When I walk into a room, people know I am black. Homosexuality, on the other hand, is private sexual behavior. Unless a person wants to put his or her sexuality on display, no one knows what they do in the privacy of their bedrooms. In fact, most people do not care until it is shoved in their faces or pushed on their children. "Coming out" is about letting people know, sometimes flamboyantly. Black people have no need to "come out." By observation, we are out from the moment of birth.

The status of being black never changes. On the other hand, I have met people who have been delivered from homosexuality. They stopped being homosexuals, raised families, and are free from same-sex attraction. I have never met anyone who has been "delivered" from being black.

The claim of widespread discrimination against homosexuals is a myth. You can't knowingly discriminate against people when you don't even know who they are. In fact, there is an interesting schizophrenia that goes on in the homosexual movement. If they are so interested in being "out," why do they call themselves "gay"? It obfuscates the issue of sexuality and suggests they are "happy," as the word used to mean. The strategy is to impact thinking by changing vocabulary. That is why we should reject the vocabulary of the LGBTQ movement. They should be referred to as what they are—homosexuals or transgenders.

Homosexual activists despise the Bible because it is the major impediment to full normalization of homosexuality. In fact, they want everyone to approve their lifestyle as virtuous and desirable. They cannot get past the fact that the most famous and beloved book in the world condemns it as an abominable sin. They have tried in every way to destroy the credibility of the Bible, but it has proved indestructible. They have lashed out at the apostle Paul, reinterpreted the story of Sodom and Gomorrah, and dismissed the

Bible as an ancient, "homophobic" text. Yet it stands alone as the most influential book in the history of the world.

Unable to censor the Bible completely, they strike at the reputation and credibility of Bible-believing Christians. High-profile individuals have been attacked because they merely belong to a church teaching what Jesus taught—marriage is a union between one man and one woman. Chris Pratt, a famous actor, faced a firestorm after it was learned he attends such a church. Chip and Joanna Gaines of HGTV fame found themselves at the center of controversy when their church, which teaches a biblical view of marriage, was labeled "anti-gay." The ultimate opprobrium leveled by the LGBTQ movement against a Christian, a pastor, or a church is they are "anti-gay." This has proved especially effective among young people, who are vulnerable to peer pressure.

You can have your Christianity and your Bible, but only if you conform to their standards. Otherwise, you will be mislabeled, vilified, and marginalized by the mainstream media. This is decidedly un-American. It is similar to the spying and shunning in communist countries against those who won't obey the dictates of the Party. Far from being discriminated against, the LGBTQ community has outsized influence in most of our institutions. It is going to take major and sustained legal, social, and spiritual action to root out the anti-Christian bigotry in corporations, sports, entertainment, journalism, and academia.

CHAPTER 37

HATE CRIMES

Hate crime laws violate the First Amendment. They criminalize thoughts and beliefs. These statutes were conceived by homosexual activists to break down remaining opposition to sexual deviancy. They were not created to protect black people from lynching, although that's how many of them were sold to the public. Hate crime laws were created to punish people for not agreeing with homosexuality. No one should be punished for ideological or philosophical viewpoints. The law properly punishes wrong behavior. If I am killed because I happen to be black, I am no more dead than if killed in a robbery gone wrong.

In a nation valuing freedom of conscience, we don't punish people for their thoughts, no matter how abhorrent those thoughts may be. It does not matter whether one is harmed because an attacker doesn't like the color of your skin or likes the car you drive and is willing to kill you for it. He should be punished for the harm done, not the thoughts held. Crime is violent action, not offensive thoughts.

For example, one day I walked into a store to buy some jewelry for my wife. The salesperson helping me was very effeminate, but I did not care one way or the other. However, when passing a jewelry box to me he deliberately slid his hand over mine. I pulled back, disgusted. Had I responded with verbal aggression, I would have been accused of homophobia. Had I pushed or punched him, it would have been treated as a hate crime. In my mind, what was done to me was an assault against which I have a right of self-defense. Had a heterosexual assaulted me and I responded with physical force, it might have been trouble for me, but when a homosexual is involved, it becomes much more serious and the consequences much graver. Homosexuals should not be bullied or attacked ever. They have the same right as other human beings to be left alone and to be safe in their persons and property. However, the claim of a hate crime should not be a shield from the consequences of unwanted sexual advances. The sexual preferences of the victim or attacker should have no bearing on the law.

CHAPTER 38

GOING ON OFFENSE

Homosexuality and other sexual categories are given protected legal status in many state and local jurisdictions, but Christians are muzzled or persecuted for their beliefs. Our First Amendment rights are being trampled. The message is "be silent or lose your reputation, your business, or your job."

I know of a young man working at a store in Boston whose manager was a lesbian. The woman kept talking about what she did with her lover, and this made the male employee feel very uncomfortable. Finally, the man said—in a non-confrontational way—he was a Christian and he would appreciate it if she would keep the details of her personal life to herself.

The manager reported him, and he was fired. What about that man's First Amendment rights? The lesbian was allowed to talk about her homosexual lifestyle in the workplace, but the young man was fired simply for mentioning his faith and asking her to stop. We have come to a place where homosexuals can openly promote their sexual lifestyle, but Christians who disagree are hauled before diversity boards or HR departments to be fired or subjected to "sensitivity training." Why aren't we putting LGBTQ employees through sensitivity training, so they are nicer to Christians?

LGBTQ activists and their enablers label you a bigot and homophobe if you do not agree with their behavior. It is clear for anyone willing to be objective, the intolerance is not coming from Christians, but from those who are pushing homosexuality on others. Christian morality is in their way. They need to destroy not only the moral principles, but the Christians who hold them.

We need to stand together and make our voices heard. Less than 3 percent of the population is homosexual, although it is increasing because of nonstop promotion in the culture. Transgender adults comprise less than 1 percent.[36] These groups' disproportionate power and influence is the direct result of Christian silence for too long. We can no longer be silent, or we will lose what liberty we have left.

We must never apologize for the truth of God's Word. We have compromised our principles in fear of offending anyone. In the meantime, our opponents offend and intimidate at will. Homosexual activists will destroy anyone to further their agenda. We must be courageous and unapologetic in pushing back. Homosexuality is not good or right or normal for those who engage in it nor for the societies which encourage it. Human beings have a right to live their private lives as they choose. They do not have a right to force the culture, laws, and the citizens of our country to bow in approval. That is idolatry. Christians must resist it by every legal, political, and spiritual means available.

CHAPTER 39

HUNTING FOR OUR CHILDREN

Because the Left in general and the LGBTQ movement in particular reject moral absolutes, especially about sex, it should not surprise us they would unapologetically go after children. Kids are suggestible and malleable because of their tender age. Normal human beings would reject exposing young children to explicit information about homosexuality, sexual identity, transgenderism, lesbianism, and masturbation. Homosexual and transgender activists not only proudly impose these ideas on preschool children, they ridicule parents who object. They have no respect for the parent/child relationship. They consider themselves morally superior arbiters of what children should know and learn. Any parent who objects faces the ultimate accusation— "bigot." You are hateful for daring to suggest that you, not school bureaucrats, know what is best for your child.

As I write, there are confrontations breaking out at government school board meetings all over the country as parents stand up and push back. It is gratifying to see. These statists who push their sexually perverse agenda on children can be traced all the way back to 1913, when Gyorgy Lukacs, a Hungarian communist, became the first Marxist to deploy sex education as a tool to assert the primacy of the state over children. Many have pursued that model over the last century, and it is being implemented aggressively right here in the land of the free.

The presumed wisdom and authority of parents to make decisions for their children until they come of age is being turned on its head. Children are now considered wiser than their parents in matters of human sexuality. If a child as young as four years old decides his or her "assigned" gender is not his or her true identity, the institutions of government will back the child in moving ahead full force. Mind you, a four-year-old and children much older have no clue what these terms mean. If they make such claims, it is because adults are coaching them.

The fact that the supporters of this sick sexual revolution would pretend a child could make such an earth-shattering decision should tell us all we need to know about the evil of this movement. That there is not a unanimous cry of defiance across the land bespeaks such confusion and cowardice as to call into question the future of freedom in America. If a society loses the will to protect innocent children, it has suffered a cataclysmic collapse of the values upholding civilization.

In liberal jurisdictions, usually by order of incompetent and activist judges, the state has removed children from the custody of parents who refuse to submit a son or daughter to hormone treatments leading to breast and genital surgery. Children cannot legally drink alcohol, drive a car, or sign a contract. Yet against parents' wishes, they may decide to mutilate their bodies with irreversible surgery. Only those who have been morally lobotomized think this is rational.

Nevertheless, there are people who support this as reasonable policy, even in conservative Texas, where a court awarded custody of a twin boy, James Younger, to his mother, who renamed him Luna and started dressing him in girl's clothes, complete with painted nails. The mother aggressively "affirmed" this boy as a girl. By age seven the boy's case was in the public domain, but according to the mother, he made his gender preference known at age three.[37]

Adults who encourage this madness—renaming a toddler and trying to reverse his or her genetic and biological gender—are emotionally abusing the child. When it results in surgery, that is physical abuse and every adult involved should be charged with a felony, spend several years in prison, and be prohibited from contact with the child until he or she comes of age.

Consider the logical extension of treating a child as if he or she can make life-altering decisions adults are then expected to rubber stamp. If a prepubescent child can decide to change his or her sexual identity, can that child also decide to have sex with an adult? If children are wiser and more aware of their own sexuality than adults charged with their care, why should their decision-making be limited? Why shouldn't they make all decisions about sexual activity? Pedophilia is the next logical step when to be free to "be" is to be free to "do."

Articles are now being written and strategically placed arguing that pedophilia is a morally neutral "sexual orientation."[38] These closet predators and their supporters try to separate sexual fantasizing about children from actual sexual contact or trafficking in child pornography. They categorize "non-contact pedophiles" as no threat whatsoever to children. According to this view, parents can take comfort that not all pedophiles are bad pedophiles. There are "good" ones too. This is the absurd thinking the Left has embraced, and it does not portend well for the future protection of America's innocents.

Salon magazine has had numerous articles by Todd Nickerson, including one titled, "I'm a pedophile, but not a monster." Salon later took all Nicholson's articles off their website. Jesse Singal, a Left-wing journalist, defended the article, saying it was a "brave and important article to publish—one the site should be proud of . . ."[39] Singal agrees with Nickerson on the mission of a group called "Virtuous Pedophiles," where the goal is to help them not to "hurt children." It's not quite clear what that means. What is clear is the group encourages pedophiles to "accept" who they are.

While it is true the *Salon* piece did not defend pedophilia, neither did it condemn the practice as inherently wrong. It left wiggle room by suggesting there is nothing wrong with "sexual attraction" to children but admitted "actualizing" is illegal. The article also suggests the age of sexual consent should vary for children and raises the monstrous idea that some children might be sexually attracted to adults, just as some adults are to children. Therefore, in the warped minds of the perverts who think this way, certain adults and children are sexually made for each other. It is sick stuff—but be warned it is worming its way toward normalization, just like homosexuality.

This is why homosexual and transgender adoption of children is so dangerous. These adoptions are political statements. The goal is not to provide a safe and loving home, but to advance the agenda of the LGBTQ movement using children as pawns.

When I lived in Massachusetts, the Gay & Lesbian Alliance Against Defamation (GLAAD) was handing out literature outside an elementary school. The pamphlet for girls had two women on the cover; the one for boys had two men. The title said, "Just do it." Their message to children was not to let anyone tell them being "gay" was not good and right and fun. The pamphlets listed celebrities and famous pop culture figures they alleged to be "gay." In other words, they were openly recruiting elementary school-children. I organized our church to counter their demonstration. We confronted them peacefully, but they were unapologetic. They said parents were not telling their children the "truth" about homosexuality, and GLAAD was going to, whether parents liked it or not.

That was forty years ago. The situation has become exponentially worse. LGBTQ radicals have become bolder as they have gained influence far out of proportion to their numbers. What was once utterly unacceptable, such as Drag Queen Story Hour for young children at public libraries, is now approved and promoted. Daring to question this or to assert a Christian perspective will likely cost you your job, your business, and your reputation in the corporate world and the many other spheres under LGBTQ domination.

They have in effect created a gigantic cult encompassing the mainstream media, public schools, colleges and universities, the corporate world, entertainment and most recently, the military. All that remains of the resistance is Bible believing churches and families. The activists' goal is to change the sexual mores of the culture and to criminalize orthodox Christians and observant Jews. Tragically, they are a long way toward achieving that end.

In the story of Sodom and Gomorrah, one of the most famous in the Bible, depravity was the rule. Here is how the Bible in Genesis 19:4–5 describes the attempt to sodomize two angels who were visiting with Lot:

"Now before they lay down, the men of the city, the men of Sodom, both old and young, all the people from every quarter, surrounded the house. And they called to Lot and said to him, 'Where are the men who came to you tonight? Bring them out to us that we may know them carnally.'"

This was not some subtle seduction, but a bold effort to do a mass rape. Spectators surrounded the house to watch. The city was wholly given to sexual degeneracy, which seemed quite normal to them. Is that really any different from Drag Queen Story Hour, where sexual deviants romp with kids? Some of the transgenders in these "shows" have been found to be registered sex offenders.[40] Yet the libraries inviting them in could not bother taking the time to check for the safety of the children. After all, advancing the sexual revolution is too important to be slowed by the effort needed to protect innocent children.

God has made clear in His Word that homosexuality and closely related transgenderism and incest are abominable sins. That is not Bishop Jackson's opinion or Christian bigotry. It is what the Bible says, and it is the truth. Christians must stand up for our faith—the faith that has protected America and our children since the day this nation was created nearly 250 years ago.

Embracing the depravity of the Left can only lead to societal collapse. If America continues to follow the LGBTQ path of moral degeneration, the day will come when the America we know and love will be no more. Instead of a shining city on a hill, we will become a dystopian wasteland of moral anarchy. Our greatness will be forever lost, and America will become a cautionary tale.

We are not a perfect country because we are not perfect people. However, standards should not be repealed because human beings are flawed. Moral principles should be upheld as the goal to which we aspire as individuals and a nation. There is plenty of room for grace and forgiveness in America, and there always will be.

As Paul wrote in 1 Corinthians 6:9–11, homosexuality is one among many sins that can be overcome with a changed heart:

> Do you not know that the unrighteous will not inherit the kingdom of God? Do not be deceived. Neither fornicators, nor idolaters, nor adulterers, nor homosexuals, nor sodomites, nor thieves, nor covetous, nor drunkards, nor revilers, nor extortioners will inherit the kingdom of God. And such were some of you. But you were washed, but you were sanctified, but you were justified in the name of the Lord Jesus and by the Spirit of our God.

There is no room for the pride and arrogance of asserting that the immorality of a few should set the standard for all. Freedom only works where virtue is upheld. It is time to reassert our identity as a virtuous people, for therein lies the only hope for a secure and prosperous future.

PART VII

EDUCATION IN AMERICA

As a Christian, I did not come to a sudden realization of the pitched spiritual battle we are in for the soul of this great nation. It happened over a period of years. Piece by piece, the puzzle came together. This is how I began to understand the need for a massive overhaul of our educational system.

The first incident I remember involved my son when he was in high school. That was thirty-five years ago. He told me his teacher was discussing "religion" with them and said the only things that are certain in life are death and taxes. God is a figment of our imaginations. I did not like hearing that but did not yet understand this was about more than one teacher expressing an anti-Christian opinion.

This was about a philosophy through the entire educational system. As parents, we were playing catch-up. There were Christian teachers in public schools, but they were few and shrinking in numbers. They too were probably not aware of the revolution taking place around them. It is painful to contemplate even fifty years ago, a teacher who objected to anti-Christian bigotry in the schools would have put his or her job in jeopardy. Even that long ago, the Marxist machine was churning, using the ACLU and the teachers unions to keep government schools moving in a leftward, i.e., "progressive" direction.

Hence, the political indoctrination of our children has been going on for a long time. Students need to be taught to read, write, analyze, and articulate their thoughts. If America is to remain at the forefront of world leadership, future generations must be able to compete and win in the global market. Too many of our children after thirteen years of public school are graduating as functional illiterates. In many urban communities, half the student population drops out[41] and only 83 percent of those who graduate can read beyond an eighth-grade level.

Federal education spending, per student, has almost tripled since 1965. We have spent $2 trillion in inflation-adjusted dollars on public education, yet 7,000 students drop out of high school each day, 1.2 million per year.[42]

Democrats want to spend more on education, but while funding has continued to increase, student performance has decreased. According to research by Andrew J. Coulson of the Cato Institute, there are no positive correlations between federal spending per pupil and test scores in reading, math, or science—and the current state of affairs in America bears this out.[43] New York State spends more than any other state school system in America—more than $25,000 per student.[44] That is twice the national average. Yet according to the Nation's Report Card, New York is below national average proficiency in every category of student performance.[45]

The National Education Association and other teachers unions have only one answer—spend more money. This enriches and empowers the teachers unions, but it does not result in better educational outcomes for the students.

Clearly, our education system needs a dramatic overhaul. The government is forcing us to pay for failed schools that graduate failing students. Educating future generations is one of the most important responsibilities we have as a nation, and we are not doing it. What we are doing now threatens the future of our country.

CHAPTER 40

REDEFINING PUBLIC EDUCATION

The United States currently ranks 18th among the thirty-six industrialized nations in secondary education, according to the Organization for Economic Cooperation and Development. This is unacceptable, and it violates American exceptionalism. Instead of spending more money for poorer results, we need to completely re-think the concept of "public" education. We now educate most of our children in government schools. It is a misnomer to call them public because they are only open to "the public" that the government deems eligible to attend. In most jurisdictions, whether your child can attend a particular school depends on where you live and how school districts are drawn.

A "public school" should mean any school open to the public, not only schools operated by the government. Taxpayers are financing schools that no longer teach their children or reflect their values. My wife and I removed our two youngest children from public school because we objected to the ideological anti-Christian bias of the system. That was forty years ago. Its values often clashed with our own. As a result, we paid twice—taxes for schools our children did not use, and tuition for their education in the school of our choice.

What should make a school public is that all children have the option of attending that school by having taxpayers' education dollars follow parents and children to whatever school they choose. My wife and I sacrificed to give our children a better education, and we do not regret it. We had the means to do so, but what about parents who do not? Their children are held captive in a system robbing them of opportunity instead of preparing them for it. The law should not mandate which school a child attends. It should facilitate the parents' choice.

If parents want a school passing out condoms, promoting homosexuality, prohibiting the Bible from being discussed, and teaching American history as a story of racism, sexism, white supremacy, and that humans are simply evolved animals, many "public" schools will happily accommodate them. This indoctrination should not be inflicted on the rest of us.

Expecting citizens to pay for the privilege of having our country, faith, and values denigrated in schools failing to teach our children to read is a travesty. American students fall further and further behind the rest of the industrialized world in math and science, but they are much more accepting of socialism. This does not portend well for the future of our country and economic competition in a global economy.

When Americans have the freedom to make educational choices for their children, schools failing to deliver will find their classrooms empty. Schools meeting the educational needs of children and affirming the values of America and its parents will thrive—and so will our society.

Competition created by an open school system will produce innovation and excellence and make quality education available to all students. Freedom and competition have put America in the forefront of the industrial, scientific, and technological revolutions of the last 150 years. We have become the greatest nation on earth not by government planning, but by free people dreaming, creating, working, and risking. Each individual seeks to maximize his or her own potential and in so doing the entire community is better off.

Top-down bureaucratic control never works; it only suppresses the innovative energies of the human spirit. Education is no different.

Under the current government monopoly, mediocre and failing schools have no incentive to improve. Local, state, and federal funding continues and increases, no matter how poor the product. Many teachers are frustrated because they want to do a more creative and effective job, but they feel hemmed-in by union rules and school bureaucracy.

My wife taught in government schools for twenty years. She was overworked, underpaid, and micro-managed. Teachers should be free to create an exceptional education experience and leave a life-long impact on children. Instead, they and their students are pawns in the never-ending quest to produce revolutionaries and good democrats. It is time to stop sacrificing students on the altar of the teachers unions and Democrat machine politics. It is time to put the children first, for they are the future of our country.

CHAPTER 41

DISMISSING MORALITY FROM THE CLASSROOM

We are experiencing an unprecedented assault on historic American values and our Judeo-Christian heritage. Whenever people reject God's authority and moral order, they substitute their own. In effect, they become their own gods. That is what the ACLU and the Left are trying to impose on America. We were established as a constitutional republic, where rights and freedom are our legacy from God.

America's Judeo-Christian culture was founded on "self-evident" truths. Any substitute will necessarily be based on self-evident lies and deception. Such an idolatrous moral order with man as his own god will not only be inferior, but destructive. This is the bondage in which the Left now holds our public schools. They are sowing the wind and our children are reaping the whirlwind. They have turned our public schools into a Petri dish for the new "morality," and they are breeding a virus of educational failure and moral decay.

What John Dewey and Horace Mann conceived for public education was never what the American people wanted. They wanted a secularized system, heavily influenced by socialism and ideas they thought of as enlightened. However, they had to overcome the moral and spiritual consensus in our country. The fundamental beliefs and values of most Americans were the same, regardless of race. We believed in individual liberty, personal responsibility, and hard work. We took responsibility for our own lives and families.

Life has never been fair in the cosmic sense, but in times past, most Americans would be insulted by the suggestion of anything that smacked of a handout. Now we live in the era of entitlement. Everyone is a victim, one way or the other, and society must address our victimhood.

The church and pastors were once respected. There is now a growing hostility, especially toward any biblical or Christian understanding of The Supreme Being. Lawsuits abound over the mere mention of God. Court dockets are filled with cases against the display of a cross, holding a public school ceremony in a church building, or the very mention of Jesus Christ in a commencement speech. Children are shown how to put on condoms but are forbidden to bring Bibles to school. They may not wear crosses around their necks or place a Bible on their desk lest someone be offended. It seems lost on the system and those who control it that without the Bible and the faith of our Fathers, there would be no United States of America.

CHAPTER 42

THE LIBERAL VIEW OF EDUCATION

A big reason for our failing schools lies with the Democrats and the politically powerful teacher unions. They vehemently oppose allowing parents and children the option of exiting their system. They claim giving parents a choice will leave too many children behind. What they really mean is there will not be enough union dues left to assure they remain politically powerful. They ignore the obvious fact that if the school system is doing its job to the parents' satisfaction and children are actually learning, parents will not want to leave.

The Left—including black elected officials who are owned by the unions—argues that since not all parents and students will take advantage of school choice, no students should be allowed to escape. That is like coming upon a sinking ship and saying, "Since we may not be able to save all the passengers, it is best to let them all drown." That is absurd.

The teachers unions and the politicians who do their bidding are not motivated by the educational interests of our kids. They are motivated by power. The dues collected from teachers all over America provide hundreds of millions of dollars for union officials. Union leaders earn six-figure salaries, and the unions make large contributions to political campaigns. The system is corrupt to the core, and our children are the victims.

Instead of developing the intellectual capacity of our children, the liberal forces dominating many schools want instead to teach them about sex, homosexuality, and gender identity. At the same time, they don't want children to recite the Pledge of Allegiance, which the Left deems racist. Public education in America is failing, and the indoctrination of American children is moving ahead at breakneck speed.

Seven out of ten parents in the District of Columbia wanted the D.C. Opportunity Scholarship Program expanded. Since its origin in 2004, the OSP provided more than 11,000 children the opportunity to attend higher performing schools. It has a 97 percent graduation rate, contrasted with an overall graduation rate in the District of just 55 percent.[46]

Despite this success, the Obama administration killed the OSP by cutting its funding and refusing to allow new students to enroll.[47] Teachers unions backed by the Democrat Party came out in full force against the program, and the Left obliged. Obama said, "I have said to [teachers unions]—we want to work with you. We're not interested in imposing changes on you."

Heaven forbid teachers unions have to change in order to educate our children. Most teachers want to educate children. That is why they became educators in the first place. Only the corrupt unions—the NEA and the American Federation of Teachers— object to reforms necessary to expand educational opportunity.

They feign concern for children, but it is obviously a charade. During the school voucher program debate, President Obama invited children who were profiled in the documentary, *Waiting for Superman*, to visit the White House. *Waiting for Superman* focuses on five children who are desperately trying to win a lottery slot to get into charter schools.

Obama attended private school. His daughters attended private school. Democrat President Bill Clinton sent his daughter to private school. Yet overwhelmingly, the Left restricts access to private education and supports the teachers unions, to keep the money flowing into poor-quality, low-performing schools. They mouth compassion, but it is all sound and fury signifying nothing. They have no empathy for children trapped in failing schools. These children will not be prepared to take advantage of the opportunities our country offers. The thirst for political power overrides what should be the only motivation for a school system—making certain every child receives a quality education.

This is a matter of great urgency for children of inner-city schools. We are losing generations of youth to a life of gang membership, prison, and early death, especially for young men. Their gifts and abilities are stunted and cast aside instead of being developed. This is a travesty with no end in sight because the Democrat Party and their union masters are unwilling to put children first.

We are out of time. America's future is at stake. Fifty years of educational decline should be enough to sound the alarm and motivate all of us to do something very different. This is not merely a political failure but a moral failure. The teachers unions are engaged in child neglect and abuse on a monumental level. It is time to remove union bosses from influence over our schools and restore parents as the final authority on the education of their children.

CHAPTER 43

PARENTAL RESPONSIBILITY

Parents must be willing to fulfill their proper role. The breakdown of the family has placed tremendous pressure on the school system. The good teachers who have a passion for education and truly care about children are faced with insurmountable odds. The job of education is ultimately a parental responsibility. If parents are not providing the support, security, and encouragement children need, even the best teachers face an uphill battle. In poor communities, many of today's students are the children of children. The parents are barely beyond adolescence. The fathers are not there to provide love, discipline, guidance, and financial support. Unless grandparents step in, teen moms and young single mothers are likely to fail as parents. Some are too busy satisfying their youthful impulses to be good parents. However, even those who put forth admirable effort are likely to find their children shaped by the values of their peers and consumed by the pathologies of the streets.

Where there is no foundation of family, teachers must be social workers, psychologists, counselors, police, and parents all rolled into one. When children come from dysfunctional families and unhealthy social environments, a teacher's task is made practically impossible. Too much time in the classroom is consumed with behavioral issues. This is why school choice is so important. Parents who are trying to do the best they can for their children should not be forced to keep their children in an educational environment disadvantageous to the child.

As a society, we are facing problems of a magnitude previous generations did not confront. Children are born to addicted parents, or they have attention deficit disorder (ADD), hyperactivity disorder, and other behavioral issues. More and more children are mentally and emotionally damaged. Sexuality and gender identity issues are now pushed on children as early as kindergarten. The breakdown in education reflects the breakdown in society. Reform of our government school system could save some of these children, but the system is intractable to meaningful change. A healthy dose of competition through parental choice is the only hope for making quality education available to every child.

Up to and including the fifth grade, I was being raised in a foster home. My foster parents were well-meaning people who loved me as best they knew how, but they were illiterate and there was little discipline. During the summer after I nearly failed fifth grade, my father took custody of me. As I related earlier, he gave me the love, support, and discipline I needed. I went from being an "F" student and truant in fifth grade, to an "A" student and fully engaged in sixth grade. The difference was my dad, not any government program. He inspired me and held me to high expectations. He revolutionized my life, and what success I have I owe in large measure to him. I wish every child could have that support.

When responsible parents have the ability to make educational decisions for their children as opposed to the government making them, we will have better results. Democrats want to take your money and "solve" your problems. Of course, the outcome is always worse than before they "intervened." To quote Ronald Reagan: "The nine most terrifying words are, 'I'm from the government, and I'm here to help.'"[48] What we get from their help is more bureaucracy, less freedom and poorer results. Bureaucrats must no longer be permitted to determine the destiny of the next generation.

The homeschool movement, for example, has faced extreme hostility from many state and local governments. As the movement was getting started, the public was told homeschooled children will be inadequately socialized. They would be socially inept creatures incapable of functioning in the wider world. There is now a record of decades to debunk that criticism. Homeschool students excel on standardized tests, do very well in college, marry, raise families, and "function" just fine. Yet in spite of homeschooling's demonstrable success—or perhaps because of it—resistance to homeschooling in "progressive" circles remains very high. Clearly the issue is not education but power and control.

CHAPTER 44

RACIAL FAILURES

One of the worst things that has ever happened to the modern black community is what President George W. Bush called the "soft bigotry of low expectations."[49] I would go further. It is the hard and destructive bigotry of racial paternalism. The elitism and snobbery of the "expert" educational professional applies across all racial lines, but it is particularly acute in its use against black parents. The Left obviously believes black parents are simply not ready for individual liberty and the right to pursue happiness as they understand it. Liberals beat their chests about how racially sensitive or "woke" they are and how those who disagree with them are racist. Not surprisingly, they oppose the policies allowing black citizens to strike out independently of the systems the liberals built for them.

Black parents loved the Washington, D.C. school choice program, but the Left turned thumbs down on it and took away the one hope of many parents that their children would get an education equivalent to America's elites. While they would never explicitly admit it, most liberals believe that black Americans do not know what is best for them or their children. White progressives will have to tell them.

The Left has its own scale of racial morality. Only liberals make the grade, no matter the negative impact their policies have on minorities. Black children are more victimized by liberals today than the black community ever was by the Ku Klux Klan. The racism is more subtle and it is wrapped in a veneer of compassion, but the control is nearly absolute. The Left does not control the black community by terror, but the subjugation is just as terrifying. Whether their votes are controlled at the point of a gun or through manipulation and deception, the outcome is the same. People are forced to act against their own interests, which produces long-term negative consequences. The liberal policies of the 1960s devastated black families, and the consequences today are nothing short of cataclysmic.

The condescension and paternalism are in substance no different from a slave master constantly telling his slaves they are much better off remaining in slavery because they are not equipped to strike out on their own. Indeed, it is betrayal of the master's kindness and compassion to want to escape. *There is nothing better out there, so it is foolish to even seek it. Stay where you are. Stay in your place and all will be well with you.*

I am so grateful my father taught me never to have low expectations. He never said to me: *You're black. Don't expect that much.* On the contrary, he expected me to give my best at all times and promised me life would reward me for hard work and a commitment to excellence. To the extent I have accomplished anything significant, it is because of the values instilled in me by my father. They are American values.

By contrast, liberals ghettoize black people and other minorities by telling them, *You are not really up to it, but we will create special programs to help you out. If you cannot pass a test, we will lower the standards. If you commit crimes, we will excuse it away as the result of poverty. Whatever is wrong in your life is the result of racism, not any of the choices or decisions you have made. You are not responsible for your life, and you cannot control your own destiny. Your life is in the hands of racists and your destiny is controlled by racism. Take heart. We will be your saviors, and you can be our dependents. Just remember at election time to vote Democrat.*

This is so condescendingly racist that it is truly amazing so many Americans of African ancestry have bought it for so long. One day, liberals are going to face a very angry and rebellious black community which realizes they have been duped for sixty years. That is the day the Democrat coalition shatters, and black Americans are set free.

CHAPTER 45

DUMBING DOWN THE AMERICAN PEOPLE

It is one thing to keep people trapped in failing schools. It is quite another to turn those schools into indoctrination camps dumbing down the people it's supposed to educate. Yet that is what is happening in schools across America today amid the rise of the woke movement and its offshoots such as Critical Race Theory, the 1619 Project, and the Black Lives Matter curricula. We will forgo an analysis of the details of these examples of pernicious academic sophistry.

All have the same overarching purpose—to convince the American people, particularly black people, that America is intrinsically, irredeemably, and hopelessly racist. It was born in racism because America was not founded in 1776 when the Founders declared independence, but in 1619 when the first slaves arrived. They came as indentured servants as did many Europeans. This is ignored because it does not help the anti-American narrative that some of those original Africans became free and owned slaves themselves.

According to this new counterfeit scholarship, America was founded on slavery, and the Revolutionary War was fought to preserve slavery. The conclusion they want everyone to reach is America is a racist and white supremacist nation. Therefore everything, and they do mean everything, is racist. I have argued that this mania is a psychological disorder—Racial Obsession Syndrome (ROS). In this sick and delusional view of the world, math is racist because of its focus on precise and correct answers to mathematical problems. Science, engineering, and technology are racist for the same reason. Literature is racist because it focuses on old white men like Shakespeare and Chaucer. Speaking proper English is a racist notion because the rules of grammar were made up by white people.

There is no "black" English or "white" English. You either speak and write it well, or you do not. You either speak and write well, according to accepted rules of grammar and contsruction, or you do not. What you may not do is use some inane and convoluted notion of "racial justice" to change the rules and lower the standards. Creating a separate standard for black students only handicaps and calcifies them in a status of inferiority.

This kind of thinking is so distorted and absurd that it is difficult to understand who so many Americans have embraced it. Those who have "drunk the Kool-Aid," so to speak, view themselves as intellectual superiors. Journalists, college professors, and even corporate leaders are seduced by the irrational.

For a long time, I have argued the cult-like nature of this extreme leftward and Marxist shift. Given the developments of the early twentieth century, it would not be going too far to say it is a cult. The Left behaves like a cult because they are a cult. All the indices are there. They divide the world into people who are in the cult and people who are not. They separate themselves from people who are not in the cult, including family members. They accept the most irrational ideas and reject those who don't share their view as insufficiently enlightened, or not "woke."

That means the public schools and many private schools to which we send our children for an education are institutions of cult-indoctrination. Left to themselves, these schools separate children not only from their parents, but from reality. They teach them to hate themselves, hate America and hate Christianity. In the meantime, they dumb them down so they cannot read, write, analyze or do math or science with any precision or accuracy lest they fall prey to white supremacy. Every American child deserves an exceptional education, and it should make us angry when children are condemned to educational ghettos and indoctrination camps.

Liberal, self-appointed benefactors are using our children as pawns in their power grab. Day by day, the children are losing and therefore America is losing. None of us expected the government to raise our children, but we were told public schools would educate them. They have failed. It is time to allow parents to choose the best school for the education of their children. Every school is public, and tax dollars should follow the parents' choice. It is time to liberate parents and children from government schools and give every child in America the opportunity to fulfill his or her God-given intellectual potential.

PART VIII

THE ERA OF AMERICAN SHAME

Iheard all my life from a variety of people in the black community that America would never elect a black president. They would never let a black man get that far, some would say. Others claimed he would be killed before he could become president. Never in all those years did I ever hear a black American say, "one day there will be a black president." Yet for as long as I can remember, contrary to conventional wisdom, I believed it was inevitable that there would be a black president. Surely there were Americans of African descent who agreed with me, but I never met one. Therefore, while the election of the first black president shocked almost everyone in the black community, it did not surprise me. However, I was deeply disappointed in who became the first black president. Let me say for the record, he will not be the last. There will be others if God allows this era of human history to continue long enough.

I did not vote for Barack Obama either time. He was as close as anyone can come to being my ideologically opposite. Nonetheless, his election confirmed my confidence in America. I still believe the era of racism is over. The citizens of our country overwhelmingly want to see each other as individuals and get on with the business of living, working, raising families, and running businesses. They want to fulfill Dr. King's dream that we not be judged by the color of our skin, but by the content of our character.

In fact, many Americans voted for Mr. Obama not because they agreed with him, but because they thought it was time for a black American to be elected president. They hoped it would catapult the country beyond racial conflict. Although an opponent of his presidency and his policies, that was also my hope. Perhaps he would surprise us and bring us a long-hoped-for unity. Unfortunately, far from ushering in a new era of national unity across racial and cultural lines, he exacerbated racial division in our country instead of healing it.

He taught us an important lesson I hope our country never forgets. Leftists are constitutionally incapable of creating unity. They do not want it. Their ideology requires resentment and division. The rich have more than they should. White people have more than they should. The rest of us must take from them what they have no right to possess. The ideology of equity, diversity and inclusion feeds on envy.

Obama comes out of that radical far-left background. He was nurtured in communism. His voting record after six years in the Illinois Senate and two years in the U.S. Senate was decidedly far Left. He associated with terrorist Bill Ayers, racist Louis Farrakhan, and his pastor Jeremiah Wright was an anti-American demagogue, not a preacher of the gospel of Jesus Christ. Obama was supported by Planned Parenthood, the ACLU, and the NEA. In spite of his feigned support for traditional marriage, he had the full backing of the LGBT movement because they knew the truth. He was always an avid supporter of homosexuality and the "gay rights movement." When he told a national audience at Rick Warren's church he opposed same-sex marriage, he was lying and those in his inner circle knew it. The man was a creature of Marxist politics through and through.

He sat for twenty years under the communist-inspired black liberation theology of Jeremiah Wright, and then claimed to know nothing about the hatred and propaganda Wright preached. Wright married Barack and Michelle and baptized their two daughters. Louis Farrakhan was Wright's close friend and helped organize his

"Million Man March." I was on C-Span the morning of that march, publicly opposing it. Barack Obama, a future president, was there supporting it. I had been denouncing Farrakhan for a long time. Obama had been commiserating with him and hiding that fact from the public as he rose in politics.

While Obama was campaigning, people said to me, "*It's time* to have a black president." I understood that sentiment. It is a testament to the goodness and decency of the American people that Obama got elected to a large extent because he is black. Americans are fair people. The mistake they made was to elect Obama based on the color of his skin, and not the content of his character. We are still paying the price for that mistake because his presidency set race relations back twenty-five years.

As I finish this book in 2022, our country is still digging out of the rubble of racial turmoil in 2020. There were over 500 riots that year. The looting, vandalism, and lawlessness of 2020 spilled over into a horrendous crime wave in 2021 which persists today. Crime, including homicides, has spiked throughout the country as police have come under attack and law enforcement budgets have been slashed. A defund-the-police movement took root among Leftist politicians and their supporters, causing a wave of retirements and resignations from police departments across the country.

Robberies, rapes, carjackings, and murder are up significantly over last year. What does this have to do with Barack Obama? He spent eight years sowing the seeds of racial division. He promoted the idea that the criticism he faced was based on race not policy differences. He and his wife Michelle, then the most powerful couple in the world, postured as victims of racism. If the leader of the free world and the First Lady of the United States are victims of racism, what black American is not?

Instead of encouraging Americans to unify and treat each other as individuals, he promoted a collectivist mindset of us against them. During the campaign, he referred to his white grandmother as having attitudes "typical" of white people. Leftists do not see the hypocrisy of such racial stereotyping. To say white people have typical white attitudes is acceptable, but to suggest black people have typical black attitudes is racist. The Left has traded one expression of racism for another.

Mind you, they have never given up racism against black people. Instead of hostility and violence, it is expressed in condescension and pandering. The root belief is the same. The Democrat Party and their elite, Leftist allies maintain the fundamental belief that black people are inferior. Instead of basing that belief on genetics and pseudo-science, they base it on sociological and racial circumstances limiting black development. Regardless how they get there, they reach the same conclusion: black people are incapable of competing against others without special help. Their lot in life is to be victims.

They define these obstacles in ethereal, intangible ways—systemic racism, implied bias, micro-aggressions. These theories infantilize Americans of African ancestry and turn us into children, incapable of making our own decisions or controlling our own destinies. Even the first black president of the United States presented himself as a victim of forces of racism beyond his own control.

In assuming the role of victim, Obama made it acceptable for every black millionaire and billionaire to play that role. They are citizens of the most prosperous nation on earth. They have become fabulously wealthy. Yet instead of promoting a vision of hope, they present a picture of despair. If Oprah Winfrey, LeBron James, and Dr. Dre, all billionaires, are hopeless victims of racism, what hope is there?

These wealthy, influential Americans should be grateful they live in a country that made their success possible. They should be teaching others how they succeeded, and how it is possible for anyone to fulfill their potential in America. Instead, they indoctrinate all who will listen with nonsense about what a terrible country this is, and how black people cannot succeed here because of systemic racism.

As for their success, they take no solace and learn no lessons. Presumably they view themselves as uniquely gifted people for whom the normal restrictions of racism do not apply. They alone are capable of defying the gravitational pull of racism, but do not try this at home kids. It would be dangerous for mere mortals. The rest of us, these black elites would say, are destined to be sucked into the abyss of frustration and failure that is American racism.

They lie to themselves and others. The biggest obstacle confronting Americans of African ancestry is not racism. It is not even in the top ten or twenty or 100. The biggest problem is these prophets of despair who have convinced impoverished black folks that the violence, gangs, drugs, and poverty holding them captive is beyond their control. In fact, it is not even their responsibility. White folks did this to them. It is the white man's fault, and only the white man can save them. When he stops being racist, all will be well.

If you accept that view, the only hope is a fantasy of some kind of violent revolution. Once we get rid of capitalism and this system created by white men for white men, we can create a socialist utopia where diversity, equity, and inclusion reign. Once we change the system, the problems will be solved.

This is the promise of communism. Marx envisioned what amounted to the Kingdom of God, except there would be no God, only communist leaders who implement his bold theories. History has left behind a long trail of bodies, people murdered as a sacrifice to this communist god of utopia.

The only revolution which actually produced freedom and prosperity is the American Revolution. That is because American principles were not intended to guarantee an equality of outcomes, but equality of opportunity. The Left is convinced as they all have been since Karl Marx that with the right amount of power, perhaps a little tyranny, you can produce the same income and outcomes for everyone. The Left's new in-vogue word today is "equity."

The Founding Fathers understood that in a world of sinful human beings, the best we can hope to achieve is freedom and opportunity for all. Let each person take responsibility for the outcome and make of his life what he or she will. Each person will be free to succeed or fail based on her unique gifts, talents, hard work, and character. Equality of outcomes is the dream which produces a bloody totalitarian nightmare. The American dream is not one of forced government redistribution of wealth, but of earned prosperity through the private decisions, interactions, and transactions of free people making their own choices. I prefer unequal outcomes with liberty rather than the fantasy of equal outcomes promised by tyranny.

CHAPTER 46

THE APOLOGY TOUR

Michelle Obama said on the campaign trail in 2008, "For the first time in my adult life, I'm proud of my country."[50] It was a staggering revelation. It is almost unimaginable a middle-aged, affluent American woman could say she never before had a reason to be proud of our country. It shows how ideologically radical the Obamas really are. There is much to be proud of in America, but she could see none of it. One would have to conclude her husband shares her utter disdain for our country. What little pride they felt was in becoming the most powerful people in the world as America's first family. So, it was about them, not about America.

It became clear during Obama's presidency his view of America was not one of pride and gratitude, but shame and hostility. A group of Georgetown University students of different racial backgrounds was interviewed by a Fox News host for the July 4th holiday. They were asked whether they were proud to be Americans. The consensus answer was "No." Indeed, they said they were "embarrassed" by America. While I do not attribute this entirely to Obama, he is the first non-patriotic president.

President Obama never expressed sincere pride in or gratitude for America because, like those students, he is embarrassed by our country. He is the first president to conduct an international apology tour, bowing and scraping before other sovereign leaders for America's alleged misdeeds. He told European nations we have been "dismissive" and "derisive."[51] He told the Muslim world something similar. He never lost an opportunity to denigrate the United States in the eyes of the world.

- To the Muslim World: "We have not been perfect" (January 27, 2009).[52]
- To France and Europe: "America has shown arrogance" (April 3, 2009).[53]
- To the Turkish Parliament: "All of us have to change" (April 6, 2009).[54]
- To the Summit of the Americas: "We have at times been disengaged" (April 17, 2009).[55]

Obama also loved to claim we have disrespected Islam, refusing to recognize what he perceived as the great contributions Islam has made to America. During his entire presidency he refused to acknowledge the obvious—our national culture is rooted in the Bible, Christianity, and Judeo-Christian values. It is precisely our Christian culture that allows us to assure freedom of religion for Muslims and other non-Christian religions. Islamic countries governed by Sharia law do not recognize freedom of speech or religion. Yet the Left consistently engages in the self-hating exercise of defending Islam and attacking Christianity and America.

When we sent troops into Iraq for the Gulf War, it was to save the Muslim nation of Kuwait from Saddam Hussein. When we went in a second time during Operation Iraqi Freedom, it was to save Iraqi Muslims from the same monster. We saved Muslims in Bosnia. We have freed millions of Muslims from brutal dictatorships and genocide. America has helped preserve Muslim culture. Islamic countries and terrorists some have financed have attacked America and Christianity.

We do not owe the world an apology! The world owes America a debt of thanks.

CHAPTER 47

HATING AMERICA

O bama is the first American president to go to the United Nations and complain about his own country. He went there and blasted Arizona for enforcing our immigration laws. This was unconscionable, and it made me wonder if he was intentionally undermining the stature of the United States.

As president, he promoted the anti-American trope we are only prosperous because we exploited other nations and people. This ignores the historical truth that America has been and remains the most creative, innovative, and inventive nation in history. We believe in hard work, personal responsibility, initiative, and sacrifice. We are 4 percent of the world's population and yet we produce 50 percent of the inventions and patents that have improved life for people all over the globe.

Americans live under the most successful governing document in history. Constitutions change on average every seventeen years. Our Constitution has lasted 235 years as of September 17, 2022. That is so extraordinary it borders on the miraculous. Yet Obama said our Constitution is flawed because it did not give government enough "positive rights." Translation? Our Founding Fathers did not give government enough power. He was particularly critical of the Constitution and the Supreme Court for failing to address what he called "redistributive justice."[56]

He is so thoroughly a creature of the radical Left that he is incapable of understanding and appreciating the founding of the United States of America. Limiting the powers of government is precisely what the Founding Fathers intended. It was not a flaw or mistake except in the mind of a someone who wants government to have expansive powers. In 1776, the American colonists were suffering under the corrupt power of King George III and the British parliament, which treated American colonists like second-class subjects. The vast distance between England and its American colonies gave them a taste of freedom, and they loved it. The Founders wanted more of that freedom for themselves and the American people. They designed our system to protect against tyranny. It has worked. What former president Obama saw as a weakness is one of our nation's greatest strengths.

CHAPTER 48

RESTORING AMERICAN PRIDE

Our country was established by gifted statesmen, not perfect men. They had lofty ideals and a grand vision for a nation of liberty. Their effectiveness must be measured by the Constitution they designed and the stability and prosperity it generated. It is difficult to find statesmen today. I believe the American people yearn for leadership like theirs to restore American pride and patriotism. This is one reason President Trump generated such enthusiasm by those who love our country, and vicious unrelenting attacks by those who hate it. His principle of America First was seen as a declaration of war—racist, xenophobic and nationalist. For most Americans it was just common sense.

When I started writing this book, there was a movement in the country to tear down our historical statues and monuments. It began with Confederate statues in the South, but many foresaw that it would not end there. They were right. The statues of George Washington, Thomas Jefferson, Abraham Lincoln, and Frederick Douglass soon came under attack.

Christopher Columbus is one of those formerly revered figures who is now attacked as a racist. It is no longer politically acceptable to celebrate Columbus Day. In many localities, it is being replaced with Indigenous Peoples Day. Columbus' incredible courage as an explorer is ignored. His mission to spread the gospel of Jesus Christ, as revealed in his journal, is defamed as "white supremacy."

All human beings are capable of virtue and vice. The Left has for some time been creating the myth of the monstrous "white man" exploiting virtuous people of color. The fact is we are all flawed. We all fall short of the glory of God. In the full light of human history, no racial or ethnic group can point the finger at another group as inherently evil or morally inferior.

As Americans, we have far more reason to be proud than ashamed. The best each of us can do is live our own lives treating others as we want to be treated. That ethic and spirit has characterized our country since its inception. God does not judge us as groups, but as individuals. We should do the same for each other.

We all owe repentance to God, but America owes no apology to the world. We have been no worse than any other country, and by most measures far better. That is the truth about American history. We must pass on our patriotic affection for America, regardless of our complexion or ancestry, so we may live and work together to make this shining city on a hill brighter and more beautiful with each generation.

PART IX

AMERICAN MILITARY SUPREMACY AND NATIONAL SECURITY

Every nation on earth pursues its own interests, whether they have a perverse or noble understanding of what those interests are. The United States of America must act in our best interests, and we owe no apology for doing so. In a dangerous world, we need a superior military. Our military strength should be second to none. The existence of the United States as a superpower is the best assurance of global peace.

We've made our share of mistakes, but America is indisputably an international force for good. We've never been a nation of conquest. Drawn into World War II, we defeated the aggressors and then helped rebuild their economies as independent nations. It is unprecedented in history for one nation to conquer another and yet not subjugate those people or claim the spoils of war.

I am a Vietnam-era veteran. Although I was prepared to fight for my country, my period of service began as American political realities were forcing a draw-down. When I joined in 1970, few were being sent into combat. Within two years after my discharge in 1973, the war was over. While our effort seemed futile, our hostility to communism was and is entirely justified. Communism is an evil ideology whose adherents seek to plunge humanity into tyranny and slavery. Communism is the arch enemy of freedom and all freedom-loving people.

The Vietnam War came to be perceived through a leftist political lens as an imperialist war by a racist America. The very people we were trying to save from the horrors of communist dictatorship were magically transformed by anti-war propagandists into victims of U.S. adventurism. The media abandoned any pretense of objectivity and became cheerleaders for the anti-war movement and radical causes in general.

Anti-American demagoguery became pervasive. American troops were portrayed as an illegal occupying force, committing atrocities against innocent people. The Viet Cong were portrayed as heroic underdogs fighting for their homeland. The lie metastasized to the point where Jane Fonda could visit North Vietnam, sit on an enemy tank, and accuse American soldiers and Marines of being war criminals. Iconic pictures of Jane Fonda sitting on a gun turret surrounded by smiling communists were seen around the world. It was the most notorious and openly traitorous act by a civilian in the history of our country. It still rankles Americans who were in the military during that time and especially those at the infamous "Hanoi Hilton" prison camp. It still disturbs me and should disturb us all. Fonda should have been tried for treason and, if found guilty, given a lengthy prison sentence.[57]

The failure to bring Jane Fonda before the bar of justice was a symptom of the decline of national self-confidence and the rule of law. We were right to resist communism. However, the Vietnam era presaged a sea change in American cultural cohesiveness. The protests, often orchestrated by the communist Weather Underground and other hard Leftists, captured the imagination of our youth and legitimized Marxist thought. A half century later, we are still suffering from the social disintegration ignited during the 1960s.

We lost the Vietnam War long before its official end. By the time it was over, we weren't sure we should ever have been fighting. Surrender began well before the shocking pictures of an American withdrawal from Saigon were seen around the world. Surrender began the moment we questioned whether our cause was just. That is not how you win a war. Vietnam was the first war in American history that ended in defeat. Even worse, honorable men who fought bravely for our country were spit on and vilified as war criminals and mass murderers.

America's prestige on the international stage was damaged for decades, which was bad not only for America but the world. The United States is the greatest symbol of freedom and human rights on earth. While we acknowledge our failings, the millions seeking to come here from across the globe speak loudly of America as a source of hope to all people.

When America is perceived as weak, the world becomes a more dangerous and volatile place. A strong United States gives our allies assurance, and our enemies pause. That balance should always be maintained. This was clear to our Founding Fathers. George Washington said, "To be prepared for war is one of the most effective means of preserving peace."[58]

After the Vietnam War, America remained a nation unsure of itself until the election of Ronald Reagan. He exuded and reasserted American self-confidence. President Reagan understood having the best trained, best equipped, and most combat-ready military force on the planet makes it far less likely we will ever have to use it.

To my knowledge, Barack Obama was the first president to view America's role in the world quite differently. He saw our country not as the preeminent force for good, but the source of exploitation, racism, and international mischief. He was not blind to danger; he simply saw America as a great cause of that danger.

I am convinced, based on Mr. Obama's background and influences, he saw the world through a Marxist lens. Capitalism therefore is an inherently unjust system of distribution of goods and resources. America, being the greatest free-market economy, is by definition the source of much of the world's evils. Poverty and all of its problems are laid at the feet of capitalism, which means America is guilty of it all.

In this view shared by many Americans and others around the world, our country is built on selfishness and greed. We have too much. We consume too much. It is America's excess causing tension, division, and war between nations. They do not attribute our unprecedented prosperity to freedom, hard work, sacrifice, innovation, and inventiveness. It is all the result of slavery, racism, and capitalist exploitation of workers. As Obama once famously said, "You didn't build that."[59]

Therefore, if America changes, other nations will be influenced accordingly. For example, President Obama refused to tackle the issue of warfare in space, believing that doing so would cause other nations to militarize space. The reality is for years, China has been developing its ability to wage war in space. They were not waiting to take their cue from the U.S.

Internationally, President Obama apologized for who we are and our achievements and took a "lead from behind" approach. Our enemies noticed and so did our allies. Nile Gardiner, in the UK's *Telegraph*, said the Obama doctrine "represents . . . the stunning abdication of U.S. leadership in an increasingly dangerous world."

Compared to President Obama's unpatriotic tone, President Trump ushered in a revolution. He was an unabashed, unapologetic patriot who was hated by the Left for his America First policies. He rebuilt our military, renegotiated our trade deals, and exited the Paris Climate Accords. He did what he perceived to be best for America without regard to what other international leaders thought. He wanted America to win in every situation. He was called racist, fascist, and xenophobic. If it bothered him at all, he never showed it.

Americans noticed, and many swelled with pride after eight years of mea culpas (America is at fault) by a president who seemed to have utter disregard for our country. World leaders took note of this new pro-American commander in chief. Some of our left-leaning allies did not like President Trump, but they knew he was going to act in what he perceived as in America's best interests no matter what. For example, he held NATO members accountable for their financial obligations to the organization. No other president had ever done that.

In the modern world, people are lulled into the false belief that war is a thing of the past. With nuclear and biological weapons, it is unthinkable that nations would take up arms against each other. The weapons have become far more sophisticated and lethal. However, human beings have not changed. We may long for the day when peace reigns as the permanent state of things, but we still live in a world where evil leaders do the unthinkable. War is abhorrent, but there are times when it is unavoidable. Few thought that Vladimir Putin would start a war with Ukraine, but that conflict is raging in 2022 and no one knows when it will end.

The world should always know if Americans are forced to choose between war and subjugation, we will fight. We will defend our freedom and destroy the forces of tyranny. It is an ugly truth of life in a fallen and sinful world, that there are times when we must destroy evil. We cannot appease it, placate it or negotiate with it. We must kill it, which sometimes means taking the horrific but necessary action of killing the human beings who represent that evil.

The mission of the military is to destroy those who set out to destroy us. To end World War II President Truman dropped atomic bombs on Hiroshima and Nagasaki. It was one of the most terrible decisions a President has ever made. In my humble opinion, it was the right one - for America and Japan. He spared both countries the ravages of a prolonged, bloody war of attrition that could have killed millions. The longer the war dragged on, the more difficult it would have been to make lasting peace. Ending the war quickly and decisively opened the door to the rebuilding process which made Japan and Germany among our greatest allies.

Our military should never have its mission diluted by concerns of political correctness and public relations. When "wokeness" becomes the primary concern of our military, national security suffers, and the nation is rendered weak and vulnerable.

It may not be charming or sensitive, but America was better off with President Trump's unapologetic toughness than with Obama's apology tour or Joe Biden's weak leadership. Groveling does not make the world love us. In the realpolitik of international relations, power matters, not apologies. Mea culpas may have made Obama personally popular with those who envy and resent America, but it only weakened our country on the international stage.

In 2021, President Joe Biden's administration followed in Barack Obama's misguided steps. Secretary of State Antony Blinken actually called for the United Nations to investigate America's human rights record on race. Inviting our adversaries to evaluate our country is to betray our country. America is not perfect, but our flaws are our business, not the business of the United Nations. It's insane for the United States to invite nations such as China, Cuba, and Russia to critique America's human rights record. In 2019, the United Nations Human Rights Council praised North Korea, one of the most brutal, repressive regimes in the world today. To open ourselves to criticism by a group filled with militarist thugs and communist dictators is an insult to the American people, and it is pathetically weak.

Peace cannot be purchased at the price of humiliation. We must always be ready to defend American sovereignty and liberty with unsurpassed military power. I pray we never again have to use it, but we must always be ready.

CHAPTER 49

SOCIAL ENGINEERING AND MILITARY "WOKENESS"

With the election of Joe Biden, the military immediately left its primary mission of securing our nation and fighting our wars. It has become a Leftist laboratory of social engineering.

President Biden immediately ordered the military to accept transgenders into its ranks. It would be bad enough to admit people who have already "transitioned" from one gender to another. It is even worse to admit people who are "transitioning" and want the military to finance their hormone treatment and surgeries. People are being allowed to join the military as men and then become women while actively serving. This introduces a confusing and controversial sexual issue consuming precious time, energy, and financial resources.

Since morale is all-important in our armed forces, a whole new set of standards and rules must be established to make military personnel accept an obvious lie. The truth is a man cannot become a woman, nor can a woman become a man. It is physiologically and genetically impossible. Modern medical technology can make a man look like a woman and vice versa, but the change is strictly in appearance. When you take away hormone treatments and surgical operations, what lies beneath is the person whose gender was established in the womb. When that person stands before God, he or she will be as a male or female based upon biological reality, not so-called "gender identity."

The mission of our military is complex and dangerous. The Left now wants our troops to embrace the radical view that gender is nothing more than a "social construct." This is at best a distraction and at worst a direct attack on military morale and esprit de corps. To be a good soldier, sailor, airman, or Marine under Biden, you must accept the abnormal as normal, reject 6,000 years or more of human history and deny a century of scientific knowledge. To add insult to injury, many are being ordered to violate their faith and their consciences.

This is directly contrary to the values that built this nation: faith, family, and freedom. This pernicious movement must be stopped.

CHAPTER 50

CRITICAL RACE THEORY IN THE MILITARY

It doesn't stop there. The top brass are also teaching Critical Race Theory and the 1619 Project. These are not scholarly works, only Marxist interpretations of American history based on radical, far-left ideology. They are highly divisive. The sum and substance of Critical Race Theory is analogous to what Karl Marx says about capitalism: America is inherently unjust. CRT says that America, rooted in capitalism, is systemically racist. Marx defined life as class struggle. CRT would say America is defined by racial struggle.

For Marx, the capitalists or owners of the means of production are oppressors and exploiters of the workers (the "proletariat"). In CRT, all white people are oppressors of all "people of color." In public schools, colleges, and universities where this is taught, the students emerge embarrassed by their own country. Some become radicalized and exude hatred toward America, our flag, our national anthem and everything else representing our country.

This hatred leads to tearing down statues honoring George Washington, Thomas Jefferson, Patrick Henry, John Adams, Abraham Lincoln, and many others. These men are condemned as racists either because they owned slaves in the early history of our country, or they did not meet the "woke" standards of today's radical Left. This hatred also leads to turning one's back on the American flag and kneeling instead of standing for the national anthem.

CRT has infected every institution of our culture. The news media, colleges and universities, arts and entertainment, professional sports, Big Tech, and the corporate world have all bought into the cultish and irrational hatred of America espoused by CRT's advocates. The teachers unions are pushing it in government schools. Students are being taught to hate themselves based on the color of their skin.

If you are white, you are by definition an evil oppressor, no matter how young or poor. The color of your skin automatically designates you as a bad person and you should apologize for who you are. More to the point, you should be ashamed of who God made you to be. If you are a "person of color" you are by definition a virtuous victim. Thankfully, many parents across the country are letting their voices be heard at school board meetings and pulling their children out of these schools to educate them at home or at private schools. They refuse to allow their children to become victims of propaganda and indoctrination.

It's bad enough to have students, the future leaders of our nation, infected with these lies. Instead of being taught what every generation has known to be true—among nations, America is the last, best hope of mankind. We are now raising generations to believe America is the worst thing that ever happened to mankind. To teach this to our troops is suicidal. You cannot have an effective fighting force if people you expect to lay their lives on the line are taught to hate their country. Why would anyone fight, bleed, and die for a nation you believe to be inherently evil?

As a pastor in the Hampton Roads area of Virginia for the last twenty years, I have had many sailors and Marines come through our doors. One young sailor was a member of my church for three years. Just before new orders sent him away, he confessed to me when he came to my church, he hated America and felt guilty about serving in the military. He read Howard Zinn's *A People's History of the United States*. That book is not history, but a Marxist interpretation of American history meant to create hatred, resentment, and racial division in our country. Teachers unions and government schools have adopted some or all of its curriculum. Zinn's book altered this sailor's attitude. As he spent time under my teaching, he came to realize he was lied to and as a Christian he should be viewing our country and his place in it with a vision for what God wants to do with him here.

CRT and Zinn's book are cut from the same ideological cloth. If that one book could turn a young sailor into an enemy of our country, imagine what years of indoctrination under CRT would do.

I am proud of my service in the United States Marine Corps. We were taught there is one color in the Corps—green. I joined in 1970. We had just emerged from the 1960s, one of the most racially charged decades in American history. It would be an exaggeration to say there were no racial incidents or issues in the Corps. The cultural and political upheaval was spilling into the military.

During my tour of duty in Twentynine Palms, California, there was self-segregation in the chow hall where many of the black Marines ate together. I had friends of all backgrounds and served as a kind of ambassador. It wasn't intentional on my part, but I hung around people I liked and didn't care what anybody else thought. As it turned out, my friends thought the same way, but few were willing to cross the imaginary social line. When it came to work and duty, however, we worked together. I cannot recall a single instance of racial fights or issues in carrying out our duties.

Today, we have military brass intentionally highlighting racial division by introducing CRT as part of military training. I believe our international adversaries are laughing at our obsession with distractions which serve only to weaken us. There should be one mission for the military, and it is not to be culturally relevant, "woke," or any other such nonsense. Our mission should be to have the best trained, technologically advanced, combat ready, and lethal fighting force on the face of the earth.

CHAPTER 51

OUR IMMIGRATION SYSTEM

Our border security and immigration policy are essential aspects of American national security. As in all such matters, our first priority should be the vital interests of our country. The entry of millions of unvetted illegal migrants into our country threatens our security and our sovereignty. President Trump is the only president in my lifetime to recognize the gravity of the situation and take action to solve it. Even Ronald Reagan, who is one of the greatest presidents of his century, was naive in bargaining away border security to the Democrat Party, which never had any intention of securing the border.

President Trump was called a racist, anti-Hispanic, and worse for his efforts to do what all other countries do with far more draconian enforcement than anything Americans have ever thought of. Increasing the border patrol, building a border wall, and deporting illegal immigrants are all reasonable policies to correct a situation completely out of control. We are a sovereign nation, and no one should be allowed to enter without our permission. The race or ethnicity of an illegal alien is irrelevant.

The Left has tried to caricature our immigration policy, particularly under President Trump, as racially motivated. The criticism is as much directed against our country as it was against Trump.

Let us acknowledge what the Left will not. We have our own unique American culture, and we have a right to preserve it.

Our culture is not defined by the skin color of our citizens, even though the Left tries to convince the world it is. Lately, we hear constant accusations of how America is racist and white supremacist. In truth, our culture is based on Judeo-Christian values and is influenced by people from all over the world. Christianity began in the Middle East among Jewish people, not Europeans. Because the Roman Empire accepted Christianity in the fourth century, it established early roots in Europe. Nevertheless, it may be more accurate to say the Middle Eastern spirituality of Judaism and Christianity influenced and shaped European civilization more than Europe influenced Christianity. Rome helped create the Catholic Church, but the teaching of the church stood in marked contradiction to pagan Roman culture.

Our America is not Roman or European, but American. Our streets, cities, and institutions are named and modeled on cultures from every continent. We draw inspiration and ideas from around the world. However, it is all recast into something uniquely American.

My wife and I, Americans of African ancestry, have vacationed in Naples, San Diego, and Portland, but we did not have to go to Italy, Mexico, or England for culinary and cultural variety. We've eaten manicotti, tacos, and fish and chips without ever leaving the country. We've watched Irish step dancing, listened to Luciano Pavarotti, and been fascinated by the lifestyle and enjoyed the food and culture of the German-descended Amish.

This is America, a mighty river of life fed by many cultural streams and undergirded by our Judeo-Christian heritage. These streams are beautiful in their own right, but they are all influenced and changed by the American experience. Frankfurters became hot dogs - German food, American style.

Instead of seeing beauty in the amalgamation, the Left wants certain cultures used as political weapons against others. Nothing our ancestors brought to America has remained what it was before they arrived. We have all influenced each other and created a unique experience of which we should all be proud. Culture cannot be owned; it is the result of a complex array of influences.

The myth promoted by the Left that our immigration system is a racist ploy to maintain a Euro-centric culture is another slanderous accusation against America. As I have demonstrated, American culture is not racial. It is a mosaic of many influences. Some of them are undoubtedly European since people from that continent were the first to settle here after Native Americans. However, there are other influences, African being among the most prominent, since Africans were the next group to arrive in America in great numbers. Music, dance, food, humor, and language have all been influenced by African culture.

As I sat in an airport lounge recently, I picked up a copy of *American Cinematography*. Inside were pictures of people of every complexion. You would not find the same variety in magazines in other places around the globe. This is America, my home—the nation I love.

I celebrate the beauty of America's unique culture, but I am profoundly concerned it could be swept away. For example, it should outrage Americans when illegal aliens flood across our borders flying Mexican or other flags. This signifies they are not coming to be part of American culture but to supplant it. They do not wish to be Americans but to take America. This should come as no surprise. The Leftist cult believes we stole the land on our southern border. This sentiment is captured in the glib saying, "aliens are not crossing the border. The border crossed them." This insidious ideology denies historical reality. Like all Marxists, American radicals must reinterpret and rewrite history in order to invent a different future.

It is pure political cynicism and racial demagoguery to charge anti-Hispanic bigotry against those who oppose illegal entry into the United States. People who favor a legal immigration system have a principled concern about a flow of illegal aliens undermining the rule of law and American sovereignty. The Democrat Party does not care about America's sovereignty or cultural hegemony. They believe illegals will eventually become citizens and vote for Democrats.

However, many who are escaping corrupt or totalitarian regimes may not be as susceptible to socialism as American Leftists think. Those who have experienced communism and dictatorship see the

Democrat Party's lurch to the far left as frighteningly reminiscent of the rise of communism in countries they escaped. They have experienced first-hand what happens when Marxists take over, and they want no more of it. That is why Americans of Hispanic background are switching their allegiance from the Democrat Party to Republicans. They do not support the lawlessness of illegal immigration because it is having devastating impact on their safety along the border. The crime, drugs, human trafficking caused by illegal immigration is affecting Hispanic Americans as much if not more than other citizens.

For me, the color of an immigrant's skin is irrelevant. Those who are not willing to endure the delays and bureaucracy of entering legally are not welcome. Those who do not appreciate freedom and admire the American Constitution and our Judeo-Christian culture are not welcome. Those who resent our country and have ill will toward us are not welcome. For example, Ilhan Omar, who represents Minnesota in the U.S. Congress, should never have been given citizenship. Her presence here is subversive. I wish her safe travel to a place she will be happy to call home, perhaps where Sharia law is in effect. America is not that place.

I would go so far as to say all naturalized citizens should be subject to having their citizenship revoked for some probationary period. Anyone who spews the divisive, anti-American demagoguery we hear from Ilhan Omar should be deported back to the country from whence they came or to any nation they choose, assuming the country will have them.

As an American of African descent, no one can credibly say my remarks are racial. My sentiment would be no different if Omar were from Britain, Ireland, or anywhere else in Europe and had the most ivory complexion imaginable. Anyone who is given citizenship and uses that privilege to attack our country and way of life should have that citizenship revoked. Immigration policy should be designed to strengthen America, not give a platform to our enemies.

If you don't view America as a land of hope and opportunity, don't come. Frankly, if you don't love this country, even if you *were* born here, you ought to leave. Find a place where you can be happy.

You should be glad to go. Those of us who love this country will be glad to see you go.

Years ago, I was at a newsstand in Massachusetts, and I heard a Middle Eastern man complaining about America. I interrupted his rant and said, "If you think America is so bad, what are you doing here?" He said, "I've got a right to be here."

He was wrong. Immigrants are here by privilege, not right. America owes them nothing, nor do the American people. Immigrants owe America for the privilege of living here. When the issue of illegal immigration comes up, the Left always argues America is a nation of immigrants. True, but life has changed since the eighteenth and nineteenth centuries. America desperately needed people in order to populate the country. Today, we have more than 333 million people. Illegal immigration threatens to overwhelm our culture, schools, economy, and infrastructure.

Immigration is also a national security issue. The Biden administration's open borders policy is allowing Islamic terrorists, gangs, guns, cartel drug dealers, and human traffickers to pour into our country. An unprecedented amount of fentanyl is killing nearly 100,000 Americans a year and climbing. One could reasonably say the Biden regime is complicit.

The first priority of immigration policy should be protecting the American people. The Left is very concerned about people who have no right to be here, but they dismiss the safety and security of Americans. They only care about people when doing so advances their political agenda. Unfortunately, we can't have an intelligent debate on this subject because anyone against illegal immigration is labeled a "racist" by the Left and the mainstream media. As I have pointed out, opposition to illegal immigration has nothing to do with race. Americans must fight for our culture and the rule of law. We must fight for America. Everyone is welcome here if they love and respect our country and come through the proper legal process. Those who cannot or will not meet these two basic requirements are neither welcome nor worthy.

We are a nation of laws. Proverbs 28:9 says, "One who turns away his ear from hearing the law, even his prayer is an abomination." When we reward people for illegal behavior, we are inviting anarchy and lawlessness. That may be why in 2020 we saw over 500 riots in over 200 locations in cities across America. When we send out the message the law does not matter, we sow the wind and then reap the whirlwind. To remain the great nation we have long been, we must always engender respect for the rule of law. Halting the flow of illegal immigrants is an important step toward that end.

CHAPTER 52

PEACE THROUGH STRENGTH

The United States is the only nation in history to finance the rebuilding of countries that attacked us without provocation and plunged the world into war. We did not seek to subjugate Japan or turn Germany and Italy into American satellites. They are free and independent nations, and we deal with them as equals. Yet it is no exaggeration to say without our help, they might never have recovered from the destructive decisions precipitating World War II.

This brings up one of the most exasperating aspects of the politics of the American Left today. They cannot seem to find anything inspiring or noble about our country. Yet one need not look far into the past to find sacrifice, courage, generosity, and a commitment to liberty even for those who made war against us. America has never been a nation of conquest and subjugation of other people. Slavery and the treatment of Native Americans will always be brought up to rebut that point. However, the settling of North America and the introduction of slavery were both part of the context of the times. You can no more call the settling of this continent an "American" policy of conquest than you can call the *Mayflower* a "warship."

The nation arising from the slow but steady arrival of Europeans to this continent feared a standing army and loved peace and prosperity. Americans wanted to raise families, start businesses, and explore and settle this magnificent land. However, like any nation, we learned from the earliest settlers the necessity of defending ourselves against hostile forces foreign or indigenous. The first responsibility of any would-be government is the safety and security of its people. Neither we nor our ancestors owe apologies for fulfilling that sacred duty.

During the Revolutionary War, a ragtag group of colonists said, in effect, *We are not going to be under the heel of King George III.* They fought desperately for their freedom. For more than five years, General George Washington and those who fought under his leadership showed great courage and steadfastness. They refused to quit.

War is not a public relations campaign. The purpose of the military is to defend the United States of America against evil. Sometimes this calls for brutal, horrifying violence. I wish we lived in a world where that is never necessary. As a Christian I believe the day will come when, "They shall beat their swords into plowshares, and their spears into pruning hooks; Nation shall not lift up sword against nation, Neither shall they learn war anymore" (Isaiah 2:4).

Alas, that is not the world we live in today. Evil cannot be wished away or appeased. We ignore it at our extreme peril. The United States seeks conflict with no one. However, it should be the stated policy of our government that those who attack us or seek to make war against us will pay a terrible price.

PART X

THE FUTURE OF
AMERICAN ENERGY

After decades of energy dependence on Middle Eastern countries who have no love for or loyalty to America, Donald
Trump led our nation to energy independence. It was a remarkable
political and economic achievement. While environmental radicals
and liberal elites predict climate catastrophe, most Americans take
a commonsense approach to the issue. Fossil fuels are going to be
here forever, and we have an abundance here in America under our
very feet.

As a result of Trump's policies on energy and fossil fuels, gas
prices dropped and stabilized. After decades of battles over drilling
in Alaska's Arctic National Wildlife Refuge (ANWR), it was opened
for lease. ANWR is over 19,000,000 acres in one of the most remote
areas of the world. Less than 8 percent of that land could produce
sixteen billion barrels of oil.

To meet the needs of our growing economy, every accessible
energy source, including ANWR, must be made available. Once
again, the free market proves more efficient than the environmental
planners and radicals who think they know best for the planet and
every person on it. We need to use fossil fuels as cleanly and as
efficiently as possible, and we need to keep getting better at it, which
we are. We all love clean air, clean water, and a beautiful

environment. What we do not buy is the apocalyptic hysteria prop-
agated by the Left and their media mouthpieces. They use fear to
make Americans submit to the massive transfer of power from the
individual to government. We should never surrender freedom for
security. As Ben Franklin said, those who do are worthy of neither.[60]

The media-created character, Alexandria Ocasio-Cortez, has
called for a totalitarian state through the Green New Deal. This
absurd "plan" would do nothing for our ecology and would be
cataclysmic for our economy. The New York congresswoman's
vision is to end air travel, limit automobile travel, and control how
much energy anyone can use in the home. The ripple effects of such
policies would be too devastating to contemplate. In the meantime,
we would surrender immeasurable economic advantages to China
and Russia.

After the United States experienced several years of energy independence and stable gas and oil prices, Joe Biden was inaugurated
president in January 2021. He immediately stopped the XL Keystone
Pipeline.[61] As an homage to the environmental radicals in his party,
he has resurrected all the energy-suppressing policies of the Obama
administration. Consequently, as this book goes to print, the price
of fuel at the pump at the pump has doubled what it was in 2020.

The Department of Interior has estimated North Dakota and
Montana have 3 billion to 4.3 billion barrels of recoverable oil, and
it could be extracted at an approximate cost to Americans of only
$16 a barrel. The U.S. Geological Survey (USGS) believes the Bak-
ken Formation in North Dakota holds more oil than the entire
Middle East.

Studies also indicate there may be more than one trillion barrels
of oil in shale—a sedimentary rock found in Wyoming, Utah, and
Colorado's Western Slope. That is nearly three times the reserves
in Saudi Arabia. Those deposits were finally being tapped to benefit all Americans. To the extent we can continue to extract resources
from private land, there is hope we can recover quickly from disastrous Biden policies with a conservative president and Congress.
This author will be working toward that end.

The energy crises we have faced have not been for lack of resources. The problem is our country has been held hostage by radical

environmentalists. It would be a welcome change if Democrats were more committed to the economic well-being of the American people than to advancing apocalyptic environmental theories. President Trump opened the energy resources of the country to exploration, and that simple policy change did more to help the poor than all the wealth redistribution schemes of the Democrat Party.

No discussion of the environment would be complete without acknowledging the utter hypocrisy of the Left. Hollywood celebrities, Al Gore, and John Kerry—now an environmental czar for the Biden administration—fly around in private jets, build outsized houses, and ride in enormous gas-guzzling SUVs for their comfort and security. Americans should be highly skeptical of people who tell us the oceans are rapidly rising to life-threatening levels, then buy oceanfront property for themselves. It reveals again the real agenda is not concern for people, but thirst for power over those people. It is always "for the good of the people," who are of course too dull to understand the exalted insights of their elite liberal masters.

CHAPTER 53

OTHER OPTIONS

Fossil fuels have built the industrial and technological marvel we all enjoy. That is why we have relied on them for so long. The coal industry provides 50 percent of the electricity of our country, but ideologically driven politicians and regulators are trying to destroy it. They have put thousands of coal miners out of work and left them to collect unemployment and welfare. The results have been disastrous for their families and the communities relying on coal as the backbone of their economy.

They're working on doing the same thing to the natural gas industry. Without fossil fuels, there never would have been an industrial or technological revolution. While China, Russia, and India use every fossil resource available, violating the Paris Climate Accords, American eco-radicals do all in their power to limit our energy resources. They offer us the pie-in-the-sky promise of efficient wind and solar. Our ancestors tried that. It did not work well for them. It certainly will not work to power a modern economy.

Alternative energy accounts for only about 8 percent of our total energy usage, and it is significantly more expensive to buy and to retrofit homes to accommodate these inefficient technologies. The Left is trying to destroy two centuries of economic and energy progress.

Investors like billionaire T. Boone Pickens have tried to develop wind power; but that technology is expensive and unpredictable. Pickens spent $80 million on TV commercials hyping his "Pickens Plan" for wind power, and $2 billion on General Electric wind turbines; in December 2010, he abandoned his plan and sold the turbines to Canada because Canadian law mandates consumers to buy renewable electricity, regardless the cost. This is where America is headed if we don't vote out the crazy Democrats who want to dictate what kind of lightbulbs we can have and the temperatures to which we heat and cool our homes. In Democratic-run California, citizens endure sky-high energy prices plus frequent blackouts and brownouts. Governor Gavin Newsome recently announced that no more gas powered vehicles will be sold in California after 2035. In almost the same breath, they asked residents not to charge their electric vehicles during certain hours because the electrical grid cannot support the energy demands. It sounds like the environmental keystone cops, and it would be funny if the consequences weren't so tragic. The sick and elderly risk heat exhaustion and death when they cannot cool their homes because of government energy policies which lead to brown outs.

The elites however, always seem to find a way around the draconian environmental regulations they want to impose upon the rest of us. The late Sen. Ted Kennedy, champion of the environment and clean energy, used his position to stop a wind farm project in Nantucket Sound that would have obstructed his view from the Hyannis Port Kennedy Compound. The environmental elitist Al Gore tells us we need to reduce our carbon footprint, but he flies everywhere in a private jet. Obama pushes green energy solutions, but he and his wife took separate government planes at taxpayer expense whenever they found it convenient. Obama used to fly his fitness trainer from Chicago to Washington every week.[62] This elitist hypocrisy is disgusting, and it is one of the reasons why Donald Trump was elected President in 2016.

Radical environmentalists believe people are the problem. The earth was just fine until we evolutionary interlopers came along and ruined it. If we could only suppress America's economic activity and rid the earth of a few billion people, the planet would be fine.

President Biden's nominee to head the Bureau of Land Management once suggested people should be limited to two children.[63] The environment can't handle more. In her younger years, she participated in spiking trees designated to be cut down for lumber. This is ecoterrorism that severely injures and kills loggers when their saws turn the spikes into shrapnel. Extreme environmentalists treasure plant and animal life, but human beings are another matter.

Despite what you hear from Hollywood celebrities and the mainstream media, the data on global warming and climate change is far from clear. Many respected scientists are coming out of the closet to say what people are calling global warming is part of a natural planetary climate shift commonplace throughout the history of the earth. We went through an ice age and warming periods hotter than today, but no cars, trucks, or factories were around to induce them. In the 1970s liberals predicted a new ice age. Scientists who are not afraid of Leftist elites say data shows the earth will remain in a cooling cycle for the next twenty to thirty years, then warm up again.

To put it politely, temperature data thrown about in support of global warming is faulty. Respected meteorologists and scientists studied 860 ground temperature monitoring stations and found 89 percent of them "fail to meet the National Weather Service's own siting requirements," which say stations must be 100 feet or more from artificial heat sources.[64] These skewed numbers are used to perpetuate the lie the planet is about to overheat like your old car and break down on the roadside of history. Oh, and of course it's all the fault of selfish, greedy Americans. According to the liberal orthodoxy, we, above all people on the earth, are destroying the planet.

Anthony Watts, a broadcast meteorologist who coordinated the study of monitoring stations, says, "We found stations located next to the exhaust fans of air conditioning units, surrounded by asphalt parking lots and roads, on blistering hot rooftops and near sidewalks and buildings that absorb and radiate heat."[65] All this simply proves we are in an ideological battle with those who seek power, not a scientific debate with those who seek truth. Those who "believe" in climate change want to shut down debate. They behave like members of a religious cult who want to silence and excommunicate heretics.

This earth and our universe have a Designer. Human beings are not evolutionary accidents. God created us and prepared the earth with humans in mind. He knew the extraordinary progress we would make because he gave us the gifts of intelligence and creativity. We are made in the image and likeness of our Creator. We have his divine endowments. He designed the earth as the perfect habitation for us. It was engineered to absorb human progress. It is not a fragile ball of dust subject to destruction by human progress or mankind's sinful and destructive tendencies. The earth is homeostatic as is all life on the planet. It has the ability to heal and cleanse itself. Oil spills thought to be the end of an ecosystem have been forgotten as the earth has restored itself to a state of normalcy.

The Left's predictions of environmental cataclysm through climate change are a reflection of their pathological god complex. They claim superior moral insight, but they celebrate the slaughter of unborn children by the millions. They will not lift a finger to save a baby, but we can trust them to save the planet. That is a staggering logical and moral inconsistency. It only makes sense when seen through the lens of their insatiable hunger for power.

Climate change hysteria isn't about saving the planet. It is about power to control the lives of the American people. The Left doesn't like our Judeo-Christian culture, the Constitution it produced, nor the individual liberty it protects. The individual is to be subsumed under the collective. The limited and enumerated powers set forth in our Constitution to restrain the power of government are misguided. The Left wants more power—much more. The utopian dream eluding dictators throughout history is surely just within their grasp. They "are the ones we've been waiting for," as Obama famously said.[66] The dream of Karl Marx, Obama's true intellectual father, has become the nightmare of humanity.

The Left wants us to obsess over the fantasy of climate catastrophe. They turn every weather event into proof climate change threatens our existence. The real threat is dependence on other countries, including hostile nations, for our energy needs. President Trump made that issue a priority and gave America energy independence. Obama heir Joe Biden took office and made climate change our top national security priority. This is not only incompetent but dangerous.

As discussed earlier, the job of the military is to protect our country from foreign threats, not to control the weather. The American Left, like communists who preceded them, are so arrogantly determined to impose their vision on the world that they're willing to inflict untold suffering and death on humanity to achieve their ends. A military incapable of fighting our real enemies, the massive loss of jobs, and confiscatory energy prices are a small price to pay to save the planet.

It is time to develop energy policy based on common sense instead of ideological extremism. The environment isn't a religion. The earth isn't our "mother." It is our home. Human beings are not earth's enemies. We're its stewards. Our existence isn't a threat to the planet. Let's protect our environment, and keep it beautiful, but maintain perspective. We're never going to control the weather or stop brutal storms and other natural disasters. What we can do is enhance the standard of living, grow our national and local economies, and have the infrastructure and economic strength to respond when inevitable disasters come. Let us cease despairing over the future of the planet and focus our attention on expanding opportunities for all Americans to live peaceful and prosperous lives.

PART XI

OUR SACRED SYMBOLS

CHAPTER 54

OUR FLAG

The flag of the United States of America is not just a piece of red, white, and blue cloth. It is the symbol of American unity. It represents this nation and our ideals. Honoring the flag is a way of honoring our country, our fellow citizens, and our veterans and active-duty military who protect our freedom.

We have heard repeatedly from the Left, and loudly from President Biden, America has never lived up to our highest ideals. That is undeniably true. The problem is the Left says this as if there is a magical kingdom on earth to which America can be unfavorably compared. The only place perfectly reflecting the highest ideals is heaven.

America has always aspired to do what is right as far as human imperfection allows us to see the right. The Left depicts us as a nation always aspiring to do wrong. Like all Marxists, they believe if they can change the system, we can produce perfect people. Utopia is within our grasp if we can only rid ourselves of the antiquated notion of individual liberty.

For patriots, our flag represents our aspirations. It represents the blood, sweat, and tears poured into building this country. I think of those who died in the Revolutionary War—like Crispus Attucks, a black patriot killed by the British during the Boston Massacre. He was the first American to give his life in a war that would change the world as no other war ever had. Our flag represents the sacrifices of the Founding Fathers, who gave their lives, fortunes, and sacred honor to bring this nation into existence. It represents Nathan Hale, just twenty-one years old, who was hanged by the British while on a covert mission. His last words were, "I only regret that I have but one life to lose for my country." The flag represents the faith, honesty, decency, hard work, and compassion of the American people. It is the symbol of our united love for this land.

From the Revolutionary War to the War of 1812, the Civil War, the Spanish-American War, to World Wars I and II, Korea, Vietnam, Iraq, Afghanistan, and other conflicts, Americans have fought, bled, and died under Old Glory. That Star-Spangled Banner represents the heart and soul of a people who have been through hell and high water to defend the cause of liberty.

When enemies arise against us and we are forced to put the lives of young men and women on the line, they fight under our flag. If they live through it, many come home with scars lasting a lifetime. They have sacrificed much in order to protect what the flag represents. We are not a perfect country, but there is more liberty and justice here than anywhere else in the world. Denigrating the flag, turning your back on it, taking a knee, and refusing to say the Pledge of Allegiance are acts of betrayal. Citizens whose allegiance is not to America should find a nation worthy of their loyalty.

Each star on the flag signifies a state with its own government and unique culture. Yet our federation of states shares a common dream and destiny. It is a picture of who we are as Americans, living together, working together, struggling together, and growing together. We believe in individual liberty and personal responsibility, but we act collectively when we need to. We do not respond well to government edicts and dictates. Our public officials have power only by the consent of the governed.

Those who want to come to this country legally are welcome, regardless of race. However, they should come only if they want to be Americans. They should come seeking to assimilate and adopt our values.

People with chips on their shoulders or who believe America is the cause of all their problems should stay where they are. Those arriving on our shores with a desire to harm us should understand we are not pacifists. We will defend ourselves. The American people are smarter and more practical about these issues than our political leaders. We resent suicidal immigration policies putting the needs of foreigners before those whom elected officials are sworn to serve and protect. We are tired of providing refuge for people who hate us and have no gratitude for the safety we provide them.

Ilhan Omar, elected to Congress from Minneapolis, says, only after arriving in America did she experience what it means to be "other." She escaped from Somalia to save her life and the lives of her family. She came to this nation where she has become an influential leader, part of "The Squad," and all she can do is express resentment and bitterness toward the nation that gave her refuge. If our immigration policy reflected the common sense of the American people, she would not be here.

People like Omar should find a place they can admire and enjoy. If no such place exists, they should stay and fight to make their country of origin a better place rather than bringing their anti-American toxicity into our country. The American people should not have to pay to take care of people who come to our country with a sense of resentment and entitlement. Ilhan Omar has supported groups that burn the flag and chant "death to America."[67]

The Left's disrespect for our flag is proof they are perfect ingrates. Colin Kaepernick has repeatedly expressed hatred for America. With the money he has made in America, including his huge haul from a Nike ad campaign celebrating his lack of patriotism, he can afford to leave. Why doesn't he? Because even though they refuse to acknowledge it, this nation has showered them with opportunities they could find nowhere else in the world. Yet they have no gratitude or affection for our country or our flag.

The flag represents our national unity. In 1989, the House of Representatives published a book called *Our Flag*, which describes its parts:

The star is a symbol of the heavens and the divine goal to which man has aspired from time immemorial; the stripe is symbolic of the rays of light emanating from the sun . . . White signifies purity and innocence, Red, hardiness & valour, and Blue . . . signifies vigilance, perseverance & justice.

Spiritual meanings have also been attached to the beautiful and respectful flag folding ceremonies given by our armed forces. Before it is stored (or presented to survivors of a veteran), it takes thirteen folds to create the final, dignified triangle we are so familiar with.

The thirteen folds—two lengthwise and eleven triangular ones, have come to signify religious principles of our nation:

First fold: a symbol of life.

Second fold: a symbol of our belief in eternal life.

Third fold: in honor and remembrance of the veteran departing our ranks, and who gave a portion of his or her life for the defense of our country to attain peace throughout the world.

Fourth fold: represents our weaker nature; as American citizens trusting in God, it is to Him we turn in times of peace, as well as in times of war, for His divine guidance.

Fifth fold: a tribute to our country, for in the words of Stephen Decatur, "Our country, in dealing with other countries, may she always be right, but it is still our country, right or wrong."

Sixth fold: where our hearts lie. It is with our heart that we pledge allegiance to the flag of the United States of America, and to the republic for which it stands, one nation under God, indivisible, with liberty and justice for all.

Seventh fold: a tribute to our armed forces, for it is through the armed forces that we protect our country and our flag against all enemies, whether they be found within or without the boundaries of our republic.

Eighth fold: a tribute to the one who entered into the valley of the shadow of death, that we might see the light of day, and to honor our mother, for whom it flies on Mother's Day.

Ninth fold: a tribute to womanhood, for it has been through their faith, love, loyalty and devotion that the character of the men and women who have made this country great have been molded.

Tenth fold: a tribute to father, for he, too, has given his sons and daughters for the defense of our country since he or she was first born.

Eleventh fold: in the eyes of a Jewish citizen, represents the lower portion of the seal of King David and King Solomon and glorifies, in their eyes, the God of Abraham, Isaac and Jacob.

Twelfth fold: in the eyes of a Christian citizen, represents an emblem of eternity and glorifies, in their eyes, God the Father, the Son and Holy Ghost.

Thirteenth fold: With this completing fold, it is a triangular shape with only the stars against a blue background, reminding us of our national motto, "In God We Trust." The shape resembles a cocked hat, similar to the ones worn by soldiers serving under General George Washington, and the sailors and Marines serving under Captain John Paul Jones.

Because the flag also represents those who have sacrificed and paved the way for us, it is an emotional symbol. When the National Football League and other professional leagues joined in the insanity of kneeling instead of standing for the flag, it caused a visceral emotional reaction among most Americans. That movement ended my interest in professional sports. I was an avid football fan, but I no longer watch professional football at all. The protest angered me so much that I simply no longer enjoyed watching. I never bought the benign excuses that it was only a protest of police brutality. It was an expression of hatred for the country and Colin Kaepernick later confirmed this by saying he would not celebrate July 4th. Other radical activists followed suit.

Roger Goodell, the most overpaid person in America, was stupid enough to appease these ingrates instead of putting a stop to it. One can only conclude he is too dense to understand the emotional impact of disrespecting the flag or so lacking in patriotic sentiment that it simply did not matter to him. For many of us, it is the equivalent of spitting in our faces. You don't spit in my face and then ask me to support your enterprise.

Roger Goodell should have been fired long ago. The NFL needs a commissioner who would say to the players, "Our success depends upon the support of the American people, the majority of whom are patriotic. We support the cause of stopping police brutality, but disrespecting the flag is the worst way in the world to communicate that message. What you will be conveying is hatred for the country and the people who made you rich. That doesn't make sense and we're not going to support that. You can do whatever you want on your own time, but the official policy of our league is we respect our country, the flag and the national anthem."

Anybody who is too cowardly or stupid to say that to the spoiled, pampered millionaire employees should not be running a lemonade stand, let alone the National Football League. Do not hold your breath waiting to hear that coming out of professional sports teams. In early 2021, self-congratulatory NBA team owner Mark Cuban decided to discontinue playing the national anthem before Dallas Maverick games. All this proves the axiom, it is possible to be brilliant and successful at one thing and be dumb as a rock when it comes to the common-sense wisdom of life. The NBA Commissioner overrode Cuban's decision and announced league policy was to play the national anthem.

Goodell should require all NFL players to stand respectfully during the playing of the national anthem, period. If their hatred for the country is such an important cause, quit professional sports and be a full-time Marxist and Black Lives Matter activist. While they're at it, they should give back the money they've made in our capitalist system. These players are like children who are given every advantage but hate the parents who provided for them.

Sadly, with few exceptions, the entire corporate world has joined the Leftist, anti-American, pro-Marxist cult. Whatever the cult says, they do. Anybody who doesn't agree is outside the cult, a bad person, and probably unemployable. The cult says disrespect the flag, and the corporate lemmings comply. The cult says there is no difference between a biological female and a man who simply states he "identifies" as a woman, and the corporate lemmings comply. Turning away from the facts and analysis they rely on to run their businesses, they become sycophants to the very people who would take away their companies if they ever gained the power to do so.

All cults lead to suicide—morally and spiritually if not physically. The institutions of influence buying into this far-left rejection of the values and symbols that unite us are committing cultural suicide. They assume siding with those who seem to be ascendant will shield them from the consequences of the revolution when it happens. Like the useful idiots in 1917 Russia, they are engineering their own doom. The cult they are supporting does not believe in liberty, free enterprise, and private property, all of which make corporate wealth possible.

The American flag is a symbol of the country I love. I respect it, fly it proudly, and pledge allegiance to it without apology. So should every American.

In 2018, while seeking the Republican nomination for the U.S. Senate in Virginia, I was interviewed by a reporter from the *Richmond Times-Dispatch*. He asked me what I liked about President Trump. I said he set a new tone of patriotism and love of country. Barack Obama never did or even aspired to. The reporter looked at me quizzically and responded, "I mean something real." He had no understanding of how real patriotism is to me and millions of other Americans.

Most journalists do not understand patriotism and love of country because they do not have it. Therefore, they dismiss it as a cover for something else, something evil. If half our citizens love our country and the other half hates it; if half our citizens respect the flag and the other half disdains it; if half our citizens stand for the national anthem and the other half turns their backs on it; then we are not one country, but two. That is dangerously close to becoming reality. This growing trend toward division that the Left has forced on the country through deception must be reversed or it will propel us into another civil war.

CHAPTER 55

THE PLEDGE OF ALLEGIANCE

The Pledge of Allegiance, like the flag, is a symbol of our ideals. It is a solemn covenant of unity and adherence to our principles. A nation as diverse as ours needs unifying symbols to remind us of our common vision and shared culture. The first version of the pledge was crafted by Francis Bellamy in 1892. It was formally adopted by Congress in 1942. In 1945, it was given its official name, "The Pledge of Allegiance." The version we use today was finalized in 1954, when the words "under God" were added to the final sentence. In one form or another, the pledge has been with us for over half our nation's history.

President Eisenhower, concerned about the rise of secularism and communism, proposed adding the words "under God" as a reminder that America has always been a nation rooted in the Christian faith. We have no official religion, but our culture is distinctly Christian. Our mores are Judeo-Christian, based on the Old and New Testament Scriptures.

Unfortunately, the Democrat Party and many of its partners are working hard to remove God, not only from the Pledge of Allegiance but from every aspect of American life. At the 2020 Democratic National Convention, the LGBTQ Caucus intentionally left the words "under God" out of their pledge, as did the Muslim

Caucus. Both groups are major constituents of the Democrat Party, and party officials did not object.

To eliminate God from our pledge and our society is to redefine America. Our nation was founded on the principle that freedom and rights are the gift of Almighty God, not granted by government. As long as that idea remains a founding precept of our nation, we are indeed one nation "under God."

The Founders believed Americans could not be a free people if freedom rested on mere political or legislative action. They wanted it to rest on an indestructible foundation, not subject to the whims of the politically ambitious and power hungry. That foundation is God, who has always been the central figure in American culture.

The original Pledge of Allegiance was published on September 8, 1892, in "The Youth's Companion" magazine by Francis Bellamy, for schoolchildren to recite on Columbus Day. That version read, "I pledge allegiance to my Flag and the Republic for which it stands, one nation indivisible, with liberty and justice for all."[68]

On Columbus Day of that year, October 12, millions of schoolchildren across the country recited the pledge to celebrate the 400th anniversary of Christopher Columbus's arrival in the Americas. Critics of the phrase "under God" like to point out it was not in the original version. While that is true, American culture was so steeped in faith that submission to God could be assumed.

The phrase was added to the pledge on June 14, 1954, by a joint resolution of Congress, in an amendment to the Flag Code. By that time, there was a growing threat of godless communism and a rising tide of secularism in America that no longer allowed us to take submission to God for granted. President Eisenhower said of the added phrase, "In this way we are reaffirming the transcendence of religious faith in America's heritage and future; in this way we shall constantly strengthen those spiritual weapons which forever will be our country's most powerful resource in peace and war."[69]

Eisenhower was inspired by a sermon given by the Scottish-born minister George MacPherson Docherty during Lincoln Day services at the New York Avenue Presbyterian Church in Washington, D.C. Docherty's sermon was called "A New Birth of Freedom." He said his children came home from school one day and proudly announced they recited the Pledge of Allegiance. When they repeated the pledge to Docherty, he was struck that there was no mention of God. He said in his sermon:

> There was something missing in this Pledge, and that which was missing was the characteristic and definitive factor in the "American Way of Life." Indeed, apart from the mention of the phrase, the United States of America, this could be the pledge of any Republic. . . . The only point I make in raising the issue of the Pledge of Allegiance is that it seems to me to omit this theological implication that is inherent within the "American Way of Life."[70]

Indeed, our "American Way of Life" incorporates moral, Judeo-Christian values into the laws and society of our culture, and we believe our Creator gave us life, liberty, and the right to pursue happiness. There is no other nation like America, and every American should be proud to recite the Pledge of Allegiance.

I pledge allegiance to the flag of the United States of America and to the republic for which it stands, one nation under God, indivisible, with liberty and justice for all.

CHAPTER 56

OUR NATIONAL ANTHEM

On June 18, 1812, America declared war on Great Britain. What precipitated the conflict was the British practice of "impressment." The British kidnapped 15,000 Americans on the high seas and pressed them into service in England's Navy between 1793 and 1812. American citizens were forced to fight in British wars against other European nations. For all practical purposes, Great Britain was kidnapping our citizens into slavery.

In the summer of 1813, Major George Armistead asked for a flag so big for Fort McHenry that "the British would have no trouble seeing it from a distance."[71] The finished flag measured thirty by forty-two feet and cost $405.90. The fifteen stars each measured two feet, point to point. It contained eight red and seven white stripes, each two feet tall.

At the time, Francis Scott Key was a young lawyer living in Washington, D.C. On August 19, 1814, the British entered Chesapeake Bay, and by August 24, they had captured Washington.

Key found out Dr. William Beanes, an elderly physician from Upper Marlboro, Maryland, was captured and being held on the British flagship *Tonnant*. Townspeople asked Key for help negotiating the doctor's release. On September 3, he and Col. John Skinner set sail for Baltimore. Upon arrival, they boarded the ship as guests.

At 7 a.m. on September 13, 1814, the British bombardment on Fort McHenry began, lasting twenty-five hours. Key and his companions were forced to watch it from a British ship. In the smoke and fire of the attack, Key could not see whether the huge flag still flew over Ft. McHenry. When dawn came, "our Flag was still there," and it inspired him to write a poem on the back of a letter he was carrying.

Copies of his poem called "Defence of Fort M'Henry" were circulated around Baltimore, and then it was printed in a newspaper. Someone set it to music and renamed it "The Star-Spangled Banner." It was adopted as our national anthem on March 3, 1931.[72] The flag that inspired Key's poem over Ft. McHenry now resides in the Smithsonian Institution's Museum of American History. It is a breathtaking display.

The Left is looking for every opportunity to reduce the impact of the flag and other national symbols. Many liberals are ashamed of America and uncomfortable with patriotism.

I was having a discussion one time on a television program. I told the host and the other people in the studio that I thought Americans were offended by our leaders going around the world apologizing for our country. The way the liberals came back at me that day told me what was really in their hearts about our nation. They said they had a problem with their patriotism being questioned. I didn't say anything about their patriotism; I simply said I didn't think it was appropriate for American leaders to go to other countries and apologize for ours. They said, well if we know we've done something wrong we might as well own up to it and accept it.

What that told me was liberals are not proud of America; they do not love America. They see this country as something for which we need to do penance. When you call them out on that view, it is like pulling the scab off a wound. The reaction is viscerally defensive because they know it is true, they do not love America. But they do not want to own up to their true sentiment or have others expose it.

The word "patriotism" comes from the Latin root *patr*, which means "father." Patriotism means a love for one's fatherland—and I don't think many liberals have that. They have a wary, disdainful attitude toward America. They are uncomfortable with American prosperity and success, and they are especially uncomfortable with American faith.

A Gallup poll in the summer of 2010 confirms this: 52 percent of conservatives said they were "extremely patriotic," while only 19 percent of liberals said they were.[73] Over five years of polling data, the percentage of liberals, Democrats, and independents who describe themselves as "extremely patriotic" has declined. While writing this book in 2021, the lack of patriotism of the Left has become open hostility toward our country. In an article about the 2021 Summer Olympics, ESPN commentator William Rhoden, upon seeing the flag unveiled said, "Nationalism is not good."[74] To him, the flag represents perverse, racist nationalism.

Remember, Michelle Obama told us that for the first time in her adult life, she was "proud" of her country when her husband was elected president. During his first presidential campaign, Barack Obama said he didn't feel the need to wear a flag pin on his lapel.[75] He wasn't comfortable with that kind of patriotism. In truth, he's not comfortable with patriotism at all. This speaks volumes about his and Michelle's attitude toward America.

After an all-too-brief Trump presidency, during which there were no apologies for putting our own country first, we have now regressed to having Obama's protege—Joe Biden—as president. The lectures have been nonstop about our not living up to our principles. It may take a generation to rescue our country from the people who have such a poor opinion of it, but it must be done.

I believe I speak for the majority of Americans when I say that under the banner of our flag, we will fight until the Marxist movement infecting our country like a plague is cast on the refuse heap of history forever. We will fight until the scourge of racial division is a distant memory. We will fight until we are, *one nation, under God, indivisible, with liberty and justice for all.*

PART XII

THE ROLE OF
THE CHURCH IN
AMERICAN LIFE

I believe the American church is in an identity crisis, and our culture is bearing the consequences. The church was charged by
Jesus Christ to be salt and light in the world. Only a remnant of the
American church is living up to that charge. Jesus said if the salt
loses its flavor, it is good for nothing but to be trodden under foot
(Matthew 5:13). Some historians say bad salt was used by the
Romans in road paving. It is no exaggeration to say in many ways,
today's church is being walked on. Even worse, it is laying down and
allowing itself to be walked on.

During the COVID-19 pandemic of 2020, churches were
ordered closed by government officials who had no legal authority
to do so. In fact, they were violating the Constitution, which protects religious liberty in the First Amendment of the Bill of Rights.
Pastors who refused to comply were threatened, fined, sued, and
arrested.

It was not that these pastors were oblivious to the dangers or
unconcerned about the welfare of their people. Rather, they were
responding to the obvious discrimination of declaring bars and
liquor stores to be "essential" services, but not churches. They were
also rebelling against the heavy-handed treatment by some mayors
and governors who began to act like petty tyrants.

Despite the pressure and persecution, the church I pastor and many olthers refused to close our doors. Most, however, went immediately to virtual services through live streaming and remained closed for much of 2020. Some are still closed.

The mayor of Louisville, Kentucky, threatened to record the license numbers of anyone caught attending a church service and fine each person $500. New York's Marxist mayor, Bill de Blasio, threatened to permanently close any church or synagogue daring to open after having been "told not to."

The church is supposed to hold government accountable, not the other way around. Unfortunately, many pastors are more concerned with fear of man than fear of God.

Christianity has lost a great deal of its influence because we have bought into the lie that churches and preachers should not be involved in politics. As a result, America is becoming increasingly secular and immoral. Pastors are afraid to openly defend our Judeo-Christian values in the public square.

If the anti-Christian forces manage to remove the church's influence from American life, our country will be lost. It will collapse under the weight of its own sin and rebellion.

We constantly hear the refrain, "separation of church and state." Few Americans realize the phrase has absolutely no legal authority. Thomas Jefferson coined the term "wall of separation" in a letter to the Danbury Connecticut Baptists to assure them of no encroachment into their affairs by the state. It was not an admonition for Christians to stay out of political issues, but an assurance the government would stay out of church affairs.[76] The Supreme Court mangled it in a 1947 ruling written by Hugo Black,[77] a former member of the Ku Klux Klan. It has been taken out of context ever since.

Our Founding Fathers did not want government in control of religious practice. That was how things operated in England, but it would not be so in America.

There was no fear of the influence of Christianity on American government and culture. In fact, the Founding Fathers welcomed it. Church had a crucial role in the development of America. The Bible was their most quoted source when speaking and writing about the grand experiment in liberty to which they pledged their "lives, fortunes and sacred honor."[78] Our Founders believed the fundamental rights of all human beings come from God. This belief is the basis of our Declaration of Independence and our Constitution.

They also believed America could not be a free, prosperous nation without the favor and guidance of Almighty God. Benjamin Franklin said, "God governs in the affairs of man."[79] Thomas Jefferson said, "God who gave us life gave us liberty."[80] George Washington said, "It is the duty of all nations, to acknowledge the Providence of Almighty God, to obey his will, to be grateful for his benefits, and humbly to implore his protection and favor."[81]

As the American colonies moved toward conflict with England, the loudest voices for freedom were the churches. John Adams said, "the pulpits thundered," and indeed they did.[82] Pastors played an essential role in the American Revolution, inspiring the nation to reject tyranny and fight for freedom. If not for their courage and persistence, there would be no United States of America.

Christians and churches were the most vehement opponents of slavery. They argued to Northerners and Southerners that slavery was a sin. It could not withstand the moral scrutiny of a just God. That truth hung in the air as a solemn warning until the Civil War, which took the lives of 600,000 Americans and brought slavery to an end. The light of liberty will always prevail in America because the darkness of tyranny cannot overcome it.

CHAPTER 57

MY CHURCH EXPERIENCE

As I have already explained, the first ten years of my life were spent in foster care. My foster parents took me to church regularly, indeed too often, in my child's mind. Life with my father was different. He was not a churchgoer until later in life and was unwilling to make me do something he would not do.

I was relieved. As a child, I found church boring and, in some cases, punishing. At the little Baptist churches I attended with my foster parents, there was nothing designed for youth. The closest thing I remember to a youth program was "Children's Day" in June, which was a worship service focused on children. I remember getting pinched or slapped on the head when I fell asleep during an evening service. It was not abuse, but it did not endear me to church.

In my immature mind, I made a decision if it were up to me, I would never go to church. Ironically, today I am a pastor. I remember vividly my childhood distaste for church and never want any children in my ministry to feel that way. Our church has the William Jackson Youth Center named for my father. I want our young people to enjoy the experience of church and remember it fondly.

One of the factors in the well-documented falling away by high school students and young adults is how they experienced church when they were children. It is incumbent upon pastors and churches to give our young people reasons to stay and great memories to anchor them.

I have no memories of organized children's activities. I remember making mischief. A few of us kids entertained ourselves with the son of the first pastor I remember—Rev. Hayes. His son Michael was a weak boy and we bullied him. Bullying was not socially condemned during my childhood. It was a rite of passage teaching you to stand up for yourself. Of course, there were kids like Michael who simply could not or would not fight back. Punching a bully in the nose to teach him a lesson is no longer an acceptable response, but it used to be quite effective.

Today, we turn to counseling, mediation, and even law enforcement. Those can be helpful in extreme situations, but there is no substitute for the fortitude developed by standing up to a bully. We are a weaker society raising a weaker generation of kids because we no longer teach or expect mental toughness. This is the new world of political correctness that produces "snowflakes" who melt at the slightest discomfort.

At some point, my foster parents figured out I could sing. I still have a great ear for music, but singing talent left me when my voice changed. As a youngster, my voice had range and strength. I became the lead singer of the adult choir and would have the congregation on their feet as I stepped out of the choir box and walked the aisles singing. I don't recall anyone teaching me to do that. It was just a gift God gave me. To this day, when I speak, I tend to leave the podium and come down from the platform. That started in Friendship Baptist on Third Street in Chester, Pennsylvania.

I was too young to be aware of church politics, but it was swirling all around me. Friendship Baptist was a split from the larger Shiloh Baptist. Then, Friendship Baptist split or closed and Rev. Hayes and his family disappeared from our lives. Mt. Levi Baptist was born under the leadership of Rev. Leslie Sapp. With each split, the church got smaller. Both these splits opened little storefronts on Third Street, and there the process began again. I left Mt. Levi when my father took me into his custody. Years later, the building was closed and to my knowledge, the church no longer exists.

I have no idea what precipitated these divisions, but the new pastors occasionally ate Sunday dinner at my foster home. No matter how scarce food was during the week, when the pastor was coming, a feast somehow managed to appear. On those occasions there were melt-in-your-mouth rolls, fried chicken, and sweet potato pie. On other occasions without the pastor, I remember there being nothing more than biscuits and syrup.

Third Street in Chester was what we would now call the inner city. When I was growing up, we called it the ghetto. Friendship Baptist Church was housed in a storefront not far from the corner of Third and Edward streets. One of the two theaters serving the black community was in that same block across the street from the church. Next to the movie theater was a shoeshine shop where the men gathered to swap stories and talk sports.

Mt. Levi was also on Third Street, but two miles east. The building looked like it might have been an old store or garage. It was a simple box shaped building of perhaps 1,000 square feet. Somehow, they managed a makeshift baptismal pool where I was first baptized at the age of nine. Without explanation, I was told it was "time." I made no decision for Christ. I simply complied with what I was told to do.

Of all the time I spent in church as a child, one incident stands out, which I talked about earlier. It happened at Mt. Levi. The minister they chose to lead this small congregation was Rev. Leslie Sapp. He had a large family with lots of boys. These were street kids from Philadelphia, and we got along just fine.

In fact, it was at their home I got my first and only "process." That was the hair treatment popular in that day among black men to straighten and wave the hair. I suppose black entertainers made it a fad. By the time I entered high school, James Brown was singing, "How you gonna get respect (when you haven't cut your process yet)." By then, the "process" was out, and the Afro was in.

Before I went to live with my father, I remember occasional moments when he exerted his influence. The "process" incident was one such occasion. He came to visit and took one look at my hair. As I recall, he said, "Boy, what is wrong with your hair?" It must have been a Saturday because I remember being taken immediately to the barber shop and having all my hair cut off. That was the only time I ever used straightening lye or anything else to change the texture of my hair.

Rev. Sapp was instrumental in the earliest spiritual encounter of my life. I cannot remember my exact age, but I believe I was about six years old. We were at an evening service, and I was sitting in the front pew as Rev. Sapp preached a sermon about Job. Suddenly, I was captivated, held in rapture. I understood every word. The message came alive for me. I had my first encounter with God. I never forgot that experience although I was very young when it happened.

It was nearly twenty years before I surrendered my life to Jesus Christ and became a Christian. When I did, memories of those days at Friendship Baptist and Mt. Levi Baptist came flooding back. I remembered hymns and Bible verses hidden deep within me. I had no conscious memory of those things until they were suddenly awakened. I realized God was working in me all the time, even in the somewhat illiterate version of Christianity to which I was exposed. He was sowing seeds in me that would one day bring the harvest of my salvation. God can indeed take a crooked stick and hit a straight lick.

CHAPTER 58

"THE BLACK CHURCH"

During the first decade of my life, Jim Crow was still alive and well in the South. I realize many in my generation who lived in the south experienced it. However, I lived just north of the Mason-Dixon line in Pennsylvania, and there was no legal segregation. I remember drinking milkshakes at the counter of the five-and-dime downtown. There was never an issue.

I often hear black Americans, particularly those who lean Left, say we are still suffering from the vestiges of slavery and Jim Crow. I believe that is true, but not in the way they mean it. They mean black people were artificially held back, are still behind, and can never catch up without special help. The Democrat Party's central tenet is "systemic racism" is the cause of every social and economic problem of the black community. This, they say, is the legacy of slavery and Jim Crow.

This is a demonstrable lie, but it is also a self-fulfilling prophecy. The past has a magnified effect when you will not let it go. It is especially pernicious when it absolves individuals from personal responsibility for their own lives and robs them of any sense of control over their own destiny. The notion that the destiny of any American of African ancestry is controlled by slavery, which ended 150 years ago, is cancerous and fatal. It must be rejected as demagoguery.

My great-grandparents were slaves and were set free after the Civil War. I have never been a slave. To talk about the issue as if it happened yesterday is to draw people into an abyss of bitterness, anger, and hatred. That is exactly what the Left and the Democrat Party want. They want black citizens bitter and paranoid. As long as people live in fear of a ubiquitous, racist enemy from which they must be saved, they are easier to manipulate and control by those who purport to be their saviors.

Democrat elites are the self-appointed saviors of Americans of African ancestry. Many black Americans have succeeded fabulously in this society. The liberal elites have no interest in showing others how to achieve as they did. They want all Americans who are not of European ancestry to see themselves as helpless victims whose only recourse is protests and riots, which destroy rather than build. These elites have constructed an industry designed to exploit the issue of race in America. It keeps Leftist elites in power by keeping black citizens captive to the psychological and emotional prison their masters have built for them.

The "black church" was originally a refuge from the harsh realities of bondage. It was the place where the humanity of displaced Africans was affirmed. Sadly, that which calls itself the black church has not matured into the fullness of the gospel. The church is not black or white. It is neither defined nor bound by the earthly limits of race and ethnicity. It is an eternal reality representing the kingdom of God on earth.

A church identifying itself by race has fallen into idolatry. It takes people captive rather than setting them free. The modern concept of the black church filled with racial animus against others on the basis of skin color is as pernicious as the antebellum concept of the white church defining itself by the superiority of its members to their black slaves.

I am not unmindful of the historical and demographic reality of black people being excluded from or segregated within predominantly "white" churches. However, the antebellum "white church" was a perversion of Christianity, turning it into a racial religion. It departed from its true mission as the repository of the gospel of Jesus Christ and the liberating truth of God's Word. It instead became an expression of the ideological need to justify slavery and racial subjugation. Repeating the same mistake by reversing the narrative betrays the good news Jesus Christ came to bring all people.

In spite of the ugly circumstances of slavery, God gave the captives a dream of freedom. They found their hope in Him. They learned God is the Great Liberator: "If God is for us, who can be against us?" (Romans 8:31). As these new Christians came to know the God who loved them, they knew they would be free.

It is amazing people could have hope in the midst of the most horrendous circumstances, and yet centuries later, their heirs, living in freedom and opportunity, could give in to despair. Although black people are still the most religious demographic group in America, their worldview has been poisoned by liberal theology and racial ideology. They have embraced the emptiness of the social gospel, which lacks spiritual power and relies on the power of the state to create "equity." It is a race-obsessed perspective informed by Marxism and collectivism.

Under "social justice" teachers, black churchgoers are taught racism is so pervasive in America not even the God who rescued the children of Israel out of Egypt can rescue them from the clutches of racism. The God who opens doors never again to be closed cannot open the door of opportunity for black Americans. He has finally found a problem He cannot solve. The hearts of "white people" are too hard and wicked, even for God to penetrate. It will take reparations or revolution to liberate poor black souls from the clutches of evil white men.

That kind of hate inspired thinking coupled with the impotent faith, which many black ministers teach today, is destructive. It is a "form of godliness but denying its power" (2 Timothy 3:5).

Oprah Winfrey, Beyoncé, Tina Turner, and many others developed their talent and found their confidence in church. All too often, black celebrities have abandoned the church for Buddhism, Hinduism, Scientology, and other exotic cults. They are much too sophisticated for the God of the Bible. The bridge that brought them over has long been forgotten as a relic of a bygone era. To paraphrase Abraham Lincoln, they "have forgotten God."[83]

The Civil Rights Movement was based in the church, which produced most of its leaders. As the Civil Rights Movement abandoned its roots and came under the influence of Leftist radicals, it lost its focus and influence. Instead of being the representative of Christ on earth, it became the representative of the Democrat Party and social grievance.

The church was not created by God to be a mouthpiece for aggrieved people, as desirable as that might be at times. The church was called and established to announce good news and proclaim God's Word. It is the herald of truth—unadulterated, absolute truth. The great struggle in America is not black against white, liberals against conservatives, or Republicans against Democrats. The American saga is the confrontation between good and evil.

Sadly, what is referred to as the black church today is making the same mistake the Southern white church made in the antebellum South. The Southern church became a symbol of racial solidarity instead of a testimony to the righteousness of God. In short, it ceased to be Christian and became a racial religion. There is no substantive spiritual or moral difference between a church of white supremacist theology and a church of black liberation theology. They are both institutions designed to justify the claims of a racial group instead of justifying the claims of Christ. They are both organizations of apostasy—an abomination to God and a stench in His nostrils.

The true church rejects the heresy of racial religion. It seeks to fulfill the ministry of reconciliation, which holds we can all be brothers and sisters in Christ. Many black Christians are taught a racial worldview, unwilling or unable to see it for the evil it is. It is a betrayal of the very gospel they claim to believe.

One reason for this departure from orthodoxy to embrace apostasy is the liberal seminaries from which many of today's pastors graduate. These institutions for the training of ministers have created a liberal theology that is spiritual poison. They convince their gullible students the application of high criticism to Scripture is a mark of intellectual superiority, when it is in fact spiritual stupidity. Marxist atheism is incompatible with biblical Christianity.

Pastors who are disciples of these institutions are more enamored of Karl Marx than the apostle Paul. Marx's destructive critique of free societies is brought to bear on the church and its underlying theology. Raphael Warnock, who won election as a Democrat U.S. Senator from Georgia, wrote in his 2021 book, *The Divided Mind of the Black Church*:

> To be sure, the Marxist critique has much to teach the black church. Indeed, it has played an important role in the maturation of black theology as an intellectual discipline, deepened black theology's apprehension of the interconnectivity of racial and class oppression and provided critical tools for a black church . . .[84]

Karl Marx was a virulent atheist who hated the church and Christianity. He saw it as a major obstacle to bringing humanity to the utopian state he envisioned. He would create the kingdom of God—but without God. Marx would be its philosopher king and creator. When his theory was finally put into practice, under the guise of seeking justice and liberation, mankind's sinful predisposition toward depravity was unleashed. Churches were closed, Christians and pastors imprisoned, tortured, and murdered and those who survived were driven underground. The pattern has always been the same. After all, to create utopia for the masses, the individual must be sacrificed.

The church is the body of Christ. It is committed to spiritual struggle, not class struggle. It is committed to righteousness, not racial identification. Racism and poverty are real problems, but they are mere symptoms of the underlying disease—sin. The antidote is not progressivism, socialism, or communism, but the blood of Jesus Christ which washes away our sin.

Marxism is not a cure for injustice. It is a far worse disease. The verdict is in. History has taught us Marx's utopian dream camouflages a tyrannical nightmare. The wellspring of justice is love, mercy, and righteousness. These come from God. There is no system that can make people compassionate; or make fathers and mothers care for their children; or make people choose sobriety over alcohol and drug addiction, or make people choose the law over criminality.

No matter how many justifications the Left creates, "socialism" and "racial justice" cannot excuse a father who abandons his children for a life of hedonism; or a young person who rejects education to run the streets, or an adult who refuses to work and chooses to rob and kill. These are not the product of the capitalist system. They are the products of a sinful heart.

The church is the arbiter of righteous justice, not racial justice. They are not the same. Racial justice implies special treatment for certain groups based on skin color. It divides people rather than uniting them. True justice, God's justice, needs no qualifier or racial classification. It is good for all. The church must herald this truth, not echo political correctness. It must be the place of high expectations and personal responsibility. There is no room for the blame game in the one institution where people know every individual is accountable to God. There is no affirmative action entrance to heaven and no racial exemption to the standard for salvation. The church must speak the truth in love no matter who happens to be sitting in the pews or listening on the airwaves.

CHAPTER 59

REMOVING GOD
FROM HISTORY
START HERE

S ecularism is on the rise, and God is no longer welcome in many precincts of society. The media, politics, science, entertainment, higher education, and even sports have expelled God.

The chairman of the House Judiciary Committee, Jerry Nadler, said on the house floor:

"What any religious tradition ascribes as God's will is no concern of this Congress."[85]

He was responding to Florida U.S. Rep. Greg Steube quoting Deuteronomy 22:5 on the wrongness of transgenderism. Congressman Steube spoke in opposition to the abominable Equality Act, which would enshrine transgenderism as a legally protected class based solely upon a person's declaration of a gender different from his or her genetic and biological gender. For Nadler, sexual perversion is a fitting matter for Congress to consider, but not what the Bible says about it.

High school football coach Joe Kennedy was fired in 2015 for praying on the field after a game. He started by simply praying alone silently. No players were asked or required to join the prayer. Many did voluntarily. The Bremerton School District in Washington State ordered him to cease and desist from praying on the field. He would be allowed to do so in a private office or space off the field or

he could wait until everyone left the field. Apparently one man praying silently on a field posed a threat to the establishment clause of
the First Amendment.

It is ironic that a man praying on the field after the game must
be stopped, but players kneeling in disrespect and repudiation of
the American Flag should be applauded and supported. In the
coach's case, everyone was leaving, and no one had to watch. In the
flag case, everyone who paid for a ticket was forced to watch.

The school district used some of the most convoluted reasoning
ever concocted, claiming they were protecting the religious liberty
of parents and students attending the game. During their departure,
they might glance at the field and notice a man praying silently.
That is apparently enough to precipitate a constitutional crisis.

Thanks be to God, the Supreme Court finally ruled 6–3 in
Coach Kennedy's favor in June 2022 and blasted the school district's
suppression of his First Amendment rights.[86]

The truth is hostility toward Christianity has been growing in
recent years, largely fueled by the homosexual lobby, which has
become a kind of political mafia. They know the Bible condemns
their behavior, so the slightest whiff of a Bible-believing Christian
is a declaration of war. Jesus defines gender as male and female
(Matthew 19:4 and Mark 10:6) and multiple texts condemn homosexuality as an abomination to God (Leviticus 18:22 and 20:13). It
also says those who practice homosexuality shall be denied entry
into heaven (1 Corinthians 6:9) unless they repent like other sinners.

One need not quote these verses or speak openly on the subject.
If you are discovered to believe the Bible or attend a church that
believes what the Bible says about sexual morality, you are a target
—a threat to "democracy."

As discussed in earlier portions of this book, the obsession with
normalizing homosexuality and punishing anyone who dares disagree
has the feel of a cult targeting heretics. Those who openly express
love and faith in Jesus Christ and believe the Bible is the inerrant word
of the Living God are met with hostility and hatred. Some of these
anti-God activists and bigots are willing to act on their hostility. The
FBI looked into a credible death threat against me, and it turned out
to be a "gay activist" who threatened to shoot me.

Given the history and founding of our country, one would not expect to find the anti-Christian bigotry which has become so virulent today. Christians have been persecuted for 2,000 years, but America is a Judeo-Christian nation where followers of Jesus have lived in relative peace and security throughout our history.

The demonic forces warring against God's people for thousands of years have been held at bay in the United States because of our Christian culture and constitutional restraints on our government. A political sledgehammer is pounding against these walls of protection. Unless we attend to the matter urgently, we could see bigotry devolve into violence.

When the first settlers arrived on the shores of the American continent, they entered a covenant with God and each other for a civil body politic by which to govern themselves. When John Winthrop spoke to the *Mayflower* pilgrims, he spoke of a city on a hill.[87] It was a distinctly Christian vision, which he borrowed from Jesus' words to His disciples in Matthew 5:14: "You are the light of the world. A city that is set on a hill cannot be hidden."

After a long, dangerous journey, it was faith that filled the travelers with optimism for the New World. They foresaw the birth of something that would represent God's kingdom on earth.

Four hundred years later, we have witnessed federal, state, and local governments targeting the Little Sisters of the Poor, Hobby Lobby, or some bakery, florist, or photography shop because they put their religious convictions ahead of the demands of the state. These actions would shock Winthrop and all the patriots who succeeded him.

Above all, America was to be the place where Christians could worship and practice their faith without governmental hindrance. There are now in our country people who believe every individual must submit his or her own conscience to the dictates of tyrannical anti-Christian forces. This would be expected of a totalitarian nation, but not in "the land of the free." Those who revere the Constitution find this abhorrent. Even more disturbing is the future it portends if we continue on this path.

The rejection of Judeo-Christian culture and principles has become more pronounced since the 1960s. Lawsuits have been filed demanding "under God" be taken out of the Pledge of Allegiance.[88] The ACLU and Freedom From Religion has demanded crosses be taken down at military cemeteries and removed from memorials to our heroes fallen in battle. At least seven times, former President Obama misquoted the Declaration of Independence, leaving out the word "Creator." President Biden seems to be following suit, acknowledging we are "endowed" with freedom and rights but refusing to state by Whom those unalienable rights are granted.[89]

Same sex "marriage" has become a sledgehammer against Christians in their work lives and businesses. You can be fired from your job, driven out of business, and made anathema by the media for asserting what most Christians know to be absolute truth—marriage is a union of one man and one woman. Christians are now punished for believing what the Bible has taught for thousands of years and the world has known even longer.

Barack Obama's administration was the most aggressive in American history (exceeding the Clinton years) to use the federal government as a weapon against Bible-believing Christians to force the perverse sexual morality of LGBTQ activists upon society. Joe Biden is following suit.

Today's totalitarian Left denies the existence of absolute morality or the Absolute Authority. Human beings, they say, can decide for themselves what is moral and what is not. They will decide for the rest of us what is right and true. The self-appointed elites are sufficiently endowed with superior wisdom and enlightenment to be our moral guides. When a nation has sinful human beings as the final arbiters of morality, the consequences will always be cataclysmic. This is where we are headed today unless there is a 180-degree turn, and it must happen soon. The clock is ticking on the moral and spiritual time bomb lit by Marxist revolutionaries in our country sixty years ago.

How did we lose our Judeo-Christian focus? George Washington and our Founding Fathers prayed for the grace and courage to establish this nation. Today, Marx-influenced professors and scholars have convinced many of our citizens that the Founders missed the mark by a wide margin. Although obviously imperfect, the truth is they were godly men of integrity and honor. The Left has reduced them to one-dimensional caricatures: slave owners.

This is intended to undermine the legitimacy of America and our way of life. After all, if the Founders were evil slave owners, the nation they produced cannot possibly be good. The Christianity they practiced is merely a white supremacist religion meant to keep Americans of African descent enslaved and themselves in power. This narrative holds there is nothing about our founding or our Founders to be admired because America's roots are rotten. The religion of Christianity, which was used to justify this rottenness, is discredited, and needs to be discarded.

Some mainstream denominations have effectively done just that. They have discarded the Bible, at least as an authoritative guide. It remains as a relic from which poetry and inspirational sayings may occasionally be found, but that aside, it is irrelevant. During one Lenten season, the United Church of Christ suggested church members do a carbon fast[90]—drive electric cars or ride bicycles to atone for their sins against Mother Earth. Many of the institutions calling themselves churches have replaced the biblical admonitions of holiness and righteousness for cultish adherence to political correctness. They have rejected the true and living God for the golden calf of Marxist ideology.

Many churches in America—Protestant and Catholic—have been seduced by doctrines of demons and robbed of their power. If America's future is to be greater than its past, the church must take its rightful and central place as a prophetic voice to the nation.

CHAPTER 60

LIFE AND GODLINESS

America is in desperate need of moral and spiritual renewal. The church must be the instrument of that awakening. As we conclude this part of the book, we should remember what Jesus said in Matthew 5:13–16:

> "You are the salt of the earth; but if the salt loses its flavor, how shall it be seasoned? It is then good for nothing but to be thrown out and trampled underfoot by men. You are the light of the world. A city that is set on a hill cannot be hidden. Nor do they light a lamp and put it under a basket, but on a lampstand, and it gives light to all who are in the house. Let your light so shine before men, that they may see your good works and glorify your Father in heaven."

God wants to be involved in every dimension of our lives. We cannot separate political issues from spiritual issues. George Washington said in his Farewell Address, "Of all the dispositions and habits which lead to political prosperity, **religion and morality** are indispensable supports" (emphasis added).[91] Therefore, we need to look at political engagement and voting as crucial ways in which we can take action to please God.

It is not acceptable for Christians, especially pastors, to hide their faith and commitment to Christ out of fear of opposition. We should expect some will be offended by our light. In fact, if you are a Christian and no one has ever been offended by your stand for Christ, perhaps you are not standing. Stand up. Step up. Speak up. Your family, your community, and your country will be the better for it in the end.

The central figure in American history and the source of our success as a nation is God. He has blessed us beyond measure and beyond what we could ever deserve. We must never forget Him or fail to promote the principles that made our nation possible.

America is at a critical moment in our history. Christians and churches must rise to the call. The church must stand for liberty and truth, just as it did during the Revolutionary War. If we don't act now, we may look back at this time and discover this is the moment we lost it.

The faith that served as the essential ingredient in the founding of America and its unparalleled success is the same faith that can lead us out of the confusion and decay threatening our continued existence. If we will remember and follow George Washington's counsel and restore the indispensable supports of religion and morality to their central place in American life, we will secure a bright future and fulfill our national destiny.

PART XIII

SECURING AMERICA'S FUTURE

*"Freedom is never more than one generation
from extinction."*

—Ronald Reagan

A world without America is unimaginable. No other country has
experienced such astounding domestic success along with
international stature and influence. There has never been a perfect
nation, and America is no exception. Nonetheless, we are the greatest place in the world to live, work, raise a family, build a business,
and pursue our dreams. That is why we don't have a problem with
people wanting to get out. We have to manage the vast numbers
who wish to make America their home. Our fellow citizens who
carp constantly about social injustice never leave because no other
country protects the freedom to hate it and publicly express
that hatred.

The early immigrants who came escaping poverty, famine, and
religious persecution were full of hope for what the New World had

to offer. They faced many dangers including starvation, violence, and death, but they persevered because the possibilities were limitless. The future was theirs to seize.

Even my ancestors, then slaves, heard the words of the Declaration of Independence and were filled with hope. They didn't experience the promise in their own lives, but I have. Americans of African descent enjoy more opportunity and prosperity than any African people anywhere in the world.

The Founding Fathers set the stage for generation after generation to grow and thrive—regardless of skin color or national origin. All of our ancestors have suffered in some way. They did not whine about life's unfairness. They got on with it.

Each person in each generation faces the challenges of establishing a set of ideals by which to live. Inherent in the concept of self-government is governing one's self. That is the great challenge every one of us faces, rich and poor alike. The better we are at governing ourselves, the safer we are from government tyranny. We should never expect the government or anyone else to do for us what we can and should do for ourselves. We should never ask or allow the government to usurp from us the right of moral sovereignty to decide for ourselves what is best for us and our families. This is the heart and soul of self- government.

John Adams said: "Our Constitution was made only for a moral and religious people. It is wholly inadequate to the government of any other."[92]

The vision of our Founding Fathers was a nation of moral virtue. It would not ultimately be the fear of government that would prevent harming our neighbor, but the fear of God and a moral conscience. In a culture of personal virtue, freedom can flourish.

This far-reaching vision has produced the greatest nation in the history of mankind. Communist China, with nearly 1.5 billion people, has allowed enough freedom to grow their economy. But their people live under the command of Communist Party leaders. They deny what Americans hold more dear than life itself—freedom. It is the God-given right of every individual. It is not our wealth that makes America a shining city on a hill. It is adherence to the fundamental principle of freedom guided by virtue.

If the light that America has lit for the world were ever snuffed out, mankind would plummet into darkness. Therefore, the flame of freedom must be kept burning bright in our hearts, not only for our sakes, but for sake of the entire world.

CHAPTER 61

THE REAL MEANING OF
FREEDOM

No group of people in America should be more committed to freedom than those of us who are descended from slaves. The constant theme of Rev. Martin Luther King was liberty— "free at last." Rarely does one hear civil rights leaders talk about freedom. Freedom is the right of every individual. A group is only free by virtue of each person having the right to determine his or her own destiny. If the group is deciding your destiny, you are not free.

So-called leaders of the black community today do not speak of freedom. They have embraced Leftist and collectivist thinking in which individual aspirations do not matter. Conforming to the collective will is the Orwellian freedom they promote. To be free, in their minds, is to bow to the established orthodoxy. To refuse is to be targeted for destruction.

Unfortunately, this trend toward cultural totalitarianism in America is growing. One would have thought, with the collapse of the Soviet Union, Marxist ideology would diminish, especially in a country such as ours. The fact it has not is proof of its cult-like hold on the human mind. When I was in college in the late '60s and early '70s, it was fashionable for students to carry *Quotations from Chairman Mao Tse-Tung*, a.k.a. "The Little Red Book." The brutality of communist revolutions and the terror of their regimes should make any thoughtful person recoil. Communists never "liberate" people; they enslave them. We should be alarmed by the ease with which the evil of Marxism has gained popularity in our country.

The communism that once frightened most Americans has taken on the camouflage of "social justice." It manifests as Critical Race Theory, "equity," "diversity" and "inclusion." Communism by another name is no less dangerous.

Is there any real danger of a violent communist revolution in the United States? I hope not, but recent polling indicates two-thirds of the American people believe there could be another civil war. The rapid cultural change is so shocking and the division so sharp that some have concluded that just as Marx believed violent revolution is inevitable, many Americans feel the Left can be stopped only through violent resistance. As Clay Higgins, Congressman from Louisiana said, "You can vote your way into socialism, but you have to shoot your way out."

I am not recommending or predicting violence. I have publicly and repeatedly denounced violence as a solution to our political problems. I have been asked many times whether we have come to the point where a violent response is necessary to right the ship of state and return our culture to sanity. My answer has always to remind my audiences on radio and online that we have not exhausted the constitutional mechanisms at our disposal. Not enough of us vote or participate in the political process. Only half of Christians are registered to vote. Only half of those registered actually go to the polls. That is where the fight must be waged.

I am praying for and expecting a third Great Awakening in our country. This is not only a spiritual revival about salvation and acceptance of the gospel. That would be wonderful. I am talking about a cultural awakening to the blessing of American freedom, prosperity, and potential, an awakening to the beauty and brilliance of our founding principles. It includes a recognition that our national success is neither an accident, nor is it born out of the exploitation of minority groups. There are principles that work in life for nations as well as individuals. America struck upon those principles and our reward is the stuff of history.

Those principles are not the invention of man but the wisdom of God. Thus, we answer to an Authority higher than ourselves, and there are rules we must follow, made for us, not by us. Each of us is accountable to that Authority in this life and the next. As such, we are responsible for ourselves and our families as the most basic building blocks of society. Collective progress is a by-product of individual progress, not the other way around. Individual achievement is the platform for the next generation of individuals to achieve the dreams that succeeding generations will inherit and build on. That is the dynamic of freedom, the formula for an ever brighter future.

Seen through the eyes of Marxism, our national success is just more capitalist exploitation, colonialism, racism, and sexism. Our Declaration of Independence, Constitution, and the laws governing our society are mere drapery hiding underlying rottenness. This Marxist poison courses like a plague through nearly every institution of cultural influence: government, public schools, colleges, sports, entertainment, journalism, and even churches, synagogues, and mosques.

If it continues unchecked, there will be no need for a violent overthrow of America. It is already happening, right before our eyes. They are well along in establishing a new cultural norm which can serve to expand the power and influence they already hold in every institution of society.

Any open attempt to subvert the Constitution and assume dictatorial powers would be met with fierce and violent resistance. However, the steady transformation we are witnessing is death by a thousand cuts. A totalitarian government taking away our freedom at the point of a gun leaves no room for misinterpretation. A totalitarian culture using social pressure, labeling us bad people for not submitting, can be excused as an over zealous pursuit of the common good. During the height of the COVID pandemic, anyone refusing to submit to the shot was accused of trying to kill people. We were labeled selfish and irresponsible. Even after the CDC admitted the so called vaccine prevented neither contracting nor spreading COVID, many institutions continued to require it. Military personnel who had served honorably were threatened with less than honorable discharges for refusing the shot. Although many adverse events such as scarring and swelling of the heart were documented, the government did not relent.

While some are looking for a violent revolution, what is happening is a long march though the culture. It is like a metastasizing cancer. The question is whether we have diagnosed it in time to cure it.

The frog is in the kettle, and the heat has been steadily turned up over time. Peaceful, law-abiding American citizens have lost jobs, businesses, and their freedom for violating the unwritten dictates of an increasingly totalitarian culture. Leftists and progressives once used the rhetoric of "tolerance." Their new vocabulary of "diversity," "equity," and "inclusion" requires intolerance toward anyone opposing the new orthodoxy. The old mantra of peaceful co-existence has been replaced with "de-platforming" anyone saying things deemed unacceptable. For example, California's legislature proposed punishing misgendering with fines and imprisonment. Proponents of the law claimed that conservatives over stated the case, but Politifact admitted that "Violations of the bill could, under limited circumstances, be treated as a misdemeanor with punishment of up to one year in jail and/or a $1,000 fine." Even in California, these anti-free speech proposals have not become law; not yet at least.

A *UCLA Law Review* article by Chan Tov McNamarah and published in 2020 said this:

> ". . . the deliberate misgendering of [transpersons] . . . [is] an arrogant attempt to belittle and humiliate." Given this, courts addressing the issue have almost uniformly found the practice hostile, objectively offensive, and degrading, and the Equal Employment Opportunity Commission (EEOC) has repeatedly held that purposeful misgendering constitutes harassment actionable under Title VII of the Civil Rights Act of 1964 (Title VII).[93]

That is where Marxism leads. Indeed, that is where they want to take us. Leftist elites are more than willing to sacrifice the freedom, blood and treasure of others for what they believe to be the greater good.

It is difficult to imagine that people who have experienced unparalleled liberty and prosperity would subject themselves to power hungry people. Yet the Big Lie has great allure. It never dies a natural death. It must be killed on the battlefield of ideas. It will not surrender to reason. I believe there are enough Americans who have not drunk the progressive Kool-Aid that we can still vote our way out.

The Bible teaches that before God openly intervenes again in human history, there will be a world dictator—the antichrist—who demands absolute obedience or death. What better groundwork could be laid than the Marxist-inspired effort to enforce group think on everyone? They ruthlessly silence speech and punish freedom of conscience. In universities, where vigorous debate should be the norm, students and faculty refuse to hear or allow speakers with a conservative viewpoint. They disrupt conservatives' meetings with violence and destruction of property.

We once believed the cure for bad speech is good speech, not censorship. It was an article of constitutional faith that good ideas will prevail over bad ideas. Freedom of conscience, which underlies the First Amendment, was once considered sacred.

Every American once subscribed to this famous quote: "I wholly disapprove of what you say—and will defend to the death your right to say it." The Left has now bought into the antithesis: "If I disapprove of what you say, I will do anything in my power to stop you from saying it."

Media, journalism, entertainment, and education have all become ideological. Most reporters are Leftist ideologues masquerading as journalists. Some have gone so far as to say objectivity is no longer an appropriate ethic. For example, they proudly declare those who do not "believe" in climate change will not be given platforms, quoted in their newspapers or interviewed on their programs. This is what passes for professional "journalism" today.

CNN, once a respected international news outlet, uses analysts only from the hard Left, and pretends they are covering the full spectrum of thought. They preach a superficial diversity. What difference does it make if people have different complexions or genders but the same ideological perspective? Today's newsrooms operate like elections in communist countries. Everyone is "free" to vote, but it had better be for the candidates and ideas the party designates. That is not freedom.

Long years of indoctrination have precipitated an American identity crisis. Olympians, professional sports figures, and entertainers disrespect and burn our flag, turn their back on our national anthem, mock patriotism, and side with those who would destroy our country if they could. Millionaire NBA players railed against America while defending the brutal dictatorial regime of Communist China. They belittle America's freedom and defend China's tyranny. Such national self-loathing is suicidal, and Americans must not drink the Kool-Aid with them.

CHAPTER 62

FROM CLASSICAL LIBERALISM TO MARXIST MANIA

Classical liberal thought in the late nineteenth and early twenti-eth centuries valued free speech and eschewed the expansion of the state to dangerous levels of power.

Today's liberals think instead like Leftist German intellectuals of the late nineteenth and early twentieth centuries. Their most prominent social writers believed German organizational genius demanded suppression of individualism for the good of the collective. Today's American "liberals" likewise want to suppress and punish all thinking and expression contradictory to their vision. Pre-Nazi German elites spoke of freedom, but they did not mean for the individual. They meant freedom to subsume every individual for the good of the state. When the Left in America speaks of equal-ity, they do not mean equal opportunity. The words "democracy" and "equality" are Orwellian code words for the Left's intention to impose their collective will on all of us.

Modern Marxists in America control almost all aspects of our culture. They have deconstructed the family, infiltrated the church, and are, as I write this book, moving to reshape the military from a warrior machine into a "woke" mob. Their control over the media is nearly absolute. There are exceptions—conservative talk shows, *The Washington Times, The Epoch Times, The New York Post, Fox News* (for now), *Newsmax*, *One America News*, and *American Family Radio* among them. We need more pro-American journalists, entertainers, professors, teachers, and corporate leaders to stop the long march of Marxism through our culture.

The entertainment industry is little more than a propaganda department of the Marxist Democrat Party. Even professional sports have succumbed to progressive ideology. The NBA, the NFL, and MLB all have sided with far-left approaches on social issues. The NBA attacked North Carolina for passing a law requiring restrooms and locker rooms be separate according to biological gender. The NBA threatened to pull its All-Star game from the state. After Georgia passed an election integrity law in 2021, Major League Baseball yanked its All-Star Game from Atlanta and played it instead in Denver. Incredibly, the move was backed by Coca-Cola, Delta Airlines, and other corporations headquartered in Atlanta.

The NFL bowed to Colin Kaepernick's America-hating insanity for years, losing some of its audience for good. As stated earlier, I have stopped watching professional sports. I want to be entertained, not insulted. I suspect many Americans share my sentiment because viewership of professional sports has decreased. How owners and managers intelligent enough to run these teams could be so stupid as to bow to these juvenile antics and treat them as serious expressions of legitimate grievances is beyond me. Kaepernick is nothing more than a misguided, half-baked, wannabe revolutionary. Thanks to Nike, he has become richer for his anti-American tantrums than he ever could have been as a mediocre quarterback.

The cult captivating so many of our institutions and seizing the imagination of so many of our people is evil. The future they have in mind for America is one we must never accept. It ends in mass social and political suicide. We must expose the cult and destroy it before it destroys us, all along with the America we know and love.

CHAPTER 63

A VISION FOR AMERICA'S FUTURE

Conservatives are often accused of trying to return America to its darkest days. It is difficult to determine whether the Left makes such claims out of ignorance or willful demagoguery. Perhaps it is both. No sane human being is interested in reinstating the mistakes of the past. No one wants to return to slavery, Jim Crow segregation, or a time when women could not vote, own property, and were considered the possession of their husbands and fathers.

Among the many mistakes the Left makes, one of the most egregious is to define our country based on the worst of our history. Americans are not perfect people. Our national sins are a function of our fallen humanity, not some unique predisposition in the American psyche. No person or people save One is without sin. It is not as if the whole world were a utopia and it was ruined on July 4, 1776. Yet that is the picture the Left paints.

The truth is the world has always been filled with barbarism, violence, conquest, and slavery. That is why the first American settlers wanted to establish a "New World." They were trying to escape the "old world" in more than a geographical sense. The Founding Fathers were born into a barbaric world, but the Declaration of Independence was one of the most civilizing documents ever published. Until that moment, wars were fought for conquest, subjugation, and power. The signers of the Declaration ushered in a new era of human history in which a war would be fought to defend the lofty principle of freedom and the right of a people to determine their own destiny.

This is one of the greatest stories in history. It is noble and heroic. Whatever our national sins and mistakes, if we are to have hope for the future, we must celebrate the virtues and triumphs of our past. To wallow in the past, as the Left would have us do, is to become ensnared in anger and bitterness over things we cannot change. Viewed in the context of the world, Americans have a history of which we can be proud and a nation for which we should be grateful.

Returning to the values that made America great is not returning to the mistakes of our ancestors. Our vision for America is a nation of freedom. We must restore the vitality of our Constitution, especially the First and Second Amendments, which are essential to liberty in our everyday lives. We must recommit to personal responsibility for ourselves and our families. The toughness and resilience of Americans is part of our legacy as pioneers, indentured servants, and yes, slaves. From Jamestown and the Pilgrims to the first Africans, to the waves of immigrants arriving on these shores, every people group has faced untold hardship. We all persevered. We are Americans.

CHAPTER 64

THE CURSE OF WELFARE

The earliest settlers to this continent found no government welfare program to sustain them and no civil rights laws to protect them. They struggled, sacrificed, and built lives for themselves. Neighbors helped neighbors, but no one asked others to do what he could do for himself. We helped each other where help was needed, but no one expected others to raise their children, bring in their crops, or feed their families. There was a fierce streak of personal pride and independence. I remember my father turning down government cheese and powdered milk that was handed out in poor neighborhoods. He worked for a living and was proud of it. He did not take handouts and was ferocious about it. That was once the cultural norm, ingrained in the American spirit. We must reclaim that spirit, rather than continuing down the road of entitlement and victimhood. No one is "entitled" to share in what another earns.

Because of our Judeo-Christian culture and heritage, Americans are the most generous people on the face of the earth. That is why there is so much volunteerism and charity in our country. One of the biggest mistakes we ever made was the creation of a welfare society. It has sapped Americans of independence and toughness. It has enslaved too many people in intergenerational poverty. It has substituted government compulsion for human compassion.

Compassion creates bonds of cooperation and friendship; compulsion engenders only division, dependency, and resentment.

We are nearly a quarter of a millennium old with more than 330 million people. It is probably unrealistic to think we can end welfare as we know it, but we can begin. No able-bodied, mentally healthy person should be on welfare longer than it takes to get the training and education to hold a full-time job. No woman should be rewarded with more welfare for having more children and no husband. The same is true for public housing. It should be temporary. There should be no such thing as lifetime residency.

This approach may seem harsh, but it is based on true compassion and respect for the dignity of every human being. After the historic welfare reform of 1996, the welfare rolls were reduced, and many people found worthwhile jobs and recovered their dignity. People need to be encouraged to reach their God-given potential. Every human being has gifts, talents, and abilities. If they are allowed to live off of others, those abilities atrophy. We need every American operating at full throttle if we're going to lead in the twenty-first century as we did in the twentieth. Welfare only weakens us.

CHAPTER 65

GOVERNMENT SCHOOL INDOCTRINATION

George Washington was highly intelligent, but he never spent a day in a classroom. He was homeschooled and tutored by his mother and those she chose to educate him. Government programs begin with the expressed intention of helping people, but often end up hurting them. Instead of being an educational panacea, "public schools" became a government monopoly. Because they are government institutions, it was inevitable public schools would become political institutions. They are the primary source of teacher union funding and power.

Teachers unions are major political partners in the Democrat machine. As a result, government schools have become a tool of the Democrat Party. They inculcate children with a Leftist worldview rendering them more likely to become loyal soldiers on the Democrat field. Recently, they have become much more explicit about it, but John Dewey and Horace Mann, fathers of American public education, were far-left progressives and Marxists at heart. In that sense, public schools are doing exactly what the originators had in mind.

Today, schools are absorbed by Critical Race Theory or its more euphemistic label, Ethnic Studies. Students in public school classroom are there to learn about homosexuality, transgenderism, and "intersectionality" (when a single person is a victim of more than one form of oppression, such as being black and transgender).

They are unlikely to learn anything positive about George Washington and the Founding Fathers. Students are more likely to know about gender transitioning than about the transition of our country from being ruled by a monarchy to being governed as a constitutional republic. They are taught to denigrate the Founding Fathers as slave owners rather than honor them as the architects of American freedom. America's students are introduced to the false "fairness" of socialism but learn little or nothing about the creativity and compassion of capitalism and the free enterprise system. They will not be told socialism has brought only poverty, misery, and death while free enterprise has raised the standard of living for everyone.

The American education system no longer reaffirms American culture and values. I envision an America where all totalitarian ideologies are cast on the waste dump of human history never to rise and trouble us again. I see an America where Christianity is affirmed, not attacked; where a traditional biblical view of family and gender is acknowledged as normal, not treated as bigotry.

Our education system should respect our Judeo-Christian values rather than oppose and attack them. It should reject all racial, cultural, and economic divisions and work to unite us in the vision of *one nation under God, indivisible, with liberty and justice for all.* Our educational system should teach each generation why we are proud and grateful to be Americans.

CHAPTER 66

RESTORING THE TRADITIONAL FAMILY

I was born into a broken home. My mother and father were already estranged when they came together to conceive me. According to my father, it was on the last occasion of my parents' intimacy. My mother was a confused twenty-two-year-old and my father was angry and bitter over a second failed marriage. Neither of them was in a position to care for a new baby. There was some back and forth between them over my care, but ultimately my father assumed control and placed me in foster care. The arrangements were temporary and informal at first, but at fourteen months old I was placed in a permanent home under the care of Rebecca and Willie Molet. I remained with them until the age of ten.

I was born in 1952. Most of the children born in America at that time came into a home with their biological mother and father. In 1960, 75 percent of black children were born to their married parents and just 25 percent into single-parent households.[94] Today, those numbers are reversed with 75 percent of black children born out of wedlock.[95] In Richmond Virginia, not far from my home, only 15 percent of black children are born into a married home—a drastic difference.[96]

The problem started in 1965 with Great Society programs intended to rescue black and poor citizens from poverty. The law of unintended consequences played out to devastating effect. There is a legitimate question whether the consequences were completely unintended. Daniel Patrick Moynihan warned of the looming crisis in the black family.[97] He was called a racist for pointing it out and told to recant. In actuality, he was prophetic. If only policymakers had listened.

My vision of America is one where we restore the centrality and influence of the two-parent, married, monogamous family made up of one man and one woman as husband and wife, father and mother. Those who choose differently would be free to construct their lives as they see fit. But the cultural consensus should be the two-parent, married family with a mom and dad, is the normal, optimal and ideal way to bring up children. This is key to a healthy America with a prosperous future.

CHAPTER 67

THE LEFTIST ATTACK ON CHRISTIANITY

In my vision of America, being true to our Christian cultural heritage does not mean running afoul of the Constitution or trampling the rights of religious minorities. Indeed, we cannot be true to our founding principles without adhering to Judeo-Christian values. How can it be unconstitutional to pray when the convention and the delegates who gave us the Constitution acknowledged the importance of prayer? America has no official religion, nor should we. That does not mean we must deny our Christian culture. It is not a violation of the Constitution to acknowledge the truth.

The Christian principle of freedom of conscience also protects non-Christians. During the 2,000-year history of Christianity, this principle has not always been practiced perfectly, but human imperfection does not invalidate the principle. Hindus are free to worship and practice their religion in America. Muslims also have the same constitutional right. Atheists are free to worship the idol of their own intellects. That said, we are not a Hindu, Muslim, or atheist culture. Every poll ever taken indicates the overwhelming majority of our people self-identify as Christians. The future of America lies in accepting that historic reality while protecting the right of others to worship or not worship as their consciences dictate.

The Left resists this approach because they want to sanitize the country of our Christian identity. Christian morality rejects homosexuality, transgenderism, and abortion as grievously sinful. In the America I envision for this century, no Christian will ever be persecuted or punished for holding to biblical teaching on sexual morality or any other issue. American culture should exalt virtue and discourage immorality. American moral ideals are informed by the Bible. Moral standards should never be set by popular whims, fads, or mob hysteria. Standards are set by Almighty God, and as such they are eternal and not subject to change. When Alexis de Tocqueville visited America, he found that the secret of our culture was in the churches:

"I sought for the key to the greatness and genius of America in her harbors . . . ; in her fertile fields and boundless forests; in her rich mines and vast world commerce; in her public school system and institutions of learning. I sought for it in her democratic Congress and in her matchless Constitution.

"Not until I went into the churches of America and heard her pulpits flame with righteousness did I understand the secret of her genius and power.

"In the United States, the influence of religion is not confined to the manners, but it extends to the intelligence of the people . . .Christianity, therefore, reigns without obstacle, by universal consent . . ."

Just as the church was a compelling force for securing our freedom, it is the best hope America has for preserving it. If the church will reassert its rightful place as the moral and cultural center of American life, our country will endure and prosper as that shining city on a hill. We must do everything in our power to it bring it to pass and rely on God to do the rest.

CONCLUSION

Why do I love this country so much? Because I believe it is a gift from God, and we are a providential nation. Being an American is a great blessing. Unfortunately, as I have explained, indoctrination has robbed too many Americans of the profound gratitude we should have for our national heritage. I wrote this book to provide reasons why I, as the great-grandson of slaves, have such patriotic affection and great hope for my country and our people.

We desperately need a Third Great Awakening. The Left is attempting to separate us from our godly heritage with devastating effect. We must rely on divine intervention to help us restore our foundational principles in the hearts of our people.

It is going to require a spiritual awakening, a rebirth of our national consciousness as a Christian culture. I believe the seeds of that awakening are already sprouting. I expect to live to see them in full bloom.

I especially want my fellow Americans of African descent to hear, understand and embrace my perspective. I also wrote this book to open their eyes to see America for what she truly is - the greatest place on earth to realize your potential and fulfill your dreams. That is why I spend time putting American history in the context of the world at large. I challenge every American to take a globe of the earth and spin it until you find a better place to live. If you find it, go there. You won't because there is no better place for the business of living.

Every nation on earth has division and injustice. It may be racial, tribal or religious, but the human impulses of selfishness, hatred and destruction have plagued every people group in the world. However, no nation has done more to affirm human freedom and dignity than the United States of America.

The root of our problems has never been race or poverty, but the human condition. Like every other nation we have a sin problem. Unlike most other nations, we have seen God as our answer and held ourselves to be accountable to Him. That is why our motto is "in God we trust." That is why it is engraved on our money and emblazoned on the wall of the Congressional Visitors Center. That is why our Pledge of Allegiance includes the words, "one nation under God." America doesn't work without God. America has worked because in spite of our national sins, we have never been without God. Millions of Americans have fasted, prayed, interceded and sought God's face on behalf of our nation. He has heard our prayers and answered.

It is my hope that a book written by a patriot who is the great-grandson of slaves would inspire all Americans to realize how blessed we are. It is time to discard the divisive racial classifications and cast aside the ancient grievances. We are fellow citizens and fellow human beings living in a shining city set on a hill.

My ancestors came from the African continent over 200 years ago, but I have never lived there. They came on slave ships and lived in bondage for several generations. I am their heir, but I have never lived in bondage. I was born in freedom, blessed with opportunity, and nurtured in the hope, the heritage and the promise of America.

I am not ashamed of my ancestral heritage, but I am not an African. I am an American. This is my native land, my country, my home. Our citizens come from every continent on earth, and I am proud to call them my fellow Americans. We are one people with a common hope and a common national destiny. Our ancestors came on different ships, but we are all in the same boat now.

Abraham Lincoln, in the closing words of the Gettysburg Address, expressed my vision for the country I know and love:

[T]hat this nation, under God, shall have a new birth of freedom—and that government of the people, by the people, for the people, shall not perish from the earth.[98]

I took the title of this book from my favorite patriotic hymn. Written in 1831 and titled "America," it came to be known as "My Country 'Tis of Thee." Twenty-four-year-old seminary student Samuel Francis Smith wrote the lyrics. As I finish this book, that song is now 191 years old, but we are still singing it. My vision is an America in which this song resonates with gratitude in every heart—regardless of race, age, religion, income or ancestral origin:

My country, 'tis of thee,
Sweet land of liberty,
Of thee I sing;
Land where my fathers died,
Land of the pilgrims' pride,
From ev'ry mountainside
Let freedom ring!

The last stanza is the closing prayer for this book and my continued prayer for our country:

Our fathers' God to Thee,
Author of liberty,
To Thee we sing.
Long may our land be bright,
With freedom's holy light,
Protect us by Thy might,
Great God our King!

NOTES

Introduction: Why I Wrote This Book

1. Letter "From John Adams to Massachusetts Militia 11 October 1798," https://founders.archives.gov/documents/Adams/99-02-02-3102.

Chapter 4: Media Attacks on My Biography

2. Candace Owens, Twitter, April 22, 2018, https://twitter.com/RealCandaceO/status/988053820004499457?ref_src=twsrc%5Etfw.
3. Tom Arnold since deleted his tweet, but the story can be found at Ryan Gaydos, "Tom Arnold goes on tirade against conservative commentator Candace Owens," Fox News, April 23, 2018, https://www.foxnews.com/entertainment/tom-arnold-goes-on-tirade-against-conservative-commentator-candace-owens.

Chapter 15: Returning to College

4. Steven A. Camarota and Karen Zeigler, "63% of Non-Citizen Households Access Welfare Programs," Center for Immigration Studies, November 20, 2018, based on U.S. Census Bureau's "Survey of Income and Program Participation (SIPP)," https://cis.org/Report/63-NonCitizen-Households-Access-Welfare-Programs.

Chapter 17: Harvard Law School Admission

5. Anna J. Egalite, "How Family Background Influences Student Achievement," *Education Next* 16, no. 2 (Spring 2016), https://www.educationnext.org/how-family-background-influences-student-achievement/.

Chapter 20: "The Boy's Gone"

6. "Woke Up This Mornin'," Public Domain.

Part III: The Constitution, Limited Government, and American Prosperity

7. "Preamble to the Constitution," Archives, gov, https://www.archives.gov/founding-docs/constitution?_ga=2.246309188.15083 16815.1659736010-1180004723.1659557630.

Chapter 25: Collectivism Over Individualism

8. "Lord Acton Writes to Bishop Creighton (1887), https://oll.libertyfund.org/quote/lord-acton-writes-to-bishop-creighton-that-the-same-moral-standards-should-be-applied-to-all-men-political-and-religious-leaders-included-especially-since-power-tends-to-corrupt-and-absolute-power-corrupts-absolutely-1887.

Chapter 27: Off the Plantation

9. Cydney Hurston Dupree, "White Liberals Present Themselves as Less Competent in Interactions with African Americans," *Yale Insights*, November 15, 2018, https://insights.som.yale.edu/insights/white-liberals-present-themselves-as-less-competent-in-interactions-with-african-americans.

Chapter 30: Affirmative Action

10. "Executive Order 10925—Establishing the President's Committee on Equal Employment Opportunity," The American Presidency Project, March 6, 1961, https://www.presidency.ucsb.edu/documents/executive-order-10925-establishing-the-presidents-committee-equal-employment-opportunity.
11. Clayborne Carson, ed., *The Papers of Martin Luther King Jr., Volume III: Birth of a New Age December 1955–December 1956* (Berkeley: University of California Press, 1997), 457.

Chapter 31: Rethinking American Slavery

12. Herbert L. Byrd Jr., *Proclamation 1625: America's Enslavement of the Irish* (Victoria, BC: Friesen Press, 2016), 10.
13. *The Nation and Athenæum*, Vol. 41 (April 30, 1927), 119.
14. *Benjamin Franklin: A Life from Beginning to End* (Hourly History, 2016), chapter 7.
15. John Jay, "Letter to R. Lushington, March 15, 1786," https://teachingamericanhistory.org/document/letter-to-r-lushington/.
16. Letter "From John Adams to Joseph Ward, 8 January 1810," https://founders.archives.gov/documents/Adams/99-02-02-5495.
17. Letter "From John Adams to William Tudor, Jr. 20 November 1819," https://founders.archives.gov/documents/Adams/99-02-02-7261.
18. Letter "From George Washington to Robert Morris, 12 April 1786," https://founders.archives.gov/documents/Washington/04-04-02-0019.
19. "Declaration of Independence: A Transcription," https://www.archives.gov/founding-docs/declaration-transcript.

Chapter 32: Dr. Martin Luther King's American Dream

20. MLK Speech – Full Text "I Have a Dream" | Paul Pop's Ponderings, http://paulpop.com/2017/01/mlk-speech-text/.

Chapter 34: The Need for National Unity

21. "Abortion Surveillance—United States, 2019," Centers for Disease Control and Prevention, November 26, 2021, https://www.cdc.gov/mmwr/volumes/70/ss/ss7009a1.htm.
22. Anthony Leonardi, "Tim Kaine: The United States 'Created Slavery,'" *Washington Examiner*, June 16, 2020, https://www.washingtonexaminer.com/news/tim-kaine-the-united-states-created-slavery.
23. Letter "Thomas Jefferson to John Holmes," (April 22, 1820), Library of Congress, https://www.loc.gov/exhibits/jefferson/159.html.
24. "Query XVIII" from Thomas Jefferson's *Notes on the State of Virginia (1784)*, https://xroads.virginia.edu/~Hyper/JEFFERSON/ch18.html.

25. Institute for Youth Policy JUNE 21, 2021 "Defund Planned Parenthood" https://www.yipinstitute.com/article/defund-planned-parenthood

26. "Tim Tebow & Mom – Super Bowl Ad 2010," https://www.youtube.com/watch?v=sw7qX1TpdNQ.

27. See results of 2004 survey by Guttmacher Institute under the section Why Do Abortions Occur in "U.S. Abortion Statistics," https://abort73.com/abortion_facts/us_abortion_statistics/.

28. "What the data says about abortion in the U.S." Pew Research Center, June 24, 2022, https://www.pewresearch.org/fact-tank/2022/06/24/what-the-data-says-about-abortion-in-the-u-s-2/.

29. "Goonies actress is slammed after boasting at a pro-choice event," *Daily Mail*, September 6, 2017, https://www.dailymail.co.uk/news/article-4858556/Martha-Plimpton-says-best-abortion-Seattle.html.

Chapter 35: The Racist Roots of Abortion

30. Margaret Sanger, "Apostle of Birth Control Sees Cause Gaining Here," *New York Times*, April 8, 1923, https://eugenics.us/margaret-sanger-on-human-weeds-real-facts-about-birth-control/615.htm.

31. "What the data says about abortion in the U.S." Pew Research Center, June 24, 2022, https://www.pewresearch.org/fact-tank/2022/06/24/what-the-data-says-about-abortion-in-the-u-s-2/.

32. Martin Luther King Jr., "Letter from a Birmingham Jail," April 16, 1963, https://kinginstitute.stanford.edu/sites/mlk/files/letterfrom birmingham_wwcw_0.pdf.

33. "The Dred Scott Decision (1857)," Digital History, https://www.digitalhistory.uh.edu/disp_textbook.cfm?smtID=3&psid=293.

Part VI: Homosexuality and Its Assault on American Values

34. Bre Payton, "15 of the Most Unhinged Responses to the Texas Church Massacre Yet," *Federalist*, November 6, 2017, https://thefederalist.com/2017/11/06/15-of-the-most-unhinged-responses-to-the-texas-church-massacre-yet/.

35. Rod Dreher, "EEOC's Enemy of Religious Liberty," The American Conservative, December 22, 2017, https://www.theamericanconservative.com/chai-feldblum-eeoc-religious-liberty/.

Chapter 38: Going on Offense

36. "How Many Adults and Youth Identify as Transgender in the United States?" UCLA Williams Institute, June 2022, https://williamsinstitute .law.ucla.edu/publications/trans-adults-united-states/.

Chapter 39: Hunting for Our Children

37. Brittany Bernstein, "Court Awards Full Custody to James Younger's Mother . . ." Yahoo News, August 8, 2021, https://www.yahoo.com/ video/court-awards-full-custody-james-161319112.html.
38. Craig A. Harper et al., "Humanizing Pedophilia as Stigma Reduction," *Archives of Sexual Behavior* 51 (February 2022): 945–60, https://link .springer.com/article/10.1007/s10508-021-02057-x.
39. Jesse Singal, "Salon Shouldn't Have Unpublished Its Article by a Pedophile Author," The Cut, February 22, 2017, https://www.thecut .com/2017/02/salon-shouldnt-have-unpublished-its-pedophilia-article .html.
40. Dan MacGuill, "Did a Convicted Sex Offender Read to Children at a Houston Public Library?" October 7, 2019, Snopes, https://www .snopes.com/fact-check/drag-queen-library-convicted/.

Part VII: Education in America

41. Sam Dillon, "Large Urban-Suburban Gap Seen in Graduation Rates," *New York Times*, April 22, 2009, https://www.nytimes.com/2009/04/22/ education/22dropout.html#:~:text=It%20is%20no%20surprise%20 that,71%20percent%20in%20the%20suburbs.
42. https://elevatetheusa.org/the-need/#2. Accessed August 8, 2022.
43. Andrew J. Coulson, "Toward Market Education: Are Vouchers or Tax Credits the Better Path?" Policy Analysis No. 392 (February 23, 2001), https://www.cato.org/sites/cato.org/files/pubs/pdf/pa392.pdf.
44. "New York keeps spending more on schools and getting less results," *New York Post*, January 30, 2022, https://nypost.com/2022/01/30/ new-york-keeps-spending-more-on-schools-and-getting-less-results/.
45. Results of 2019 Assessments, https://www.nationsreportcard.gov/.

Chapter 40: Redefining Public Education

46. "Poll: Families Support DC Opportunity Scholarship Program," American Federation for Children, updated June 28, 2022, https://www.federationforchildren.org/poll-families-support-dc-opportunity-scholarship-program/.

47. Penny Starr, "Administration Again Cuts Funding for Scholarship Program That Helps DC Low-Income Kids," February 8, 2010, CNS News, https://www.cnsnews.com/news/article/administration-again-cuts-funding-scholarship-program-helps-low-income-dc-kids.

Chapter 43: Parental Responsibility

48. Ronald Reagan quote from August 12, 1986 news conference; https://www.reaganfoundation.org/ronald-reagan/reagan-quotes-speeches/news-conference-1/.

Chapter 44: Racial Failures

49. For the transcript of George W. Bush's speech to the NAACP on July 10, 2000, see https://www.washingtonpost.com/wp-srv/onpolitics/elections/bushtext071000.htm.

Chapter 46: The Apology Tour

50. Andrew Romano, "Is Michelle Obama Fair Game?" *Newsweek*, May 20, 2008, https://www.newsweek.com/michelle-obama-fair-game-218940.

51. Jake Tapper and Karen Travers, "President Obama Says America Has Shown 'Arrogance,'" ABC News, April 3, 2009, https://abcnews.go.com/Politics/story?id=7246844&page=1.

52. Firouz Sedarat and Lin Noueihed, "Obama says ready to talk to Iran," Reuters, January 27, 2009, https://www.reuters.com/article/us-obama-arabiya/obama-says-ready-to-talk-to-iran-idUSTRE50Q23220090127.

53. Tapper and Travers, "President Obama Says America Has Shown 'Arrogance,'" https://abcnews.go.com/Politics/story?id=7246844&page=1.

54. White House Press Release, "Remarks by President Obama to the Turkish Parliament," April 6, 2009, https://obamawhitehouse.archives.gov/the-press-office/remarks-president-obama-turkish-parliament.

55. "Obama at the Americas Summit," CBS News, April 17, 2009, https://www.cbsnews.com/pictures/obama-at-the-americas-summit/.

Chapter 47: Hating America

56. "Obama's 'Redistributive Justice': 2001 NPR Interview," YouTube, https://www.youtube.com/watch?v=NTCNK7v3J6w.

Part IX: American Military. Supremacy and National Security

57. "VFW Calls for Jane Fonda to Be Tried for Treason," AP News, August 26, 1988, https://apnews.com/article/b7746cb614f357c0dd2f3c0e3ea4fa98.

58. George Washington's First Annual Address to Both Houses of Congress, January 8, 1790, https://www.mountvernon.org/library/digitalhistory/quotes/article/to-be-prepared-for-war-is-one-of-the-most-effectual-means-of-preserving-peace/.

59. Barack Obama, Campaign Speech, July 13, 2012, YouTube, https://www.youtube.com/watch?v=9GjqdP6KSOE.

60. Ben Franklin's original quote from "Pennsylvania Assembly: Reply to the Governor, 11 November 755" is "Those who would give up essential Liberty, to purchase a little temporary Safety, deserve neither Liberty nor Safety." See https://founders.archives.gov/documents/Franklin/01-06-02-0107#:~:text=Those%20who%20would%20give%20up,deserve%20neither%20Liberty%20nor%20Safety.

61. Alicia Acuna and Kelly David Burke, "Biden's Keystone XL pipeline cancellation is gut punch to small businesses," Fox News, February 3, 2021, https://www.foxnews.com/politics/biden-keystone-xl-pipeline-cancellation-gut-punch-small-businesses.

Chapter 53: Other Options

62. "Meet the White House personal trainer that the Obamas fly in from Chicago—and even share with their staff," *Daily Mail*, February 11,

2011, https://www.dailymail.co.uk/news/article-1361575/Meet-White-House-personal-trainer-Obamas-fly-Chicago--share-staff.html.

63. Tristan Justice, "President Joe Biden's pick to lead the Bureau of Land Management is an ecoterrorist who advocated Americans limit their number of children," *The Federalist*, June 25, 2021, https://thefederalist.com/2021/06/25/biden-land-management-nominee-is-an-ecoterrorist-who-demanded-chinese-style-child-cap/.

64. Anthony Watts, "Is the U.S. Surface Temperature Record Reliable?" SurfaceStations.org, 2009, https://wattsupwiththat.files.wordpress.com/2009/05/surfacestationsreport_spring09.pdf.

65. Watts, "U.S. Surface Temperature."

66. "Obama 'We are the ones we've been waiting for,'" YouTube, February 19, 2008, https://www.youtube.com/watch?v=mol WTfv8TYw.

Chapter 54: Our Flag

67. Sam Kumar, "Congresswoman Ilhan Omar's Anti-Americanism," *Reno Gazette Journal*, November 14, 2019, https://www.rgj.com/story/opinion/columnists/2019/11/14/congresswoman-ilhan-omars-anti-americanism-kumar/4186849002/.

Chapter 55: The Pledge of Allegiance

68. "The Pledge of Allegiance—Changes Through the Years," http://americanflagfoundation.org/wp-content/uploads/2011/02/Official-versions-of-the-Pledge-of-Allegiance.pdf. Accessed August 11, 2022.

69. "This Day in History—July 30, 1956," https://www.history.com/this-day-in-history/president-eisenhower-signs-in-god-we-trust-into-law.

70. To read Docherty's original typed sermon "A New Birth of Freedom" from February 7, 1954, see https://old.post-gazette.com/downloads/20020820sermon.pdf.

Chapter 56: Our National Anthem

71. "The Great Garrison Flag," National Park Service, https://www.nps.gov/fomc/learn/historyculture/the-great-garrison-flag.htm. Accessed August 11, 2022.

72. "This Day in History—September 14, 1814," https://www.history
.com/this-day-in-history/key-pens-star-spangled-banner#:
~:text=On%20September%2014%2C%201814%2C%20Francis,
during%20the%20War%20of%201812. Accessed August 11, 2022,

73. Lymari Morales, "One in Three Americans 'Extremely Patriotic,'"
Gallup, July 2, 2010, https://news.gallup.com/poll/141110/one-three-
americans-extremely-patriotic.aspx.

74. David Rutz and Brandon Gillespie, "Media push narrative that
patriotism is 'adjacent to something evil,' analysts say," Fox News,
September 15, 2021, https://www.foxnews.com/media/patriotism-
media-pride-country.

75. Stanley Renshon, "The Political Mind: Obama denounces flag-pin
patriotism," *Politico*, October 23, 2007, https://www.politico.com/
story/2007/10/the-political-mind-obama-denounces-flag-pin-
patriotism-006502.

Part XII: The Role of the Church in American Life

76. "Letters Between Thomas Jefferson and the Danbury BapNormaltists
(1802)," https://billofrightsinstitute.org/primary-sources/danbury
baptists.

77. *Everson v. Board of Education of Ewing TP.* et al, 330 U.S. 855, 67 S.Ct.
962 (1947).

78. "Our Lives, Our Fortunes and Our Sacred Honor," https://founding.
com/our-lives-our-fortunes-and-our-sacred-honor/. Accessed August
11, 2022.

79. "The Constitution of the United States," https://providenceforum.
org/story/declaration-independence-2/. Accessed August 11, 2022.

80. "Quotations on the Jefferson Memorial," The Jefferson Monticello,
https://www.monticello.org/research-education/thomas-jefferson-
encyclopedia/quotations-jefferson-memorial/. Accessed August 11,
2022.

81. "Washington's Thanksgiving Proclamation, October 3, 1789," https://
www.revolutionary-war-and-beyond.com/george-washingtons-
thanksgiving-proclamation.html#:~:text=In%20George%20
Washington's%20Thanksgiving%20Proclamation,in%20
modern%20times%20that%20the.

82. John Adams quoted by Charles Sumner in *Speech of Hon. Charles Summer on the Night of the Passage of the Kansas and Nebraska Bill* (Washington, DC: Buell & Blanchard, 1854), 5.

Chapter 58: "The Black Church"

83. Original Lincoln quote was from his proclamation in 1863 appointing a National Fast Day, https://www.abrahamlincolnonline.org/lincoln/speeches/fast.htm.
84. Raphael G. Warnock, *The Divided Mind of the Black Church: Theology, Piety, and Public Witness* (New York: New York University Press, 2014), 83–84.

Chapter 59: Removing God from History

85. Andrea Morris, "'God's Will Is No Concern of This Congress,': NY Dem Jerry Nadler Rejects God During Equality Act Debate," CBN News, March 3, 2021, https://www1.cbn.com/cbnnews/us/2021/march/gods-will-is-no-concern-of-this-congress-ny-dem-jerry-nadler-rejects-god-during-debate-over-equality-act.
86. Andrew Binion, "'I haven't stopped smiling once': Joe Kennedy reacts to Supreme Court decision in prayer case," *Kitsap Sun*, June 27, 2022, https://www.kitsapsun.com/story/news/2022/06/27/former-bremerton-high-coach-joe-kennedy-reacts-supreme-court-decision-prayer-ban-case/7746195001/.
87. "John Winthrop Dreams of a City on a Hill, 1630," https://www.americanyawp.com/reader/colliding-cultures/john-winthrop-dreams-of-a-city-on-a-hill-1630/.
88. Kathleen Hopkins, "Lawsuit challenges 'under God' in Pledge of Allegiance," *USA Today*, November 19, 2014, https://www.usatoday.com/story/news/nation/2014/11/19/lawsuit-challenges-under-god-in-pledge-of-allegiance/19295203/.
89. Bradford Betz, "Joe Biden botches Declaration of Independence quote during Texas rally," March 3, 2020, https://www.fox32chicago.com/news/joe-biden-botches-declaration-of-independence-quote-during-texas-rally
90. "New Lenten Practices Redefine Tradition," United Church of Christ, March 8, 2011, https://www.ucc.org/new-lenten-practices-redefine/.

Chapter 60: Life and Godliness

91. George Washington "Farewell Address, 1796, https://www
.americanyawp.com/reader/a-new-nation/george-washington-
farewell-address-1796/.

Part XIII: Securing America's Future

92. "From John Adams to Massachusetts Militia, 11 October 1798,"
https://founders.archives.gov/documents/Adams/99-02-02-3102.

Chapter 61: The Real Meaning of Freedom

93. Chan Tov McNamarah, "Misgendering as Misconduct," *UCLA Law
Review*, May 11, 2020, https://www.uclalawreview.org/misgendering-
as-misconduct/.
94. Spencer Rich, "Single-Parent Families Rise Dramatically," *Washington
Post*, May 3, 1982, https://www.washingtonpost.com/archive/
politics/1982/05/03/single-parent-families-rise-dramatically/cc4afac4-
2764-419e-8bda-66f14bad3dd0/.
95. 2020 U.S. census information found in the article "Percentage and
Number of Children Living with Two Parents Has Dropped Since
1968," April 12, 2021, https://www.census.gov/library/stories/2021/04/
number-of-children-living-only-with-their-mothers-has-doubled-in-
past-50-years.html#:~:text=Fewer%20than%20two%2Dfifths%20
of,in%20this%20arrangement%20in%202020.
96. Information from the 2010 census and from the 2012–2016 American
Community Survey, https://statisticalatlas.com/place/Virginia/
Richmond/Household-Types.
97. "(1965) The Moynihan Report: The Negro Family, the Case for
National Action," https://www.blackpast.org/african-american-
history/moynihan-report-1965/.

Conclusion

98. "Gettysburg Address delivered at Gettysburg, PA, November 19,
1863," https://www.loc.gov/resource/rbpe.24404500/?st=text.